"*Neoliberalism, Ethics, and the Social Re__
Dialogues at the Edge* brings us up close to the exciting work of interdisciplinary iconoclasts in several fields as they talk informally about their work with iconoclastic colleagues. Each dialogue is truly 'at the edge,' opening readers' minds to questions and ideas that the writers' home disciplines too often police, appropriate, suppress. Each writer also offers a personal story that reveals the costs, bravery, and, sometimes, the loneliness of challenging dominant Eurocentric, neoliberal, individualistic, and universalizing paradigms, of breaking disciplinary boundaries. No matter in what discipline you comfortably or uncomfortably reside, this book will challenge you to rethink what you know about subjectivity and its discontents."

Lynne Layton is author of *Toward a Social Psychoanalysis: Culture, Character, and Normative Unconscious Processes*

"This book is a portrait of psychology in the heart of the beast. It is a remarkable collection of challenging and hopeful responses to psychology's collusion with toxic forces that threaten American society. Several of psychology's great interdisciplinary thinkers spell out the dangers and opportunities that confront the profession as it both flees from and engages its ethical responsibilities."

Philip Cushman is a retired teacher, psychotherapist, and semi-retired writer, his recent publications include *Travels with the Self: Interpreting Psychology as Cultural History* and *Hermeneutic Approaches to Interpretive Research: Dissertations in a Different Key*

Neoliberalism, Ethics and the Social Responsibility of Psychology

This volume encompasses deeply critical dialogues that question how the field of psychology exists within and is shaped by the current neoliberal political context. Spanning from psychoanalysis to post-colonial theory, these far-reaching discussions consider how a greater ethical responsiveness to human experience and sociopolitical arrangements may reopen the borders of psychological discourse.

With the understanding that psychology grows in the soil of neoliberal terrain and is a chief fertilizer for neoliberal expansion, the interviews in this book explore alternative possibilities for how this field of study might function. By offering their own unique responses regarding the current condition of their respective disciplines, these scholars critically consider the current conceptual frameworks that set the theoretical boundaries of psychology and contemplate the ethical responsibilities currently affecting the field.

This book will prove essential for scholars and students across several disciplines including psychology, philosophy, ethics, and post-colonial and socio-cultural studies, as well as practicing mental health professionals with an interest in the importance of psychological and social theory.

Heather Macdonald is a core faculty at Fielding Graduate University in their Clinical Psychology program. Dr. Macdonald's scholarly research focuses on the interface between culture, social justice, relational ethics, clinical practice, and post-colonial thought.

Sara Carabbio-Thopsey is a licensed clinical psychologist serving children and families in greater Boston. Her interests include the historical, cultural, and neoliberal complexities that impact children.

David M. Goodman is Associate Dean for Strategic Initiatives and External Relations at the Lynch School of Education and Human Development at Boston College, where he also serves as the director of Psychological Humanities and Ethics.

The Psychology and the Other Book Series

Series editor: David M. Goodman
Associate editors: Brian W. Becker, Donna M. Orange
and Eric R. Severson

The *Psychology and the Other* book series highlights creative work at the intersections between psychology and the vast array of disciplines relevant to the human psyche. The interdisciplinary focus of this series brings psychology into conversation with continental philosophy, psychoanalysis, religious studies, anthropology, sociology, and social/critical theory. The cross-fertilization of theory and practice, encompassing such a range of perspectives, encourages the exploration of alternative paradigms and newly articulated vocabularies that speak to human identity, freedom, and suffering. Thus, we are encouraged to reimagine our encounters with difference, our notions of the "other" and what constitutes therapeutic modalities.

The study and practices of mental health practitioners, psychoanalysts, and scholars in the humanities will be sharpened, enhanced, and illuminated by these vibrant conversations, representing pluralistic methods of inquiry, including those typically identified as psychoanalytic, humanistic, qualitative, phenomenological, or existential.

Recent titles in the series include:

Self and Other in an Age of Uncertain Meaning
Communication and the Marriage of Minds
Edited by Matthew Clemente, Bryan J. Cocchiara, and Timothy D. Stephen

misReading Plato
Continental and Psychoanalytic Glimpses Beyond the Mask
Edited by Matthew Clemente, Bryan J. Cocchiara, and William J. Hendel

For a full list of titles in the series, please visit the Routledge website at: www.routledge.com/Psychology-and-the-Other/book-series/PSYOTH

Neoliberalism, Ethics and the Social Responsibility of Psychology

Dialogues at the Edge

Edited by Heather Macdonald,
Sara Carabbio-Thopsey and
David M. Goodman

Routledge
Taylor & Francis Group

LONDON AND NEW YORK

Cover image: Getty Images | Jasmina007

First published 2022
by Routledge
4 Park Square, Milton Park, Abingdon, Oxon OX14 4RN

and by Routledge
605 Third Avenue, New York, NY 10158

*Routledge is an imprint of the Taylor & Francis Group, an informa
business*

British Library Cataloguing-in-Publication Data
A catalogue record for this book is available from the British
Library

Library of Congress Cataloging-in-Publication Data
A catalog record has been requested for this book

ISBN: 978-1-032-24770-0 (hbk)
ISBN: 978-1-032-24771-7 (pbk)
ISBN: 978-1-003-28003-3 (ebk)

DOI: 10.4324/9781003280033

Typeset in Times new Roman
by Apex CoVantage, LLC

Contents

About the Editors

Heather Macdonald is a core faculty at Fielding Graduate University in their Clinical Psychology program. Dr. Macdonald came to academia after years of practice as a clinical psychologist whose work involved clinical assessment and individual therapeutic services. Macdonald's work has led to scholarly research on the interface between culture, social justice, relational ethics, clinical practice, and post-colonial thought.

Sara Carabbio-Thopsey is a licensed clinical psychologist. Throughout her education, training, and practice, she has served children and families. Her interests include the historical, cultural, and neoliberal complexities that impact children. In addition to her theoretical curiosities, her clinical interests encompass neuropsychological evaluation as well as individual and family therapy. Dr. Carabbio works in the greater Boston area, primarily serving individuals involved with child services.

David M. Goodman is Associate Dean for Strategic Initiatives and External Relations at the Lynch School of Education and Human Development at Boston College. He is also the director of Psychological Humanities and Ethics at Boston College. Dr. Goodman has written and edited over a dozen books exploring the intersections among the fields of psychology, philosophy, and theology. He serves as series editor for the Psychology and the Other Book Series with Routledge.

Contributors

Sunil Bhatia is an internationally known professor in the field of psychology and human development. He specializes in understanding the development of self and identity within the contexts of racism, migration, globalization, and formation of transnational diasporas. His second book, *Decolonizing Psychology: Globalization, Social Justice and Indian Youth Identities* (Oxford University Press, 2018) received the 2018 William James Book Award from the American Psychological Association and an "honorable mention" for its Outstanding 2018 Qualitative book award. He has received the American Psychological Association's 2015 International Humanitarian Award and the 2017 Theodore Sarbin Award for distinguished contributions to psychology.

Sam Binkley is Professor of Sociology at Emerson College, Boston. He has published articles on the historical and social production of subjectivity in varied contexts – chiefly through a theoretical engagement with the work of Michel Foucault – and an empirical interest in popular psychology. He is a co-editor of *Foucault Studies* and author of *Getting Loose: Lifestyle Consumption in the 1970s* (Duke University Press, 2007) and *Happiness as Enterprise: An Essay on Neoliberal Life* (SUNY, 2014). His current research considers the wider problematic of anti-racism, understood as governmental imperative. His research is available at sambinkley.net.

Mark Freeman is Distinguished Professor of Ethics and Society in the Department of Psychology at the College of the Holy Cross. His writings include *Rewriting the Self: History, Memory, Narrative*; *Hindsight: The Promise and Peril of Looking Backward*; and *The Priority of the Other: Thinking and Living Beyond the Self*.

Sue Grand is faculty and supervisor at the NYU Postdoctoral Program in Psychoanalysis and Psychotherapy; faculty, the trauma program at the National Institute for the Psychotherapies; faculty, Mitchell center for Relational Psychoanalysis. She is an associate editor for *Psychoanalytic Dialogues and Psychoanalysis, Culture and Society*. She is the author of *The Reproduction of Evil: A Clinical and Cultural Perspective* and *The Hero in the Mirror: From Fear to Fortitude*. She has co-edited books on trans-generational transmission with Jill Salberg. Sue Grand is in private practice in NYC and in Teaneck, NJ.

Derek Hook is the author of *Six Moments in Lacan* (Routledge, 2017), a co-editor of the three-volume commentary series *Reading Lacan's Écrits* (along with Stijn Vanheule and Calum Neill) (Routledge, 2018) and a co-editor (with Calum Neill) of the Palgrave Lacan Series. Derek was previously a lecturer at the London School of Economics (in Social Psychology) and at Birkbeck College (in Psychosocial Studies) at University of London before taking up the post of Associate Professor at Duquesne University in Pittsburgh. He has published books in the areas of critical psychology and postcolonial theory – the best examples being *A Critical Psychology of the Postcolonial* (Routledge, 2011) and *(Post)apartheid Conditions* (Palgrave, 2014) – and the topics of race and racism, alongside the work of Frantz Fanon, remain abiding concerns in his research career. He recently published a collection of prison letters by the anti-apartheid South African and Pan-Africanist intellectual Robert Mangaliso Sobukwe entitled *Lie on Your Wounds* (Wits University Press, 2018). The field of Lacanian psychoanalysis – both as mode of clinical practice and as form of social theory – has proved the overarching and unifying theme in his teaching and research for the last 20 years. Derek was a trainee psychoanalyst at the Centre for Freudian Analysis and Research in London between 2006 and 2013 and today acts as a clinical supervisor and occasional psychotherapist, at Duquesne University's Psychology Clinic. In addition to his graduate teaching commitments (courses on Lacan, Fanon, psychology as a human science, and approaches to psychopathology) Derek has, since 2016, taught an annual summer school course *Lacanian Psychoanalysis: Theory and Practice* at Birkbeck College in London.

Adrian Johnston is Distinguished Professor in the Department of Philosophy at the University of New Mexico at Albuquerque and a faculty member at the Emory Psychoanalytic Institute in Atlanta. He is the author of *Time Driven: Metapsychology and the Splitting of the Drive* (2005), *Žižek's Ontology: A Transcendental Materialist Theory of Subjectivity* (2008), *Badiou, Žižek, and Political Transformations: The Cadence of Change* (2009) and *Prolegomena to Any Future Materialism, Volume One: The Outcome of Contemporary French Philosophy* (2013), all published by Northwestern University Press. He also is the author of *Adventures in Transcendental Materialism: Dialogues with Contemporary Thinkers* (Edinburgh University Press, 2014). He is a co-author, with Catherine Malabou, of *Self and Emotional Life: Philosophy, Psychoanalysis, and Neuroscience* (Columbia University Press, 2013). His most recent books are *Irrepressible Truth: On Lacan's "The Freudian Thing"* (Palgrave Macmillan, 2017), *A New German Idealism: Hegel, Žižek, and Dialectical Materialism* (Columbia University Press, 2018), and *Prolegomena to Any Future Materialism, Volume Two: A Weak Nature Alone* (Northwestern University Press, 2019). With Todd McGowan and Slavoj Žižek, he is a co-editor of the book series *Diaeresis* at Northwestern University Press.

Suzanne R. Kirschner is Professor Emerita of Psychology at the College of the Holy Cross in Worcester, MA and a visiting scholar in the Department of the History of Science at Harvard University. She has published numerous articles and chapters on the sociocultural contexts of psychology, subjectivity, and other metatheoretical themes. She is the author of *The Religious and Romantic Origins of Psychoanalysis: Individuation and Integration in Post-Freudian Theory* (Cambridge) and a co-editor (with Jack Martin) of *The Sociocultural Turn in Psychology* (Columbia). She is a fellow of the American Psychological Association and a past president of both the Society for Theoretical and Philosophical Psychology (APA Division 24) and of the Society for Qualitative Inquiry in Psychology (a section of APA Division 5). Her awards include the APA's 2019 Theodore Sarbin Award in Critical and Narrative Psychology.

Jack Martin is a fellow of the Canadian and American Psychological Associations, former president of the Society for Theoretical and Philosophical Psychology (STPP) and recipient of the STPP's Award for Distinguished Lifetime Contributions to Theoretical and Philosophical Psychology.

Frank C. Richardson is a professor in the Department of Educational Psychology at the University of Texas, Austin. His early research focused on cognitive-behavioral approaches to the treatment of stress and anxiety. For two decades, his scholarly interests have centered on the philosophy of social science and various topics in theoretical and philosophical psychology. He is past president of the Division of Theoretical and Philosophical Psychology of the American Psychological Association. He has published numerous articles and chapters on such topics as the cultural and moral underpinnings of modern psychology and psychotherapy, determinism in social science, and hermeneutic approaches to social theory and inquiry.

Jill Salberg, Ph.D., ABPP, is faculty at NYU Postdoctoral Program in Psychoanalysis. She is editor of *Good Enough Endings: Breaks, Interruptions and Terminations from Contemporary Relational Perspectives*. She co-edited two books with Sue Grand, *The Wounds of History* and *Transgenerational Trauma and the Other*, both of which won the Gradiva Award for 2018. She's in private practice in Manhattan.

Jeff Sugarman is a professor of education and psychology at Simon Fraser University. His major interests are the psychology of personhood, the sociopolitical influence of psychology, the psychology of neoliberalism, and the historical ontology of psychological objects. His most recent book is *A Humanities Approach to the Psychology of Personhood* (Routledge, 2020).

Thomas Teo is a professor of psychology in the Historical, Theoretical, and Critical Studies of Psychology Program at York University in Toronto, Canada. He has been active in the advancement of critical-theoretical psychology and considers his research program to be contributing to the psychological humanities.

Dennis C. Wendt is an assistant professor in the Department of Educational and Counselling Psychology at McGill University. He collaborates with indigenous communities in exploring, developing, and evaluating culturally relevant interventions pertaining to mental health, substance use, and community wellness. He is also interested in philosophical aspects of clinical/counseling psychology.

Acknowledgments

We are all now living in a world shaped by the ideologies and logic of global capitalism, which in turn has also reshaped human subjectivity in a profound manner. The logic of such global economies, with an unbridled growth as the main driver, has dehumanized and monetized our ways of being in the world and our intersubjective capacities. The manner in which we can transcend these forces is made possible through thickly lived and nourishing communities. These acknowledgements are meant to point to such communities in our lives – groups and people who have enabled and expanded our imaginations.

We cannot be exhaustive of the many conversation partners who have touched these pages. From the scholars and practitioners whose work has inspired the interviewers and interviewees to the editors who have combed through these words to give them greater clarity to the students and patients who have challenged our notions of how livable this world is – these are all individuals unnamed (and many others) who direct our attention to the call for something beyond the present arrangement. We are grateful for the wisdom they have inspired.

One concrete community we will name directly is the Psychology and the Other Conference community, both those who bring the logistics to life and those who engage in these transformative conversations every other year. It is this event and the growing community therein that provided the context and space for the interviews here to come into being. Over the years, this community of students, scholars, clinicians, and friends have come together to find nourishment and critical, ethical explorations.

Another group of individuals whose work has buoyed the conversations seen in these pages is the Society of Theoretical and Philosophical Psychology (APA, Division 24). Though often living at the margins of the

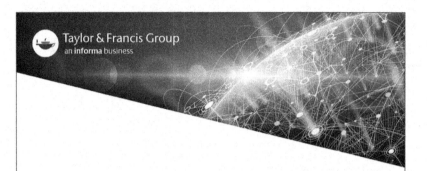

field of psychology, this Society has brought forth generations of curious students and theorists who foster dialogue in barren spaces.

We are especially grateful to our interviewers: Jeff Sugarman, Mark Freeman, Sunil Bhatia, Suzanne R. Kirschner, Derek Hook, Dennis C. Wendt and Jill Salberg. This project would not have been possible without their time and thoughtful input infused into these conversations.

Sara Carabbio-Thopsey

While I am grateful to my family and friends for their continued support, the psychological community has graced me in ways that I can only describe as cosmic. I have had the unique pleasure to learn from remarkable and critical thinkers so early on in my career. I am grateful for my experiences at Lesley University and the Psychology and the Other conferences; while my career into psychology began before college, Lesley was the home that deepened my thinking, sparked my curiosity of personhood, and questioned what it means to be myself and in relationship to the Other. Brian Becker, David M. Goodman, and Heather Macdonald have been remarkable mentors. Heather, you continue to be a transcendental force in my life – thank you for your endless wisdom and guidance. It is an honor to work on this book with people I greatly admire and feel indebted to as they have helped shape my path both personally and professionally.

Heather Macdonald

For this volume, I am indebted to some of my early mentors, Bill Adams, Deb Adams and Dott Kelly for believing in and nurturing my own scholarly growth and the mission of the Psychology and the Other programs. I am also grateful to the Seattle University psychology department, which has served as my intellectual home, in various forms, for over 20 years.

David M. Goodman

These volumes are a herculean effort. The editors and authors pile the project and its many moving parts on top of their already overflowing plates. This case is no different. I am deeply indebted to my co-editors who carried this work forward, amidst a global pandemic and through the wastelands of everyone's academic and clinical schedules, to see this come to fruition. Their patience and persistence is a testament to their characters, and their playfulness an ongoing inspiration to me. I am grateful for their friendship and for keeping these types of conversations alive in my life.

Lastly, as we write, an exciting and growing initiative is taking shape under the title of *Psychological Humanities and Ethics* at Boston College. With the generous support of Dean Stanton Wortham (Lynch School of Education and Human Development), a future is unfolding that we believe can be radically transformative to the realities about which this volume is so critical. May we find the heart and motivation to engage in such change and swim against the current.

Introduction
Manic Societies and Overfunctioning Sciences

David M. Goodman, Heather Macdonald, and Sara Carabbio-Thopsey

Introduction: Psychology as a Parentified Child

As with most things "modern," the discipline of psychology is often taken out of context. In a manner similar to Alasdair MacIntyre's opening pages of *After Virtue* (1984), we frequently wonder how scholars and scientists in 2221 will understand the psychological sciences of 2021. Future scholars and scientists will, of course, have the benefit of hindsight to illuminate the unique horizon and clearing that gave birth to this field, along with the forces that shaped its evolution. In its first century and a half of life, modern psychology was assembled in a "clearing" quite unique in human history, with intersecting factors that contributed to its complex function in human life, a function that remains prominent to this day.

Modern psychology's inception follows closely from the periods of the Renaissance and Enlightenment. A promise was in the air – humans were finally to transcend the strictures of traditional perspectives and travel, instead, in the territories of universals and purer forms of reasoning (Taylor, 1989; Toulmin, 1990). The development of the modern psychological discipline was a global process with contributions coming from Germany, Britain, Russia, France, and the United States. The rapid exchange of ideas about the science and discipline of psychology exploded into life at the height of colonialism, during which time designated forms of life and ways of thinking were hierarchically defined, endowing some qualities with higher values and others as more "primitive" and "base." Religious and community life transformed rapidly and individual subjectivity came into vogue as a new locus of identity and nodal point of meaning (Cushman, 1995; Dueck, 1995; Danziger, 1990; Fromm, 1955; Rieff, 1987; Taylor, 2007). Medical advances were intoxicating, and neurological discoveries

DOI: 10.4324/9781003280033-1

were utterly revolutionizing paradigms. Such advancements reconstituted the languages that humans had for their experience (Danziger, 1997; Rose, 2007). A technological revolution ushered in a sustained period of life-altering changes in rapid succession and in a manner incomparable with any other time in human history. From railroads to gene therapies, technology's eruption brought with it new forms of warfare, advertising, industrial capacities, forms of work, and clustering of social networks (urbanization, etc.) that had enormous repercussions on the human condition in a short period of time.

As a young discipline, psychology had much to manage. Whether the plight of returning soldiers from two brutal World Wars, the prospect of nuclear destruction, the identity loss and alienation from post-traditional/ communal life, the dehumanization of McDonaldized workplaces (Ritzer, 2011), or the forward charge of a manic, capitalist marketplace (Peltz, 2006), the subject under psychology's jurisdiction was exhibiting distress and dysfunction in an ever-changing manner. Psychology was deployed to manage the effects of these rapid reconfigurations, simultaneously as a method for understanding *and* intervention (Cushman, 1995). Barely an adolescent in its development – methodologically, theoretically, and institutionally – this new discipline had to manage the dysfunctional home of Euro-American existence (Goodman, 2012, 2015; Goodman & Marcelli, 2010).

In many ways, psychology – as an emerging discipline – had to over-function in a way typical of a parentified child and has the baggage to show for it. It was forced to carry far more than its maturity might have healthfully allowed. As a result, one might argue that it has some blind spots and over identifications that are on display for those looking critically and closely. As with most parentified and overfunctioning persons, identity is forced to become rigid and clear. Authority must be established for survival's sake – decisiveness, ownership, and certainty are necessary traits. This is the only means of managing when one is existing beyond one's capacity. One must overreach and double down. If one is to take up the mantle of parenthood, then one must affix oneself to the seemingly stable and established identifications that allow for authoritative and effective living. It has been argued extensively that psychology's identification with and commitment to objectivistic, medical, and natural scientific paradigms provided this young field the means of sustaining its overfunctioning capacities (Slife et al., 2005). Of course, this is all at a cost.

One profoundly dangerous byproduct of a parentified psychological discipline is the risk of losing its fidelity to the full dimensionality of human life. In seeking legitimacy and stability, psychology became increasingly myopic, both in terms of conceptualization and operationalization. Its commitments to particular forms of legitimization contributed to a decontextualized, non-reflexive, and universalized set of methodologies. Akin to the biological and medical sciences, psychology worked within normative, generalizable, and operationalizable principles to ensure its authority. This gave it (and continues to give it) enormous capital and cultural currency, but with a rigidity and unidimensional quality to its analytic ability. This deprives the discipline from achieving more dynamic, complex, and sociopolitically sophisticated engagements with questions of human identity, suffering, and potential. Kirschner and Martin (2010) capture this well:

> For despite a promising beginning that followed the founding of disciplinary psychology, constitutive sociocultural theorizing in psychology per se was overcome, for the most part, by the new discipline's longing for scientific credibility, a desire that took the form of powerful methodological commitments to objectivist theories of knowledge (Bernstein, 1983), operational definitions, and quantified measurements. Such ways of framing the subject matter and procedures of psychology left little room for the study of complex social and cultural phenomenon and processes that could not easily be molded to fit such methodological penchants, at least as practiced by new generations of self-proclaimed psychological scientists.
>
> (p. 4)

Among the risks involved with decontextualization and its resultant myopia is that psychology becomes a mere reflection of and means for reinforcing ideologies, sociopolitical realities, and economic arrangements, with no capacity to be otherwise (Cushman, 1995). Unbeknownst to itself, the psychological discipline becomes an agent in the formation of persons – directed by the values of dominant sociopolitical and economic forces, rather than from a reflexive or critical wellspring.

The only way to upset this "managers of the status quo" arrangement (Cushman, 1995) is to contextualize the field back to its originating horizons so that we have a clearer sense of what we are thinking with and from. Historically situated disciplines allow for the possibility of developing a more dimensional and full (and, dare we say, scientifically accurate) formulation of life. Such actions provide the possibility of liberatory and critical conceptualizations as well as praxis. The soil from which modern psychology sprouted has a very particular set of nutrients, has been irrigated through a distinct method, and has baked under the sun of a unique climate. However, truth claims and knowledge sets from the field of psychology are rarely placed within their own framing. This is an essential step.

One of the fundamental purposes of this volume is to call forward a significant contextual factor often omitted in psychology's self-understanding, its formulation of persons, or its designs for intervention and care. The omitted contextual element referenced here is the rise of neoliberal arrangements that have utterly altered the nature of human life. At this point in its development, psychology grows in the soil of neoliberal terrain and also is a chief fertilizer for neoliberal dissemination and expansion. Neoliberalism is arguably the most prevalent governmental configuration and architect of present-day life. Yet, its shape, trends, forces, and assumptions are largely absent from any psychological considerations coming from the mainstream of the field.

As an economic system, neoliberalism (or neo-liberalism) is a term used to describe the 20th-century resurgence of ideas associated with economic liberalism and free-market capitalism that were articulated during the 19th century. In general, Friedrich Hayek and Milton Friedman are viewed as two of the primary architects of this form of economic logic, which supports the deregulation of the market as well as corporations. It is a logic that favors privatization at the expense of defunding welfare and the dismantling of services that are aimed at the public good.

Scholars such as Wendy Brown (2015, 2019) have suggested that neoliberalism, as it has evolved, has become much more than a regulatory economic regime communicated through a transatlantic network of businessmen and politicians who want to capitalize on the conditions of possibility for economic growth. Brown argues that neoliberalism is now also a form of governance, reasoning, and most importantly of self-organization. As neoliberalism operates through dispersed networks of discourses that are cross-disciplinary in nature, the economic logic of neoliberalism aims to treat the self as though it were a financial portfolio: diversified in its interests and secure in its profitability. In Brown's (2019) newest book, *In the Ruins of Neoliberalism: The Rise of Antidemocratic Politics in the West*, she highlights how the market conditions that favor entrepreneurial endeavors have come to dictate how one defines self-hood and subjectivity. An entrepreneurial understanding of the self means ongoing self-fulfillment and personal growth, investing on increasing skill sets that are of value to the market, as well as producing and achieving goals as a means of self-regulation. Many scholars have also argued that psychology as a science and discipline has been complicit in contributing to neoliberal subjectivity where the "autonomous" self is wholly responsible for enhancing its own value. If it fails to strive for outward marketability, then a considerable amount of individual diagnoses may be applied to account for this "lack of self-development." The possibility of self-actualization happens through one's own labor and self-definition that is removed from any context.

As relationships among the ideology of neoliberalism, subjectivity, and market values continue to inform one another, it becomes more difficult to ignore the fact that current economic systems will not meet the needs of most people but only of a few. It also seems clear that psychology needs to deeply engage these psycho-political intersections in order to work against forces that erode human well-being. Whether the framework be neoliberalism, colonialism, technology, or otherwise, psychology as a discipline frequently disregards how such frameworks impact individuals and the field at large.

This Volume: Contextualizing Dialogues

With these concerns and this backdrop in mind, one goal of this volume is to closely consider alternative ways that psychology might be able to function. The purpose of seeking a realignment is to open back up the borders of psychological discourses in such a way that may allow for the development of greater ethical responsiveness to human experience and sociopolitical arrangements.

In the spirit of contextualization, we will briefly explain how the following pages came about. With the goal of understanding the ways that particular esteemed scholars' works have been understood by the current field of psychology, a series of one-hour interview sessions were held at the *Psychology and the Other* conference in 2015. The *Psychology and the Other* conferences foster a space for meaningful conversations and difficult dialogues to consider how entrenched languages and paradigms might give way to fuller cross-disciplinary possibilities (Goodman & Freeman, 2015). These particular interviews were ultimately published in *Dialogues at the Edge of American Psychological Discourse: Critical and Theoretical Perspectives* (Macdonald et al., 2017). The conversations were tremendously rich and provided considerable insight into the condition of the field of psychology.

In this second volume, the aim is to continue this interview project, but this time with a more specific theme and question in mind – "What is an ethics of psychology when interpreted in the context of a neoliberal political order?" (Sugarman, 2015, p. 103). Each interview captures a distinctive approach to engaging this question. Eight interviews were conducted involving sixteen scholars and practitioners whose dialogues aimed to critically examine psychology's current practices. The contributors' disciplinary backgrounds were far ranging and included sociology, ethics, psychoanalysis, critical psychology, postcolonial theory, philosophy, history of science, qualitative studies, collaborative and therapeutic assessment, theoretical psychology, and hermeneutics.

As a framework for these conversations, we established a series of broad-based questions. In this way there is some structure to the interview but also creative space to expand and widen the conversation. A sample of the questions include:

- What have been the resistances and impediments to your work being received in the contemporary discipline of psychology?
- Viewed within the context of neoliberal, neo-capitalistic world order, what would the field need to do to right its course?
- The overall social arrangement in our society is grossly unjust and yet many of us assume that all people, regardless of the conditions in which they live should arrive at the same moral conclusions as those people who have wealth and power. How should psychology take up the issue of civic obligation and the freedom to make choices when the conditions are so unjust?
  How should psychology promote psychological freedom within both personal and political domains?

As with the first set of interviews, the conversation between scholars was tremendously rich and the breadth of scholarship, thinkers, and historical narratives drawn upon was quite impressive. Many broad themes were readily apparent in the responses to these questions. Most of the scholars in this volume clearly suggested that one way for the discipline to "right its course" is to increase its capacity for interdisciplinary exchange. Drawing from a wide variety of theoretical traditions such as continental philosophy, relational psychoanalysis, and post-colonial theory would open up possibilities for creative solutions and new languages with more capacious ethical potential.

In all of these conversations there is also a steady call for more sustained engagement with work that is to be done at the intersections of the psychopolitical and a demand for the psychological discipline to engage with the overlapping temporalities of and entangled histories that comprise psychological epistemologies. Along these lines, one area of particular thematic focus centered on racism and its relationship to the logic of neoliberal and neo-capitalistic structures.

Chapter Summaries

The remainder of this introduction provides a brief background to each of the interviews. This is not designed to rigidly place each scholar in a particular "camp" but rather to provide some framing around crucial themes of discourse that are taken up in the interviews and important, ongoing scholarship of these thinkers.

The Personal Is Political: A Conversation with Jeff Sugarman
Interviewer: Mark Freeman

Sugarman frames the major problem in psychology as one where there is a fundamental lack of focus on personhood, selfhood, and human agency in psychological discourse. He also discusses the need for a focus on the history of psychological phenomena, which calls for the encompassing of social, cultural, moral, ethical, political, economic, educational, and religious features. He states, "Arguing that history and its contingency are vital to psychological constitution runs counter to the naïve naturalism of mainstream psychology that psychologists believe is necessary for the discipline to attain the status of a science" (this volume). He sees "psychology through a Foucauldian lens by looking at productive possibilities within historical circumstances; how certain conditions of possibility have enabled the emergence of psychological capacities." Sugarman uses Foucault's concept of governmentality to understand how neoliberalism shapes individuals to be the kinds of persons who function in a way that the market requires and how neoliberalism harnesses choice as a means of control – choice is managed through consumerism. People are expected to be self-reliant, flexible, and mobile – neoliberalism reconstitutes what it means to be a person. Psychology is complicit with maintaining the socio-political and economic status quo, which puts responsibility on the individual rather than considering the context within which the person is situated.

Subjectivity and the Critical Imagination in Neoliberal Capitalism: A Conversation with Thomas Teo

Interviewer: Dennis C. Wendt

Thomas Teo and Dennis C. Wendt enter a dialogue about psychology's entanglement with society, culture, and the history of psychology. Their discussion highlights important aspects of Teo's recent scholarship that aims at defining a critical psychology agenda that works to disrupt the epistemological violence and 'epistemological grandiosity' that structures psychological discourse. In his scholarship, Teo also identifies psychology as a *"hyperscience,"* a discipline that uses strategies to hide the fact that it is not a natural science (Teo, 2020). In order to do that, one inflates and complicates one's methodological activities, conceals the temporality and contextuality of psychological phenomena, and incessantly refers to one's discipline as a science. Their conversation explores the ways in which psychology has shaped, controlled, and adapted people through its relationship with neoliberal capitalism, subhumanism, and economic Darwinism. Together, they question the ethical and ontological practices of psychology.

Culture, Context, and Coloniality: A Dialogue Between Sunil Bhatia and Suzanne R. Kirschner

Sunil Bhatia and Suzanne R. Kirschner both examine and critique the ways the psychological discipline has been influenced by and continues to operate from largely Eurocentric assumptions and epistemologies.

Throughout Kirschner's career she has explored indigenous psychologies through a post-Freudian psychoanalytic psychology. Bhatia provides both a personal and scholarly view of the field of psychology that is post-colonial in nature and states, "The psychological canon had largely reinforced a narrative that people of color had a deficient humanity, and their lives or stories did not matter and were not worthy of studying." Their work explores the complex intersections between individual subjectivity and wider cultural contexts. They discuss the need for psychology to address and richly involve transnational perspectives, theoretical frameworks for thinking about selfhood in an immigration context, the influence of neoliberalism, as well as globalization. Furthermore, they call for a focus on indigeneity and an anticolonial and antiracist psychology, which addresses the marginalization of people of color. Together, Bhatia and Kirschner illuminate the ability for change and encourage movement away from Eurocentric thinking and practice.

Psychology as Apparatus: An Interview with Sam Binkley

Interviewer: Derek Hook

In this interview, Sam Binkley, using Foucault's constructivist view of neoliberalism, outlines how subjectivity gets produced in the contemporary context of neoliberal logic with a particular emphasis on the discursive effects. He and Hook discuss how selves are constructed in a cultural/ political moment – particularly in the era of populism and nationalism. Towards the end of the interview Binkley reflects on how racism evokes shame on an ontological level that leads to the exposure of an overdetermined whiteness. In further developing the theme of shame, Binkley draws upon Bakhtin's notion of the carnivalesque – where all are shamed and also redeemed, without spectators or objects; shame is a performative offering to the other who is also spectator and participant. Binkley remarks, "I've been very interested in Foucault for a long time. I'm very interested in the notion that these discourses are produced, they circulate, and they colonize us in such a way that we take these discourses and we use them to produce our own selves, our own subjectivities" (this volume).

Infinite Greed: Marx, Lacan, and Capitalism: An Interview with Adrian Johnston

Interviewer: Heather Macdonald

Adrian Johnston's interview focuses on a psychoanalytic (particularly Lacanian) return to Marx in order to show how a synthesis of Marxist historical materialism and Lacanian metapsychology allows for powerful criticisms of the liberal and neo-liberal ideologies of capitalism. The narrative of the interview moves in and around five broad themes: 1) Psychoanalysis and the analytic drive would not have been possible without capitalism, 2) Marx's theory of historical materialism anticipates Freudian drive theory, 3) "The consumption drives of libidinal economies are *symptoms* of the production drives of the political economies (and not the other way around)," 4) *Plus-de-jouir* is the residue of lost *jouissance* with each and every instance of *objet petit a* (in this sense Marx's theory can be seen as a theory that exposes, over and over again the *objet petit a*), and 5) Marx's historical materialism rebuts the liberal assertion of a capitalism that is directly correlated to self-interested egocentric consumption of goods because at its root capitalism is about *surplus value* – the maintenance of which requires us to "unlink" from our own facticity in order to perform a kind of fantasmic self-sacrifice to the Big Other or the "invisible hand of the market" or to the "Economy as God." The crucial point here is that, when capital becomes a means of quantifying a *surplus jouissance*, there emerges a coordination of both fantasy (or the imaginary) and capital operating to mask the lack.

On Destructiveness: A Conversation with Sue Grand

Interviewer: Jill Salberg

Grand and Salberg engage in a reflective and critical conversation with regard to psychoanalytic theory and practice. Through their dialogue they tackle some of the complicated intersections of politics, psychoanalysis, theology, and neoliberalism. In particular, they ask critical questions around notions of Otherness in relationship to broader political systems and psychotherapy. Grand describes the concept of evil in its relation to psychoanalysis as a means for understanding historic and current sociopolitical dilemmas from individual to global levels. Together, they discuss the powerful use of language and call for social justice origins and I-thou ethic in psychoanalysis.

Taking Persons Seriously: A Conversation with Jack Martin

Interviewer: Jeff Sugarman

After encountering the methodological restraints of traditional experimental research in psychology, Jack Martin has focused his scholarship on the development of a psychological and philosophical anthropology as a means to study persons and their lives. Martin states, "it's the complacency induced by the scientist-practitioner model that I think prevents psychology from adequately investing in what I believe ought to be its subject matter – persons as self-interpreting moral and rational agents" (this volume). He then examines how in the last decade of his work he has been writing about what he calls Life Positioning Analysis (LPA) and applying it to particular people. LPA focuses on the socio-physical, sociocultural, and social-psychological positions that individuals occupy and exchange as they coordinate interactively with others throughout the lifespan. LPA is a way to restore "the reality of persons as historically and socioculturally embedded and dynamically constituted within the normative interactions, conventions, practices, traditions, and ways of life of persons' families and communities as well as their broader society and culture" (this volume). Toward the end of the interview Martin notes that neoliberalism and neo-capitalism reduce and devalue people rather than empower a perspective that views persons as socioculturally situated, culture-capable agents of possible change. He further argues that psychology has a civic and moral responsibility not to contribute to societal inequality and injustice.

Philosophical Hermeneutics and Psychological Understanding: A Conversation with Frank C. Richardson

Interviewer: Jeff Sugarman

Frank C. Richardson's vast work encompasses an array of cross-disciplinary interests, including but certainly not limited to philosophical hermeneutics, moral philosophy, and relational ontology. In this chapter,

Richardson and Sugarman embark on a rich conversation of Richardson's career trajectory and what it means to be a theoretical psychologist. They continue on to discuss limitations and constraints in the "mainstream" scientific and technological psychological discipline. Much of Richardson's more recent scholarship takes a multidisciplinary approach in contextualizing the problems of psychology within the neoliberal order. Richardson provides readers insight into alternative ways of thinking about psychology by citing discourse in virtue ethics, hermeneutics, theology, and social theory.

Conclusion

An overfunctioning science that serves the purpose of managing the effects of manic socioeconomic structures is hardly being scientific. Furthermore, by functioning in this manner, it loses it ethical potential and transformative quality. In this volume, our hope is that the dialogues provide some ideas for the resituating of the psychological sciences. The objective is to allow the field of psychology to function as a science rather than as a miscalibrated agent in our social structures. In doing so, it has the opportunity to mature, grow, and evolve into a discipline that can serve in a liberatory and critical manner – participating in deeper human flourishing rather than merely reflecting the present order.

References

Bernstein, R. (1983). *Beyond objectivism and relativism: Science, hermeneutics, and praxis*. University of Pennsylvania Press.

Brown, W. (2015). *Undoing the demos: Neoliberalism's stealth revolution*. Zone Books.

Brown, W. (2019). *In the ruins of neoliberalism: The rise of antidemocratic politics in the West*. Columbia University Press.

Cushman, P. (1995). *Constructing the self, constructing America: A cultural history of psychotherapy*. DaCapo Press.

Danziger, K. (1990). *Constructing the subject: Historical origins of psychological research*. Cambridge University Press.

Danziger, K. (1997). *Naming the mind: How psychology found its language*. SAGE.

Dueck, A. (1995). *Between Jerusalem and Athens: Ethical perspectives on culture, religion, and psychotherapy*. Baker Books.

Fromm, E. (1955). *The sane society*. Henry Holt and Company, LLC.

Goodman, D. (2012). *The demanded self: Levinasian ethics and identity in psychology*. Duquesne University Press.

Goodman, D. (2015). The McDonaldization of psychotherapy: Processed foods, processed therapies, and economic class. *Theory & Psychology, 26*(1), 77–95. DOI: 10.1177/0959354315619708.

Goodman, D., & Freeman, M. (Eds.). (2015). *Psychology and the other*. Oxford University Press.

Goodman, D., & Marcelli, A. (2010). The great divorce: Ethics and identity. *Pastoral Psychology, 59*(5), 563–583.

Kirschner, S. R., & Martin, J. (2010). *The sociocultural turn in psychology*. Columbia University Press.

Macdonald, H., Goodman, D., & Becker, B. (Eds.). (2017). *Dialogues at the edge of American psychological discourse: Critical and theoretical perspectives*. Palgrave Macmillan.

MacIntyre, A. (1984). *After virtue* (2nd ed.). University of Notre Dame Press.

Peltz, R. (2006). The manic society. In L. Layton, N. C. Hollander & S. Gutwill (Eds.), *Psychoanalysis, class and politics: Encounters in the clinical setting* (pp. 65–80). Routledge.

Rieff, P. (1987). *The triumph of the therapeutic: Uses of faith after Freud*. The University of Chicago Press.

Ritzer, G. (2011). *The McDonaldization of society* (6th ed.). Pine Forge Press.

Rose, N. (2007). *The politics of life itself: Biomedicine, power, and subjectivity in the 21st century*. Princeton University Press.

Slife, B. D., Reber, J. S., & Richardson, F. C. (2005). *Developing critical thinking about psychology: Hidden assumptions and plausible alternatives*. APA Books.

Sugarman, J. (2015). Neoliberalism and psychological ethics. *Journal of Theoretical and Philosophical Psychology, 35*, 103–116.

Taylor, C. (1989). *Sources of the self: The making of the modern identity*. Cambridge, MA: Harvard University Press.

Taylor, C. (2007). *A secular age*. The Belknap Press.

Teo, T. (2020). Theorizing in psychology: From the critique of a *hyperscience* to conceptualizing subjectivity. *Theory & Psychology, 30*(6), 759–767.

Toulmin, S. (1990). *Cosmopolis: The hidden agenda of modernity*. University of Chicago Press.

1

The Personal Is Political

A Conversation with Jeff Sugarman

Interviewed by Mark Freeman

Mark Freeman and Jeff Sugarman

Introduction

What a privilege and pleasure it was to interview Jeff Sugarman. That's partly because he and I are good friends who have cavorted in numerous locales across the country, from Little Havana in Florida to Austin to Nashville, places where we caught some terrific music, all the way to San Diego, where we had some great feeds with other friends and, on our final day there, found ourselves wandering through the city's famous zoo, marveling at all of our feathered, finned, and furry brothers and sisters doing their animal thing.

It's been like this from the start. In fact, one thing that really stood out to me about Jeff, from the get-go, is that, despite having come from (the wilds of) Saskatchewan, he had much the same sort of self-deprecating humor and sense of irony that I found in many of my (fellow) New York Jewish friends. How was that possible? Wouldn't he be out hunting and trapping? Why did it seem to me that he could have been from Brooklyn or Queens, the kind of guy I might run into at the local deli or bagel place? Was there something about the matzoh or gefilte fish we ate across a distance of thousands of miles (kilometers, sorry) that somehow gave us this brotherly bond, this shared sense of tradition?

Lest you suppose that I will remain in this tongue-in-cheek mode, let me hasten to add that the other reason this interview was such a privilege and pleasure is that I have always had tremendous respect and admiration for Jeff as a scholar and human being. I can't recall when I first came across his work, but it was a long time ago, when he did much of it alongside Jack Martin (e.g., Martin & Sugarman, 1996, 1997, 1999, 2001; Sugarman & Martin, 2004, 2010). Given that the two of them were frequently in cahoots together, I didn't really have a sense of Jeff's distinctive intellectual voice except for

DOI: 10.4324/9781003280033-2

the one I heard in all the restaurants and bars and jazz clubs we went to. That one I came to know quite well, and I found it extraordinarily wide-ranging and intellectually venturesome; unusually attentive to large social, cultural, and political matters; and, not least, permeated by enough sarcasm and wit to let me know that, through it all, he wasn't one to take himself too, too seriously. A wonderful combination, indeed: high intellectual seriousness leavened with an appropriate dollop of droll humility and play.

Eventually, Jeff's own distinctive voice as a scholar would come through too, loud and clear. I am thinking of his innovative work on agency and personhood (e.g., Sugarman, 2006, 2014). I am thinking of his work on historical ontology (e.g., Sugarman, 2009, 2013, 2015a), which was and remains truly groundbreaking and significant. I'm also thinking of his more recent "signature" work on neoliberalism (e.g., Sugarman, 2015b, 2019; Sugarman & Thrift, 2020) – which, I think it's fair to say, helped to inaugurate an entire subfield within theoretical and philosophical psychology and has proved to be immensely important both for expanding the reach of the field and for building bridges to other disciplines and schools of thought: history, sociology, political economy, and more. This work is not only intellectually significant but ethically and morally significant, too. For, this more recent work, along with just about everything else Jeff has done through the years, is animated by deep care for the well-being of others and for the general good.

I'm not sure he's always seen it this way. Years ago, when we would have impassioned late-night exchanges about his work and mine, he tended to rest with the rhetoric of critique; he was there, he in effect said, mainly to disclose, in a Foucault-like manner, extant discourses and framings of selfhood and subjectivity, both within the discipline of psychology and in the wider world. But I always knew that lurking behind the moment of critique was this other moment, the one that told him that there are in fact better, more fully human ways of being in the world than those enshrined in neoliberalism. I hope he doesn't mind my saying so, but if I look across the vast expanse of his work and see where much of it has led, I find him ultimately to be a kind of humanist, a *critical* humanist – by which I mean someone deeply attuned both to those social, cultural, and political currents that run throughout the particularities of time and place and, at the same time, to those features of human reality, human *being*, that are most worthy. You will see this deep attunement in the pages to follow, permeated, as always, by Jeff's sharp intellect and wit.

It's great to be part of this exchange and great to be Jeff's co-conspirator and friend. Maybe we should open a jazz bar someday – call it The Ivory Tower and have it be as intense and free and fun as intellectual life can be when it's not taken too seriously. Jeff, are you in?

Mark Freeman (MF):   Before I proceed to interrogate Jeff, I figured some of you may want to learn just a little bit more about his background and achievements. But first, I have a question. Is your name actually Jeffrey or is it Jeff? We need to know this. And even if it's not Jeffrey, is it okay for us to call you that?

Jeff Sugarman (JS):   Absolutely not. Not even my mother called me Jeffrey.

MF: I had to ask that. In his own words (stolen from his university website), Jeff has stated that his scholarship is concerned with the psychology of personhood, selfhood, and human agency; the socio-political dimensions of psychological development; the influence of psychology on educational institutions and practices; the development of a critical psychology of education; and the application of hermeneutics and historical ontology to psychological inquiry. So, a lot of stuff.

What that description, of course, doesn't say, for obvious reasons, is how excellent this work is, and how outstanding Jeff's contribution to theoretical and philosophical psychology, as well as to the discipline more generally, has been. As for his many articles, chapters, encyclopedia entries, conference proceedings, and so on, suffice it to say that they comprise a really extraordinary range and depth of inquiry.

JS: Why do I feel like I'm being buttered up before the conceptual chainsaw?

MF: No! It might be noted that, alongside Jeff's academic gig at Simon Fraser University, where he's been teaching and, no doubt, corrupting young people's minds since 1998, he's an accomplished keyboard player as well as a fun-loving nature enthusiast who regularly gets together with some of his old friends to plumb the depths of being.

So, this is just my way of noting that, as academically accomplished as Jeff is, he does a bunch of other things too, which I think is a good thing for the likes of us. As a first question, it might be good to ask, what do you see your theoretical and philosophical work in psychology as being most fundamentally about? And how did you come to do it? I'll put it even more pointedly. Why aren't you just a "regular psychologist"? What pushed you into this territory?

JS: I pursued my graduate degrees at Simon Fraser University. As a doctoral student in education, I was compelled to take a couple of courses with all of the other doctoral students in education. As it turned out, I was the only one studying educational psychology in these courses. There were philosophers, sociologists of education, historians of education, curriculum theorists, people studying language arts – a range of things.

Every once in a while, someone would raise issues about psychology and turn to me. "So you're a psychologist. You have instruments and measures. You have a self-esteem instrument. If I score 10 on this thing and you get nine, does that mean I've got more of this stuff than you do? What else can you do this with? Can you do this with love?" "Can you measure everything?" They asked very pointed questions for which I was completely underequipped to respond, having been trained in the canons of psychological critique, which are very narrow and insular.

I made a good friend who was a philosopher of education, who put me on a diet of hermeneutics and other philosophical texts that he was reading. Gradually, I got interested in philosophy, and in conceptual and historical matters with respect to psychology. I also was very fortunate that, at the time I entered doctoral work, Jack Martin returned to the Faculty of Education at Simon Fraser after 15 years at the University of Western Ontario, and I ended up with the consummate mentor whose interests in philosophy and history were blooming at that time. I am deeply grateful for Jack's mentorship.

MF: Well, take a step back. Presumably, at one point, you had to encounter mainstream psychology, with its instruments and its tools and so on. What was your response to that like? This is a kind of strange way to put it: Did you have to learn to be alienated? Or, were you alienated from the start?

JS: I was like most people who went into psychology in the 1970s. It was the great new frontier. I wanted to know more about what it was to be a human being, to be a person, to understand myself and others better, and maybe do some good in the world. But very quickly you find out that psychology programs are not about that. They're about null hypothesis testing and alpha levels. There's a bait-and-switch that happens.

As a naive undergraduate student, I went along with it. But in graduate school in education, people were calling me on the carpet, or calling psychology on the carpet, with the expectation that I was there to defend it. I started to question psychology and look for ways to get back to what I really wanted to know, which was the human condition.

MF: Can you sketch out for us a little bit of the trajectory you've gone through, though? You have such a wide range of interests. I can recall, way back when, seeing words like "metaphysics" in some of the things that you wrote about. Of course, the work in historical ontology has been longstanding. But it would be good to get more of a sense of the storyline, so to speak, that characterizes your work and how that came about.

JS: Much of my early work, that took place over the course of a decade and a half, was coauthored with Jack Martin (e.g., Martin & Sugarman, 1996, 1997, 1999, 2001; Martin et al., 2003, 2010). At that time, we were trying to identify what the proper subject matter of psychology ought to be, which we concluded was personhood, and we tried to develop an account of it. A big problem in psychology is an inherent contradiction between an attempt to explain psychological phenomena using a deterministic philosophy and the assumption of individuals' free will. When you look at the traditional, received view of scientific inquiry as adopted by psychology, it's based on a philosophy of determinism. Determinism asserts that every event has a cause. It follows that if we can stipulate the antecedent determinants of an experience or behavior, then we can predict and control it.

However, if you go to see a psychologist, most psychologists, at least implicitly, hold the belief that people have free will. If individuals don't have free will, if they can't think about their situations and make changes based on their own volition, then what's the point of going to therapy? The same applies for education. What's the point of educating people if they don't have agency?

So, there's this inherent contradiction in psychology. That prompted us to start looking at the phenomena of interest to psychologists, the ways in which they were being studied, and to try to develop what we thought were more viable conceptions of the subject matter of psychology – personhood, selfhood, and human agency – and marshal arguments about how the techniques and methodologies that were being employed by psychologists were inappropriate to that subject matter if strict determinism doesn't hold. We presented an argument for compatibilism, that is, human agency as self-determination.

But that took us into fairly broad, abstract questions of metaphysics, ontology, and epistemology. We did a lot of what I now look back on as abstract work by comparison with what I do now, although it was strongly grounded in what we formulated as a developmental theory of psychologically capable human beings. That's what a lot of philosophy misses – that people develop. And considering the contexts of development is crucial to any adequate understanding of what persons are. We investigated the work of Vygotsky and Mead and other socioculturally oriented developmentalists to try and flesh out this developmental picture that would give us a clearer portrait of the subject matter of psychology, namely, persons.

MF: Say a little bit, if you can, about how we might think about agency and also think about sociocultural context, sociocultural constitution. How do we do those two things at the same time?

JS: I think that human psychology or, more specifically, psychologically capable reflexive human agency is a developmental accomplishment. It has biophysical and sociocultural origins. Once it emerges, individuals' linguistically enabled interpretations become active in anything they do. But, importantly, once it emerges, the psychologically capable reflexive agency responsible for those interpretations can't be reduced back to its sociocultural and biophysical origins. It's a theory of the underdetermination of agentive psychological being by the conditions that provide for its possibility. That's it, in a nutshell.

It's very difficult to make an argument for human agency. Jack's and my argument is an argument by elimination (see Martin et al., 2003). Our strategy is to rule out the possible explanations for human agency that exclude the agent's own self-determining capabilities. Once you rule out that human agency can be reduced entirely to our neurophysiology, or to sociocultural processes as some social constructionists have proposed, or to the contingency of evolutionary drift, and so forth – if you cannot reduce persons down to one of those things solely or in combination – then the only thing left to account for human action and experience is agency or self-determination.

That abstract work became supplanted by increasing recognition of the importance of history and its contingency – of the specific histories of psychological phenomena, or what Danziger (1993b) calls "psychological objects" and the particularity of their formation. Danziger (2003) describes his historical work as biographies of psychological objects. Biography is a nice way of capturing that psychological phenomena have a history that can be told in ways analogously to how you would tell the story of a human life with all its contingency and happenstance. This is the case whether you're giving an account of memory or motivation, as Danziger (1997, 2008) has done, or psychological disorders, in the way Ian Hacking (e.g., 1995a, 1998) has described. The features of human psychology develop in history. They all have particular historical trajectories that are the product of specific constellations of social, cultural, moral, ethical, political, economic, educational, and religious features of their historical contexts, and they bear the marks of their eras. To understand something like memory, or behavior, or social anxiety disorder, or trauma, you have to go back and trace the history of those concepts and the particular ways they developed. I follow in the tradition of Foucault (1984) and Hacking (2002), looking at concepts as archeological sites where layers of meaning and use have to be excavated to see how they have been transformed over time. When you do this kind of work, the contingency and possibility for things to have been otherwise become glaring.

So, over time, my work has become much more concerned with history, a specific kind of history. I've become more focused on the particularities produced by the historical, sociopolitical, and economic contexts in which personhood is shaped. And the term for this kind of historical work, which follows a tradition that descends from Foucault, is "historical ontology" (see Sugarman, 2009, 2015a).

One thing that I would say is that you have to understand the difference between influence and constitution. Most psychologists will admit that contexts influence human psychology. But to say that context constitutes human psychology is a much bolder claim. It's to say that the stuff of which our psychology consists is social, cultural, moral, ethical, political, economic, and so forth – that these things actually constitute the forms human psychology takes. It's not as if our psychology is fully formed and these are merely external influences – that context can just be another variable in the regression equation. It's a much more profound claim about the nature of human psychology.

MF: A quick question about constitution: How would you differentiate that from construction? I mean, I know, generally, you probably wouldn't consider yourself a constructionist. You're more comfortable using constitution. What is it that separates those in some meaningful way, in your estimation?

JS: Well, again, I want to defend that there is a distinctive subject matter of psychology. The big problem for psychology is that, if you can reduce reflexive agency to a cultural artifact – as many social constructionists have – and everything is just socially constructed, then there really is no psychology, and we might as well just close the door on the discipline, become cultural theorists, and forget about psychology. The same holds for neurophysiological or evolutionary or computational reductions.

I want to retain a space for a sui generis psychological subject matter. And I think that personhood and all that it comprises – agency, selfhood, identity, and so forth – are genuinely psychological phenomena that comprise a distinctive psychological subject matter irreducible to these other things. So, I suppose that I want to use constitution rather than construction to separate myself from certain folks that just see us as manifestations of our cultures and nothing more.

MF: Let me ask you one other question having to do with history and particularity. You said you became fascinated with the history of the concepts that psychology often uses. But I know you're also interested in the way in which those concepts themselves sometimes become constitutive of certain aspects of psychological function – as in the looping effect. Can you say a bit about your interest in that?

JS: Part of the shift in my thought was a consequence of encountering Ian Hacking's work (e.g., Hacking, 2002). Hacking is a Canadian philosopher who's done extraordinary historical studies. The idea of the looping effect comes from him (Hacking, 1995a, 1995b). Here's how the looping effect works. There's a psychological description in use. We appropriate it. We start to understand our lives in the terms that it sets. This gives rise to the possibility of new actions and experiences that, in turn, promote new descriptions that then get appropriated. This prompts new possibilities for action and experience that lead to new descriptions, and so on. This kind of recursive looping effect is continuously generating new descriptions and possibilities for human action and experience.

Because we live our lives through psychological descriptions and they provide possibilities and constraints for the kinds of persons that we can be and become – how we conceive of ourselves – they are absolutely integral to our psychological self-understanding and any attempt to explain it (see Sugarman, 2009, 2015a).

MF: Great. Thank you. So, I think we can begin to address the question that was supposed to be the first one, which is, How has psychology as a discipline, how has the field, responded to your work? I mean, you became a theoretical and philosophical psychologist. That's not the traditional path. Has it been a challenge, uphill? How have you navigated your career and the kind of challenges and demands that careers pose?

JS: Well, the first thing is, never tell anybody at a party that you're a theoretical psychologist. All kidding aside, I've been deeply gratified by the ways in which my colleagues in theoretical and philosophical psychology have taken up my work, both affirming it and being highly critical of it, which is terrific for a scholar. As you know, the greatest gift your colleagues can give you is the most trenchant critique of your work that they can muster. That's moved me forward in all kinds of ways.

Interestingly, my work has been taken up in applied disciplines. So, counseling psychologists read it, people in nursing, in social work, in education, in business. I recently had correspondence with an eye surgeon who thinks that my work on neoliberalism applies to his field. There's been a handful of philosophers who have read it. Yet my work hasn't managed to penetrate the psychological mainstream. I think there's a number of reasons for that.

MF: Have there been impediments to you doing your work? You're in a place that has accepted you and your work. Have there been trials and tribulations along the way for you trying to stay your own course, maintain your own ideals, and so forth? Or has it been basically okay?

JS: Sometimes I wonder if there's something wrong with me that I have to do what I have to do. You know, I just can't do it any other way. These questions arise for you, and you feel driven to pursue them. Fortunately, I have a job that allows me to do that. But when I think of the field generally, there's impediments like naïve naturalism. Kurt Danziger (1993a) has a lovely allegory to describe it. He calls it the "Sleeping Beauty model of science," the belief that everything psychological is there fully formed in nature, like natural objects. They're all waiting for the prince researcher to come along and awaken them with the magic kiss of his research. It's the assumption that the psychological furniture is fixed. But psychological forms and functions are not static. As products of history and discourse, they shift and mutate with the social and cultural resources within which they're constituted as those resources also shift and mutate. I think that's one problem. Arguing that history and its contingency are vital to psychological constitution runs counter to the naïve naturalism of mainstream psychology that psychologists believe is necessary for the discipline to attain the status of a science.

I think one of the deepest prejudices in contemporary mainstream psychology is its ahistoricism. When psychologists tell the story of the discipline's history, it's either what Nikolas Rose (1996) calls "sanctioned history" or "lapsed history." It's either a series of triumphs by which we have arrived at the pinnacle of psychological epistemology and explanation or it's a history of errors that were gradually overcome by triumphs.

There is a second form of historiography that derives from the neo-Marxist critical theorists – that history is full of oppression and that once we uncover these oppressive structures and become aware of them and their effects, there's the possibility of emancipation. I tend to see history through a third, more Foucauldian lens by looking at productive possibilities within historical circumstances. This is not to deny that historical oppression has taken place but instead to focus on how certain conditions of possibility have enabled the emergence of psychological capacities.

So, I think psychology's bias against history has been a problem. There is another problem. I think "psychologism," a term that I have borrowed to describe a style of thinking or style of reasoning, is a problematic assumption on which most mainstream psychology operates (Sugarman, 2017). The term "style of reasoning" originates with a historian of science named Alistair Crombie. Crombie (1994) identified a variety of "styles of thinking." For those of you with a lot of time on your hands, he wrote a book called *Styles of Thinking in the European Tradition* that's three volumes and about 2,500 pages. I've read every page. No, I haven't. Crombie charts, in magnificent detail, the history of scientific thought, from the ancient Greeks to the 19th century, when it really exploded.

His thesis is that, over that period of time, scientific thought congealed into six dominant styles of thinking: mathematical postulation, experimentation, hypothetical modeling, taxonomy, probabilistic thinking, and historical derivation. Ian Hacking picked up the idea. But Hacking (2002) doesn't like the phrase "styles of thinking" because he thinks it puts things too much inside the head, when scientific practice is very much a public activity. So, Hacking calls them "styles of reasoning" to draw attention to the ways in which there's demonstrations, there's argument, there's consensus, and so forth – the public practices by which science is conducted.

I've tried to make the case that psychology has invented another style of reasoning that I call "psychologism." Psychologism, as a style of reasoning, works like this. You watch fully functioning, integral people acting in the world. Then you notice that they're doing something, some feature of their action. You say, "They seem to be monitoring what they're doing." And you give it a name. You call it "self-regulation." Then you stick it inside the head of the individual. You attribute causal efficacy to it. You say that the reason why the person seems to be monitoring what they're doing is because of this thing in their head called self-regulation. Or, her opinion of herself is caused by her self-esteem. Or, her degree of confidence is caused by her self-efficacy. Or, the reason she doesn't try to do things is caused by her fear of failure. Or, her conception of herself is caused by her self-concept, and so on, conveniently forgetting that something can't be the cause of itself. Then, you invent an instrument that supposedly taps this feature, usually composed of questionnaire items, sidestepping entirely the question of whether what you're measuring actually exists. But, nevertheless, you proceed to make claims about it, its structure and function, about how it's correlated with other supposed psychological entities. You advise people to pay attention to it and develop technologies to intervene with it. And write it up and publish it, which adds to its seeming legitimacy.

I read recently that psychologists have discovered a new personality trait called "need for drama" – the degree to which you feel the need to create drama in your life or insert yourself into it. Of course, there's a scale that measures how much of this you've got. There are all kinds of pseudo-empirical claims, like people with a high need for drama are prone to gossiping. They're more likely to live chaotic lives. They have a tendency to inflict contrived crises on others. Notice how none of these claims are at all empirical. They're true by logical necessity. Beyond the question of whether such a thing as need for drama exists, what would it mean if the researchers found that people with a high need for drama were less prone to gossiping or less likely to live chaotic lives or less likely to inflict invented crises on others? The findings are analytically entailed by what's meant in ordinary language by a need for drama. Psychology is full of this kind of pseudo-empiricism.

Individuals are more likely to be surprised when an alternative outcome is expected. We tend to repeat the things we find pleasurable. Individuals who have a history of repeated failure are less likely to attempt things. Those who are predisposed to taking risks are more prone to practicing unsafe sex. Children who have yet to develop the idea of one-to-one identity can't determine if two different arrangements of the same number of objects are equivalent. All of these are published claims made by psychological researchers who have said that they are evidenced by empirical studies. It's nonsense on stilts. They're not empirical claims. They're logical claims. Not one of those studies ever needed to be conducted. Pseudo-empiricism is a byproduct of psychologism.

There's more to psychologism than this. But psychologism as a style of reasoning has been in place in psychology for a very long time. When you look at the study of attitudes or personality or the study of self-regulation, they all take this kind of form as a style of reasoning. A key feature of styles of reasoning is that they're self-authenticating. By this I mean that they determine the kinds of propositions that are going to be counted as true. Styles of reasoning determine the criteria for what counts as a legitimate question and the kinds of answers considered appropriate. By being self-authenticating, they create this insular way of maintaining their authority.

If you go back in history and look at Wundt's "method of introspection," belief in an inner private mental theater validated the logic of a methodology of introspection, and introspection validated the idea of an inner private mental theater. The self-authenticating character of psychologism creates these symbiotic relationships between methodology and subject matter. Moreover, because of the self-authenticating features of psychologism – its insularity and circularity – in order to critique it, and this holds for any style of reasoning, you have to step outside of it and gain perspective from another vantage. You can't critique a style of reasoning from within that style of reasoning. That's why history and philosophy are useful to psychology. But mainstream psychology is averse to history and philosophy, and to critique that would shake its foundations.

I'll mention one other impediment to the kind of work I do. Contemporary psychology, and particularly the American Psychological Association, which is supposed to represent us and our interests, is determined to have psychology recognized as a Science Technology Engineering and Math (STEM) discipline. I recently came across a report published by the American Psychological Association (2010), the rationale for which was to provide a basis for establishing psychology as a STEM discipline. The report concludes by saying that psychology is a STEM discipline by virtue of its technological and scientific innovations.
So, when you look at that mission to establish psychology as a STEM discipline, the kind of work that I do that's historical or philosophical and the kind of work that you do in narrative studies, what we do is seen by the APA as an obstacle to validating psychology as a bona fide STEM discipline. There's institutional antipathy towards what we do. I think this is another impediment to getting my work recognized, or maybe my work just isn't that good. I don't know.

MF: It's ironic; the kind of self-fulfilling dimension that you talk about is so axiomatic that other views are seen as impositions, right? So, people who hold those views aren't aware of holding them. It makes the whole institutional structure very, very recalcitrant in a way. For years, I've tried to imagine ways of breaking into that, but I'm less inclined to try to do it at this point. But we'll talk about the APA and how much we should care about all of that stuff a little bit later.

Let's shift back to some of the work that you've done for which you've become widely known, on the neoliberal self, the entrepreneurial self, and so on. How did that work emerge as part of this trajectory that you've been describing?

JS: I teach an upper-level undergraduate course called "Self, Psychology, and Education" that I inherited from Jack Martin. The course is organized around two themes, the first of which is that education is about people-making. Societies require people who not only know certain kinds of things but who also are capable of being certain kinds of persons. Education is not simply about knowing. It's about being. If you go back in history, societies have always required certain kinds of people. And education produces people of those kinds. For example, if you pick up any historical text on Sparta as it existed in the seventh century BCE, it will have nothing nice to say about the place. Sparta is described as brutal. It was an armed camp. It was politically stagnant, economically stagnant, and culturally stagnant. But they produced tremendous warriors. This is what their education system was designed to do. Every Spartan male started his military training at age 7. He was taught combat, how to build strength, survival skills, the virtues of courage and self-denial, the endurance of pain, and so forth. After 13 years of military training, at the age of 20, he became a full-fledged Spartan warrior. Their whole education system was designed around the preparation of warriors because those were the kinds of persons their society valued and wanted to produce.

If you went down the road to Athens, they wanted a different kind of person. They wanted citizens who knew about art and literature, who could exercise their political obligations responsibly, who could debate, and who were cultured. Those were the kinds of citizens their methods of education were designed to produce. Early American psychologists like Dewey and Thorndike were intimately involved in shifting education in America from the English model, which was designed to create a cultural elite, to one that would produce a nonclassed, democratic citizenry. You can consider any culture or society, and when you look at their education system, it reflects the values of the society and the kinds of people the society wants or needs to produce. Education is about people-making.

The second theme that I draw out in the course is that psychology has infiltrated education such that the kinds of people we believe our education systems ought to produce are psychologized in a variety of ways. Up to the 1920s, people sent their kids to school to learn how to read and write, do math, and become responsible citizens. Now, we not only want them to know these things, but we also want them to be self-regulated learners. We want them to have high self-esteem and high self-efficacy and strong self-concepts, to be self-expressive, to be creative, to be intrinsically motivated, and so forth. It was the dawning of organized psychology in the early 20th century, and the march of psychology into the schools, that placed a whole new set of demands on teachers and students that are, in some ways, in conflict with the traditional aims of education. These are the two themes around which the course is structured. However, there is much required to argue and connect these two themes. I don't want to take the time to go into all of it. But I need to make one point to address your question. If you want to make people of certain kinds, you target their selves – what they think they are – and notions of self are intimately tied to our understanding of fulfillment.

One of the things I get students to do is to read a series of pieces that tie subjectivity and selfhood to our notions of fulfillment. After reading these pieces, I ask students: "What would make for a fulfilling life for you?" About five years ago, the first response I started to hear was, "Money." Now, if you would have gone back a previous decade and somebody would have said that in the class, there would have been a collective sigh of disbelief and horror. But over the course of three or four years, this response has been increasingly affirmed by other students in the class.

So, you ask the next logical question: "Well, what would you do with the money?" The kinds of responses that you get are disheartingly shallow. You don't hear anything like, "I'd like to start a school in Afghanistan" or "I'd like to develop effective interventions for autistic children" or "I'd like to build community gardens in impoverished neighborhoods." It's, "I wouldn't have to work. You know, I'd have a car." I started to understand just how much my students are not at all like me. The biggest mistake that I can make in teaching is to walk into a classroom and think, "These people are just like me." They are very different from me.

I came across Phil Cushman's and his former student Peter Gilford's (2000) insightful piece in the now defunct journal, *The Psychohistory Review*, in which they put their fingers on the pulse of American society and wrote about an emerging kind of selfhood in 2000. It was a prescient article. I also read Richard Sennett's (1998) interesting little book called *The Corrosion of Character*, in which he talks about the ways in which the contemporary sociopolitical and economic climate was reconstituting people's understanding of themselves, particularly in view of the context of globalization and the effects it was having on employment. These writings really got me thinking about who my students were and what made them different from me.

As I got further into readings on related topics, I began to realize the importance of politics and economics to psychology. Politics is concerned with the exercise of power and control over people. It also is concerned with the ways in which our subjectivity is constituted by that power and control, and this happens within certain kinds of economic arrangements. Again, if you want to make certain kinds of persons, you target their conceptions of self (Cushman, 1990). I started focusing my reading on political theory and economic theory, for which I was, admittedly, completely underequipped.

But because I'm a psychologist and I'm interested in personhood, I started to appreciate just how much the personal is political. But when I use the term "personal," I'm talking about personhood, that personhood is inescapably political. You cannot talk about the psychology of personhood without addressing political and economic issues and their formative influence on our psychological constitution. This was what led me to neoliberalism.

MF: Political issues, ethical issues, moral issues, and so on. Let me ask a question that you and I have talked about before, but I want to get your latest read on these issues. You've not only been interested in the emergence of, or the description of, the neoliberal self, you've been critical of it as well. As I've suggested to you before, it seems to me that in order to be able to offer the kind of critique that you offer, you've got to be working with some more ideal conception of things, perhaps some vision of the good or at least the better. Can you say what animates your critique? Is it a vision of human nature? Is it an ethical vision? In other words, what is the foundation, so to speak, that allows you to say, "This is really not an optimal form of being human. It's a somewhat corrupted form."

I don't know if you would use those words. Maybe I'm overreading what you're doing. But, what's the ground of your critique?

JS: When I talk about neoliberalism to audiences of our age – folks in their 60s – they nod and immediately get it. But when I talk to younger audiences, they think I'm criticizing them and that I'm elevating the merits of my generation. Consequently, I have to be quite careful. I take my lead from Foucault. I'm looking at the productive possibilities, not just critique. But there is critique there. I worry about the future. I'll get to that in a moment. Foucault wrote an insightful paper written in 1984 called "What Is Enlightenment?" He borrowed the title from a piece published 300 years earlier by Immanuel Kant with the same title.

Kant was solicited by a magazine in Germany to write a piece for them – the English translation of the title of the magazine is *The Berlin Monthly*. They had this marvelous idea of going around to the famous minds of the time and asking them to write about what it's like to be living now. What's it like to be living in the Enlightenment? Kant writes this essay on what it's like to be a citizen of the Enlightenment. What he says is that the motto of the Enlightenment is to use your own reason, that people in the Enlightenment had stopped blindly accepting authority and started thinking for themselves.

But another thing that Kant does is that he says this is what differentiates his present from the past. Kant differs from his contemporaries in that he uses the past as a point of contrast with which to interpret the present. Other commentators had not done this. They interpreted the present as portending the future. Foucault picks up on this and notes how remarkable it is that, for the first time, somebody uses the past to critique the present. This historical strategy became emblematic of Foucault's work. I suppose I'm involved in the same kind of method of critique of the present. But it's not simply critique. It's critique intended to open up new possibilities.

As you know, Kant was interested in uncovering the transcendental conditions of human thought and experience. Foucault was interested in which of these conditions are dispensable, which of them are not necessarily transcendental but could be subject to change. By doing Foucauldian critique, it opens up the possibility to think that you might be otherwise – persons and subjectivities of different sorts with different psychological features – if the sociopolitical institutions within which we're constituted are otherwise. This is connected to what I think is a major problem in psychology. Psychologists have mistakenly been fixing features of persons to an assumed essential human nature rather than to the institutions within which we become persons.

So, yes, I think that people can read me as being highly critical. But I think that it's in the service of trying to open the door, to create the room to think about other possibilities.

MF: Let me push just a little. I would still imagine that there are some possibilities that you'd be more on board with than others.

JS: Absolutely.

MF: So, if we were to just ask, in the most basic way, what's the problem, so to speak, with the entrepreneurial self, how would you respond to that? And what else might we be? What possibility might we embrace that would somehow liberate us from the kind of fixity, the kind of captivity, in a certain sense, that you've described many of us as being caught in?

JS: I think to understand the entrepreneurial, neoliberal self, again, you have to understand the political context (see Sugarman, 2015b). Foucault's concept of governmentality is very useful here. Governmentality refers to the processes and functions of sociopolitical institutions that regulate our attitudes and our conduct. With respect to the neoliberal self, two of the most important features of neoliberal governance are market rationality and the provision of choice. Neoliberal philosophy attempts to impose market rationality on every feature of human existence, every human endeavor, including our most intimate relationships.

Neoliberalism is not a theory that tries to describe the way things are. It's a theory or a model that's being imposed on the world. In neoliberalism, the function of the market is not to cater to the wants and needs of individuals. It's, conversely, to compel individuals to be the kinds of persons who function in a way that the market requires. These are individuals who take up the values of market rationality. The consequences of elevating market rationality and neoliberal policies that put profit above all else and allow corporate capital to roam the world and enslave workers, are glaring. We see rampant poverty. We see increasing income disparity. There's rapid depletion of resources, irreparable damage to the biosphere, the destruction of democratic institutions, value framed instrumentally in terms of assets and liabilities. I don't see these consequences as the price of progress. They're symptoms of decline.

The second feature has to do with choice. Choice is neoliberalism's answer to the question of governmentality. How do you control people politically for whom freedom is a highly valued and essential feature of who and what they think they are? Neoliberalism solves this by harnessing choice as a means of control. It creates a field of action and experience through which people are channeled so that they have an experience of their freedom by making choices, even though, in actuality, it's choice that is highly constrained. How is our freedom enacted? Well, we can buy this product or we can buy that product. Our choice is controlled by channeling it through consumerism. That's part of it.

We all think that when we have more choice, we have more freedom. But the way choice is controlled and constrained is often overlooked. For example, there's an endless variety of credit cards that you can get, but try and do something without a credit card. Try and come to this conference without a credit card. Try to book a hotel. Try to book a flight. You need a credit card. The choices are restricted.

Another tactic of neoliberalism is to reduce government welfarist programs. This transfers the burden of risk from the state to individuals. If you go back to the late 19th century, the poor depended on charity. Government realized that private charity was not going to cut it. So, all kinds of social programs were implemented. But in the 1970s, with Reaganomics and Thatcherism, you had the beginnings of the reduction of the social welfare state. The services and protections provided by state-run social programs have gradually been curtailed, and responsibility for individuals' welfare is being placed onto the individuals themselves. There is the privatization of services and user-pay structures. So, matters of healthcare, matters of the education of children, matters of dignity in old age have now become individual responsibility, with the focus not only on choice but also self-reliance.

If you don't have enough money to send your kid to college, or you don't have adequate health insurance, or you don't have enough money to retire, whose responsibility is it? It's yours and yours alone. Many of the choices with which we're faced now were choices we would not have been faced with 30–40 years ago, and we are all expected to embrace choice and risk with an entrepreneurial spirit. The constitution of the neoliberal self is a product of sociopolitical and economic conditions. It has changed certain characteristics of people. You're now expected not only to be self-reliant, flexible, mobile – light on your feet, good at "multi-skilling," willing to take risks. But if you're going to be competitive and successful, you need to be confident, bold, exuberant, self-promoting. You have to be out there networking with your antennae tuned to opportunity.

What happened to shyness and humility? Shyness and humility became pathologies. You used to be shy; now you have social anxiety disorder. You have humility? You better go see a clinician, right? Neoliberalism is reconstituting what we think it is to be a person.

With respect to what might liberate us, or alternatives, I'm a big believer in liberal deliberative democracies. In order to be a citizen in a deliberative democracy, you need not only to know things but also to possess certain virtues. You need civility. You need to be tolerant. You need to have respect for the truth. You need to be able to engage with others respectfully. You need to be open-minded. You need to be articulate enough to express your beliefs and courageous enough to stand behind them. And, when called for, you need to be able to subordinate your interests or desires to the collective good. But, how and where do we cultivate these virtues to create a democratic citizenry? Don't look to psychology. Psychology is concerned with the enhancement and empowerment of individuals. The implicit assumption held by psychologists is that stronger, more capable individuals make for a better society. The healthy society is an aggregate of efficacious individuals. But collective interests are not necessarily served by individual interests. Often, interests conflict and, in a liberal deliberative democracy, sometimes individuals need to put the interests of others above their own. This requires civic virtue, and psychology doesn't promote civic virtue. It promotes the strengthening of the individual and their ability to pursue their self-interest. Psychology might contribute to bolstering individuals' self-regulation, their self-esteem and self-efficacy, mindfulness, and so forth. This might help me pursue my self-interests more successfully. To take an extreme example, what if I want to be an ax murderer? Psychology will help me to be a more self-regulated, efficacious, happy, mindful ax murderer. But, because of its focus on individuals and its attempt to remain neutral with respect to individuals' interests and values, I don't see psychology as much help at the level of political change. Education, particularly public education, has a broader mandate than psychology, which is to prepare people who have a sense of collective responsibility and civic virtue, who can contribute to the collectivity in ways that are concerned with more than just personal self-interest. I put my faith in education.

One of the other big influences in my life, that I didn't mention, was becoming a parent. I was very cynical before becoming a parent. Once I became a parent, I realized that cynicism is a luxury of the childless. Once you have a child, you need to have some hope. I started to think more about my role as a professor of education. I'm in the hope business. I have a responsibility to be hopeful. And I think that if we are to have hope for the future – for political progress – education is the place to invest your hope.

What makes me hopeful in addressing the neoliberal condition and the neoliberal self in my course is that when I find that I am convincing and compelling to students, and they become aware of what they are and their condition – how they see themselves and their lives in a broader context – interesting things happen. When asked about my philosophy of teaching, I say that I try getting students to think outside the box. It's a terrible cliché. But to think outside the box, you first of all have to realize that you're in one. I try to show students the ways in which our sociopolitical and economic context creates a box that constrains their thinking in all kinds of ways. Then, once you can start to see the contours of the box, and the contingency of these contours, that opens up some room for seeing things differently and maybe being otherwise. Perhaps, at the end of this particular class I teach, if I asked again, "What's your conception of fulfillment?" it won't simply be money. It would be something more profound than that.

MF: I have a few more questions. I wanted to shift more towards the discipline. Viewed within the context of the neoliberal, neocapitalist world order, what would the field of psychology need to do to change?

JS: Wow, okay. As I've said, psychologists need to pay attention to history, to language, to culture, to society, to economics, to education, and so forth, which would demand a graduate education that would look very different from the kind that most graduate schools in psychology purvey. So, that's the first thing. You're talking about righting the ship, so to speak?

MF: Yeah. In other words, what the discipline of psychology is, and what the neoliberal self is, those two are intimately related in some way. And we can see that in particular institutions, not only in the United States but also, as Sunil Bhatia has pointed out in some of his work, in India. And we can see it in Latin America, and so on. In a sense, psychology is an accomplice or, even more, it's a *creator* of certain forms of subjectivity and selfhood that need to be opened up in some way. But, of course, the APA is a monolith. The discipline is a monolith. So, yeah, it's a righting-the-ship question. I know there's no simple answer. But where should we throw our energy?

JS: Psychologists need to understand the history of their discipline and the functions it's served. Once this is understood, we can see our role, and it is a role that ought to be questioned. Donald Napoli published a book in 1981 entitled *The Architects of Adjustment* in which he traced the history of the professionalization of psychology. The historical and current aim of psychology is largely promoting conformity and adjustment to social norms. Psychology got a foothold in North America through education. The early role of psychologists in education is largely connected to Fordism. Henry Ford built his factory in 1913, and the model of production he implemented dramatically changed the way in which we made things. What steered his model was the goal of increasing efficiency and production, and his model was seen as the way to improve education as well as the operation of many institutions. It was a way to scale up people-making. There was a new echelon of educational administrators created and employed to align schools with Henry Ford's factory model.

These administrators wanted a scientific rationale for instituting and defending the changes they wanted to implement to make schools more efficient. Psychologists stepped up and said, "We can help you do that." As the self-declared experts in measuring human characteristics and functions, they designed instruments – notably, intelligence tests – with which to measure people. With these measurements, they created norms. But the norms they created were simply reflective of how the institutions function. So, when people do what they are supposed to be doing according to the functions for which the institution is designed, then they're normal. When people act in ways that make the institution not function well, they're abnormal or deviant. And now we have a rationale for instituting procedures to administer them. This is how psychology got its start in America and, soon, their expertise was applied to business, the military, and other governmental institutions. This stimulated the invention of new tests with which to administer to people – personality tests, aptitude tests, vocational tests, and so forth. All of this testing validated institutional norms that became standards of behavior, and it created classifications with which to administer people – normal, disordered, educable, employable, legally responsible, fit for command, and so forth.

To continue the story, in the 1960s, people used to talk about maladjustment. Why is this person a criminal? They're maladjusted. Why is this kid not doing well in school? He's maladjusted. Why are African Americans poor and committing crimes? It's because they're maladjusted. Many psychologists were making those kinds of claims in the 1960s.

In 1967, the American Psychological Association invited Martin Luther King to give an address to the assembled. King (1968) admonished the American Psychological Association attendees for blaming African Americans for their poverty and for their difficulties and calling them maladjusted. King said, "There are some things concerning which we must always be maladjusted if we are to be people of good will. We must never adjust ourselves to racial discrimination" (pp. 10–11). After what amounts to a potent critique of psychology for its racism, he calls for establishing an International Society for the Creatively Maladjusted. It's a terrific talk. I encourage folks to go back and look at it.

But the fact of the matter is that psychology is a very conservative discipline. We are the architects of adjustment. Psychology functions as what Nikolas Rose (Miller & Rose, 2008) calls "government at a distance." It is not a government institution, but it is complicit with maintaining the sociopolitical and economic status quo. By telling people that your problems are your responsibility, a consequence of your psychological states or characteristics or your feelings, rather than looking at the conditions of broader sociopolitical and economic contexts, as Sunil Bhatia so beautifully illustrated today in his talk, psychologists are perpetuating the real source of many problems by ascribing them to individuals. They are perpetuating the problem by making people think, "I'm failing because I'm not sufficiently self-reliant. I'm not sufficiently strong psychologically. I don't have enough self-regulation. I don't have enough self-esteem. I'm not sufficiently self-efficacious. I'm not creative or self-expressive enough," and so forth. This situates the problem in the wrong place – in the individual rather than in the institutional structures that are creating a hypercompetitive world and a philosophy of being that elevates individualism far above collective interests and civic virtue.

Again, I think that psychologists need to look closely at the kinds of explanations that they offer people. When do you go into a psychologist's office, tell them about your problems, and they talk to you about sociopolitical and economic matters that situate your problem in a much broader context of tensions you are forced to navigate that are not of your own choosing? I know that psychologists deal with individuals' suffering, as my colleague Roger Frie has pointed out to me. Suffering is real and phenomenologically individual. But, at the same time, the cause of that suffering and the way it ought to be addressed may not be individual.

MF: Sure. So, as a kind of corollary to that, we're to begin to look more in a truly social direction. Psychology would also need to look more, on the other side, at matters of social justice. It would need to look at matters of gross inequality, and wealth, and any one of a number of other things. Is that also a direction that you're interested in pursuing? Where are you in terms of addressing some of the large problems that you're talking about? Where does psychology belong in that set of issues?

JS: Social justice seems to be on everybody's lips these days. It's become this soothing mood music with which you can lull yourself into good feelings. But if you ask psychologists, "What is social justice?" you don't typically get a very clear answer. I've recently been doing a historical ontology of social justice. Where did the term originate? There's a very long story to this. You have the French and the American Revolutions in the 18th century, where people start to become concerned about inequality, particularly the distribution of wealth. But social justice, as a term, doesn't appear until the middle of the 19th century. And it comes from a very unlikely source – a Jesuit philosopher. His name is Luigi Taparelli, and his coining of the term took place against the Italian Risorgimento, which is the political and intellectual movement that was responsible for the unification of Italy. Taparelli was distressed by the oppressive working conditions endured by a great many. But even more, he was concerned with the despotic regimes of the Napoleonic and Austrian empires that were trying to centralize governmental control over people.

Taparelli made the argument that the smaller affiliations that bind people – family, church, guilds, and so forth, the relations through which they live out their daily lives – are part of natural law. They are divinely given. Disrupting them subverts divine intention. Therefore, there should not be intrusion into these affiliations by larger political powers. At the same time, Taparelli wanted to maintain the authority of the Catholic church. So, his vision of social justice, and his purpose in introducing the term, was to separate social justice from legal justice, to protect the integrity of communities, and to sustain the authority of the church. There is no mention of redistribution of wealth in Taparelli's conception of social justice.

After Taparelli, another Catholic philosopher, named Antonio Rosmini, who was strongly influenced by John Locke and Adam Smith, claimed that God has provided for people to acquire property. The possession of property is divine will, and the acquisition and transfer of property should be a private affair in which the state has no business. Rosmini defended not only that there should be no distributive justice, but also that the redistribution of wealth is unjust – benevolence by extortion. In fact, he believed franchise should be proportional to the amount of wealth that you have. People with the most property should have the most franchise. If you don't have any money, then you shouldn't have any vote whatsoever because Rosmini was concerned about the poor abusing power to appropriate stuff from wealthy folks that they have no God-given right to. This was his vision of social justice.

Then, there are others. You have the Victorian Christian socialists, who said, "We should distribute resources to the poor because it's in keeping with tenets of Christianity like compassion, charity, and so forth." Their notion of social justice has a heavily Protestant connotation.

MF: What's yours? Or is that an unfair question? I mean, it's a wonderful intellectual project to be able to chart this trajectory and to understand the remarkable variation in meanings. But I want to get a sense of where you are, also, in terms of where your commitments might be at this point, because whatever conception we're talking about, there's still suffering, and gross inequality, and so on. And so?

JS: I think, well, without telling the whole story, it's going to seem a little bit out of place. But just let me mention three more views of social justice, so I can contextualize it a bit more. Let's jump to the 1970s. There are two Harvard philosophers who set the stage. There's John Rawls's notion of distributive justice. Rawls decides that social justice is entitlement to certain basic rights. And also, that you should only create conditions of inequality in those rights when they benefit the least advantaged. For Rawls, there are grounds for distributive justice.

There's another Harvard philosopher, Robert Nozick, whose conception of social justice reiterates Rosmini's idea that the state has no business in the acquisition and transfer of property and that you have a just society when the state doesn't interfere in the dealings of individuals. Then, in 1980, you have a feminist named Iris Marion Young at the University of Chicago who insisted that social justice is the mitigation of dominance and oppression.

We need to understand that there are conflicting ideas regarding what social justice is. My initial impulse is that we need to go back to the 17th century and concerns about distribution of wealth, particularly as it has taken shape in the neoliberal context and, as Sunil pointed out today, about the great disparity in economic resources. The exploitative working conditions of many in the Third World are the product of a consumptive Western culture that relies on cheap labor because we're unwilling to pay the true cost of goods and neo-liberal economic policies that, as I've mentioned, allow corporations to have free reign and to subjugate workers. The demand for cheap labor and the desperation of the poor results in masses willing to work for next to nothing in conditions that are nothing less than obscene – a situation likely to get much worse by advances in technology and automation that will make hundreds of millions of jobs redundant. Anyone who's traveled to places like India and Africa can describe degrees of poverty that are arresting in their severity. Half of the world's population lives on less than $5.50 a day (World Bank, 2018). Income inequality is at staggering proportions. One percent of the population controls 44.8% of the world's wealth (Matthews, 2019). I think we have to talk about redistribution. Of course, nobody wants to talk about paying more taxes. I also think Martha Nussbaum's (2011) capabilities approach to social justice has a lot of merit. But this is a longer conversation.

MF: We'd better move towards a close. Final question on my end: What's your latest project? I know you are doing the social justice thing. Do you have an image of what the next one might be?

JS: The topics in which I'm interested these days are the ways contemporary psychological life is being changed by sociopolitical and economic structures. I just recently published a paper with one of my former graduate students, Erin Thrift, on the ways in which our conception of time has been transformed dramatically by neoliberalism (Sugarman & Thrift, 2020).

If you go back to the 1970s and you asked people, "What's your biggest problem?" many would have said, "My life doesn't have meaning. I'm going off to a happiness camp for the weekend to learn how to find fulfillment." Or, "I'm going to go talk to my psychotherapist." Or, "I'm going to try LSD to expand my mind." Or, "I'm reading Viktor Frankl." If you ask people now, "What's your biggest problem?" they'll say, "I don't have any time." Shifts like this can prove telling. I immersed myself in readings about time – the sociology of time, the phenomenology of time, the economics of time, among others – to look at how the sociopolitical context, particularly aided by technology, has shaped our situation such that there is an explanation for why we are experiencing a time famine.

In answer to your question, I'm interested in how our psychology, our subjectivity, our personhood are being shaped by neoliberalism, the specific kinds of problems it presents for contemporary life, and in looking to possible alternatives to our current situation.

MF: Thank you.

References

American Psychological Association. (2010). *Psychology as a core science, technology, engineering, and mathematics (STEM) discipline: Report of the American Psychological Association 2009 Presidential Task Force on the future of psychology as a STEM discipline.* Author.

Crombie, A. C. (1994). *Styles of scientific thinking in the European tradition: The history of argument and explanation especially in the mathematical and biomedical sciences and arts.* Gerald Duckworth & Co.

Cushman, P. (1990). Why the self is empty: Toward a historically situated psychology. *American Psychologist, 45*, 599–611.

Cushman, P., & Gilford, P. (2000). From emptiness to multiplicity: The self at the year 2000. *The Psychohistory Review, 27*, 15–31.

Danziger, K. (1993a). *Constructing the subject: Historical origins of psychological research.* Cambridge University Press.

Danziger, K. (1993b). Psychological objects, practice, and history. In H. V. Rappard, P. J. Van Strien, L. P. Mos, & W. J. Baker (Eds.), *Annals of theoretical psychology* (Vol. 8) (pp. 15–47). Springer.

Danziger, K. (1997). *Naming the mind: How psychology found its language.* SAGE.

Danziger, K. (2003). Where theory, history and philosophy meet: The biography of psychological objects. In D. B. Hill & M. J. Kral (Eds.), *About psychology: Essays at the crossroads of history, theory and philosophy* (pp. 10–33). SUNY Press.

Danziger, K. (2008). *Marking the mind: A history of memory.* Cambridge University Press.

Foucault, M. (1984). What is enlightenment? In P. Rabinow (Ed.), *The Foucault reader* (pp. 32–50). Pantheon.

Hacking, I. (1995a). *Rewriting the soul: Multiple personality and the sciences of memory.* Princeton University Press.

Hacking, I. (1995b). The looping effects of human kinds. In D. Sperber, D. Premack, & J. Premack (Eds.), *Causal cognition: A multi-disciplinary approach* (pp. 351–382). Clarendon Press.

Hacking, I. (1998). *Mad travellers: Reflections on the reality of transient mental illness.* University of Virginia Press.

Hacking, I. (2002). *Historical ontology*. Harvard University Press.

King, M. L. (1968). The role of the behavioral scientist in the Civil Rights Movement. *Journal of Social Issues, 24*, 1–12.

Martin, J., & Sugarman, J. (1996). Bridging social constructionism and cognitive constructivism. *Journal of Mind and Behavior, 17*, 291–320.

Martin, J., & Sugarman, J. (1997). Societal-psychological constructionism: Societies, selves, traditions, and fusions. *Journal of Theoretical and Philosophical Psychology, 17*, 120–136.

Martin, J., & Sugarman, J. (1999). *The psychology of human possibility and constraint*. State University of New York Press.

Martin, J., & Sugarman, J. (2001). Interpreting human kinds: Beginnings of a hermeneutic psychology. *Theory & Psychology, 11*, 193–207.

Martin, J., Sugarman, J., & Hickinbottom, S. (2010). *Persons: Understanding psychological selfhood and agency*. Springer.

Martin, J., Sugarman, J., & Thompson, J. (2003). *Psychology and the question of agency*. State University of New York Press.

Matthews, D. (2019, January 22). Are 26 billionaires worth more than half the planet? The debate, explained. *Vox*. www.vox.com/future-perfect/2019/1/22/18192774/oxfam-inequality-report-2019-davos-wealth

Miller, P., & Rose, N. (2008). *Governing the present: Administering economic, social and personal life*. Polity.

Napoli, D. S. (1981). *Architects of adjustment*. Kennikat.

Nussbaum, M. (2011). *Creating capabilities: The human development approach*. Harvard University Press.

Rose, N. (1996). Power and subjectivity: Critical history and psychology. In C. Graumann & K. Gergen (Eds.), *Historical dimensions of psychological discourse* (pp. 103–124). Cambridge University Press.

Sennett, R. (1998). *The corrosion of character: The personal consequences of work in the new capitalism*. W. W. Norton.

Sugarman, J. (2006). John Macmurray's philosophy of the personal and the irreducibility of psychological persons. *Journal of Theoretical and Philosophical Psychology, 26*, 172–188.

Sugarman, J. (2009). Historical ontology and psychological description. *Journal of Theoretical and Philosophical Psychology, 29*, 5–15.

Sugarman, J. (2013). Persons and historical ontology. In J. Martin & M. Bickhard (Eds.), *The psychology of personhood: Philosophical, historical, sociodevelopmental, and narrative perspectives* (pp. 81–100). Cambridge University Press.

Sugarman, J. (2014). Neo-Foucaultian approaches to critical inquiry in the psychology of education. In T. Corcoran (Ed.), *Psychology in education: Critical theory-practice* (pp. 53–69). Sense Publishers.

Sugarman, J. (2015a). Historical ontology. In J. Martin, J. Sugarman, & K. Slaney (Eds.), *The Wiley handbook of theoretical and philosophical psychology* (pp. 166–182). Wiley Blackwell.

Sugarman, J. (2015b). Neoliberalism and psychological ethics. *Journal of Theoretical and Philosophical Psychology*, *35*, 103–116.

Sugarman, J. (2017). Psychologism as a style of reasoning and the study of persons. *New Ideas in Psychology*, *44*, 21–27.

Sugarman, J. (2019). Neoliberalism and the ethics of psychology. In D. Goodman, E. Severson, & H. Macdonald (Eds.), *Race, rage, and resistance: Philosophy, psychology, and the perils of individualism* (pp. 73–89). Routledge.

Sugarman, J., & Martin, J. (2004). The political disposition of self as a kind of understanding. In W. Smythe & A. Baydala (Eds.), *Studies of how the mind publicly enfolds into being* (pp. 145–198). Edwin Mellen Press.

Sugarman, J., & Martin, J. (2010). Agentive hermeneutics. In S. Kirschner & J. Martin (Eds.), *The sociocultural turn in psychology: Contemporary perspectives on the contextual emergence of mind and self* (pp. 159–179). Columbia University Press.

Sugarman, J., & Thrift, E. (2020). Neoliberalism and the psychology of time. *Journal of Humanistic Psychology*, *60*, 807–828.

World Bank. (2018, October 7). *Nearly half the world lives on less than $5.50 a day.* www.worldbank.org/en/news/press-release/2018/10/17/nearly-half-the-world-lives-on-less-than-550-a-day

2

Subjectivity and the Critical Imagination in Neoliberal Capitalism

Conversation with Thomas Teo

Interviewed by Thomas Teo and Dennis C. Wendt

Introduction by Dennis C. Wendt

Much in the world has changed between the day I was invited to interview Thomas Teo for this volume (January 24, 2020) and the day the interview took place (May 30, 2020). The COVID-19 pandemic had disrupted our original plan to meet in Toronto during the Native American and Indigenous Studies Association conference I was planning to attend. Instead, we "met" using Zoom video-conferencing in our homes (he in Toronto and I in Montreal) on a Saturday afternoon while my wife and children played in the park. In addition to the pandemic, our interview, which occurred five days after the murder of George Floyd, was in the context of protests against anti-Black systemic racism and police brutality across the globe.

I have been acquainted with Dr. Teo and his scholarship for the past 15 years, primarily through our involvement in the Society for Theoretical and Philosophical Psychology (Division 24 of the American Psychological Association). We share many concerns about the discipline of psychology and its applications, including the many ways that psychology reflects and perpetuates societal inequity and a neoliberal capitalist order. As a leading critical psychologist with a global mindset, Teo challenges many of the ontological, epistemological, methodological, and ethical assumptions and practices within mainstream psychology in North America (Teo, 2010b). Our interview covers many aspects of this work. It begins by contextualizing Teo's scholarship in light of his early entanglement with an "Americanized" psychology during his training in Germany. We then discuss at length his scholarship concerning an "ontology of subhumanism" (Teo, 2020a), including its intersections with social Darwinism, racism, and neoliberal

DOI: 10.4324/9781003280033-3

conceptions of "dieability." Next, we discuss Teo's ideas for revealing hidden assumptions in psychology that reflect and perpetuate a neoliberal political order, as well as the importance for critical interrogation about and democratic community engagement in psychology research. We discuss how the discipline has responded to Teo's scholarship, and several ways that Teo has attempted to influence the discipline through developing accessible concepts for a general audience and interrogating hermeneutic deficits within psychology. This task is a difficult one, in light of psychology's neoliberal penchant for rewarding "epistemological grandiosity" (Teo, 2019a). We discuss how we see in psychology reasons to hope for change, along with reasons to be pessimistic. Finally, we discuss anticipated future directions for Teo's scholarship, in terms of developing a critical theory of subjectivity and providing a space for the psychological humanities.

In reviewing the transcript from our interview now, I am struck by the sheer importance of Teo's voice in the current moment. Given the myriad ways that the pandemic has illuminated societal inequities and the many vulnerabilities of a neoliberal capitalist order, especially in light of a swelling chorus calling for widespread reforms within psychology to address systemic racism, more and more psychology educators and students will inevitably need to turn to Teo's work. What remains to be seen is the extent to which this moment of reckoning will lead to recognition of psychology as a "problematic science," as well as open new directions for a more inclusive, global, critical, and socially just psychology.

Biographical Background and Knowledge Contexts

Dennis C. Wendt (DW): Thank you so much for meeting with me, Thomas. I am excited to talk about your work and how it applies in particular to an ethics of psychology in the context of a neoliberal political order. I thought we could begin by your briefly summarizing your body of work and what you feel holds it all together.

Thomas Teo (TT): For understanding academic subjectivity, perhaps the best way to begin is to consider some biographical information. When I began studying psychology at the University of Vienna in Austria, it was very apparent to us, as students, that a lot of what was proposed as psychological knowledge and practice was actually not what we expected, was not really relevant, was not really practical, was not really *emancipatory*, if you want to use this terminology. Very quickly, we realized that there was a problem with psychology at the university and in society, specifically in the 1980s.

In hindsight, we dealt with a psychology, its research and applications, based on what has been called the consequences of the Americanization of German-speaking psychology after the Second World War, particularly in West Germany and in Austria. This applied to content, and it also meant that students and scholars from, for instance, West Germany went to the United States to study, received their education there, came back, and imported Americanized psychology into a German-speaking context. You could make the historical argument that this Americanization was successfully completed in the 1960s. Due to this sociopolitical import of American psychology, the fact that German-speaking psychology had its own strong traditions, and the cultural changes in many Western countries at the same time, alternative approaches developed that sought to challenge Americanized psychology based on what I have called indigenous intellectual German sources (Teo, 2013). This effort was combined with political ideas for a better organization of society.

The University of Vienna was even further behind other German-speaking universities. In the psychology department, we encountered, for instance, a social psychology that was already outdated in an international context. The behaviorist social psychology we were expected to learn was not what we students believed psychology could be. Controlling behavior and adapting people to the status quo, the emphasis on quantification, neglecting the subject matter of psychology – this was not our vision for psychology. Students founded the Society for Critical Psychology, which still exists today in Austria. I participated on the editorial board of the Society's journal, and this is where we studied alternative psychologies and articulated a critique of Americanized mainstream psychology. I was working early on, during my student days, with the intuition, to use this simplified explanation, that the way psychology was being taught and researched didn't really make sense and that it only promoted a science of control in a capitalist economy.

Looking for forms of explanation to make sense of why this was the case and for alternatives, I was influenced by German critical psychology (Holzkamp, 1983). I started at the University of Vienna, got my master of science there, doing quantitative empirical work, and then moved to the Free University in Berlin during my doctoral studies. In fact, for my dissertation, I was enrolled at the two universities at the same time, which was possible in the German-speaking system because you don't pay tuition – neither the University of Vienna nor the Free University of Berlin charged fees. I got exposed to German critical psychology in West Berlin as well as to Western and Eastern Marxism in a city still divided when I moved there in 1988. I wrote my dissertation on German critical psychology, studying in Berlin, but finished my program at the University of Vienna. Similar to many who are interested in an alternative academic psychological career, my first job was in a traditional psychology department because for many critical psychologists that is the only way to get an academic position. I worked at the Max Planck Institute for Human Development in Berlin as a postdoc and as a research scientist before moving to Canada. Traditional research experience at the so-called highest level provided me with concrete knowledge about the varieties, possibilities, and limitations of psychological research. I applied for and accepted a tenure-track position at York University in Toronto, where I have worked since 1996. Geographical and cultural changes have opened up new horizons to me. Indeed, I developed new perspectives in the North American context, sublating German-speaking experiences. For example, although I had worked on racism in Germany (Mecheril & Teo, 1997), the topic was treated very differently in the North American context as it drew on different sources and lived experiences by racialized groups. The intellectual task for me was, and it still is, to integrate those various intellectual and cultural experiences into a meaningful whole. What guided my critical work was an understanding and realization that psychology was and is a *problematic science*, as some historians in the English-speaking world have called it (Woodward & Ash, 1982). In addition, I considered it necessary to develop the possibilities of an alter-psychology that is doing justice, global, and inclusive, and that addresses socially relevant issues that impact mental life.

We know historically that psychology has always tried to emulate the natural sciences. This has been the case because it's "better" to align yourself with something that is successful and brings money and is associated with power. Something that was already perceived in the second half of the 19th century by many as being subordinate – meaning the humanities and social sciences, historiography for instance – were no models for psychology. Psychology has become what I now call a *hyperscience*, a discipline that uses strategies to hide the fact that it is not a natural science (Teo, 2020b). In order to do that, you inflate and complicate your methodological activities that conceal the temporality and contextuality of psychological phenomena, and you incessantly refer to your discipline as a science. In the end, you have a *hallucinatory resemblance* (Baudrillard, 1988) to a natural science in order to make up for substance and content. Certainly, psychology can produce scientific studies, but psychology is clearly not a science in a traditional sense. In constructive hindsight, one could call psychology a unique science that should actually have its own epistemology, based on its particular ontology, and its own ethical-political necessities.

I still think that there is something deeply problematic with the discipline and profession of psychology, and in my work I have analyzed critiques of psychology (Teo, 2005) as well as the ontological, epistemological, and ethical-political assumptions that guide the discipline in order to make sense of what is happening and in order to imagine alternatives (Teo, 2018b). I have used historical, theoretical, and critical work to make the case for a different psychology. From a critical perspective, one cannot detach psychology from the study of society, culture, and history. I understand that it is hard for people invested in the project of psychology to recognize or acknowledge substantive flaws in the existing project and to envision a theory of subjectivity that could bring sciences and humanities together and make sense of existing knowledge.

Ontology, Subhumanism, and *Dieability*

DW: I wonder if you might talk about some of your recent work as well and how it has developed. In particular, I'm thinking about your work on subhumanism.

TT: In my latest monograph (Teo, 2018b), I divided philosophical, or critical-theoretical investigations in psychology, into ontological, epistemological, ethical-political, and aesthetic studies. When it comes to ontology, we can identify psychology's implicit machine model in which humans are conceived as things that react towards stimuli. There is no conceptualization of the possibility that human beings can actually change the stimuli themselves. This means that psychology captures how the subject could adjust and operate within an existing environment, controlled by someone else, but not how the subject could actually change presented conditions. In an experiment, the subject is asked to do certain things, but in reality, they can walk out of the experiment. That is within one's capability as a human being, part of our human nature, if you like, part of our ontology. A subject can challenge the experiment during an experiment, can have a conversation about the experiment and argue that it doesn't make sense, and can ask, Why have you given me only five options in this condition? The experimenter cannot cope with these questions or actions – the subject would be considered atypical or an outlier whose responses need to be deleted from the data set. Our human nature also allows us to challenge and change the societal conditions of life, a possibility which needs to be part of a scientific study. This would be one stream of reflection when it comes to ontology.

In theoretical psychology, scholars have developed relational ontologies, which are clearly doing more intellectual justice than individualistic ontologies. But, as is often the case with my interests, I ask, What is missing in relational ontologies? In a negative dialectical move that I picked up from German critical theory (Adorno, 1990), I ask, for instance, What is missing when we talk about empathy? What happens with empathy when it is applied selectively towards people that "I" perceive as similar to me but not towards human beings that are very different from "me" or that have been Othered? What happens with empathy when it comes to people that are radically different from "myself"? What is missing, indeed, is an ontology about people that are not conceived as humans.

Thus, when it comes to migration, I have tried to understand how it is possible that we treat people in the way we have treated them. I think about the European but also about the North American context. In the European context, in reality, people have been left dying in the Mediterranean Sea or have been refused entry at the harbor, and activists who have come to their rescue have been put on trial for helping humans in desperate need. Boat captains have been put on trial for helping migrants. At the American-Mexican border, you also have people aiding migrants by putting out water then ending up in courts for what we can call humanitarian behavior. I have asked myself: How can we explain that? There is a history of human rights and of liberal democracy in the European context, in the United States, and in Canada. In contrast, we have the reality that thousands of people have died in the process of migration, have been mistreated, and have been excluded from international law while children have been separated from their parents. How can we explain that from a psychological point of view?

I suggest that we need to go beyond a relational ontology in the sense that it seems that we continue to divide humanity into humans and subhumans. My thesis is that we operate with an ontology of sub-humanism when it comes to migrants. This ontology connects with fascist thinking, with precursors of American eugenic thought, and with precursors of Nazi ideology where subhumanism has played an important role to justify actions against groups of people who have been *Othered*. What is important in this ontology – it was also an insight for me – is that subhumanism is not primarily a rational, intellectual, or cognitive process. It is very much an affective and symbolic process. I gained this insight to a certain degree from Nazi German material on subhumans, which does not use scientific tables, graphs, and discourses. Rather, the material operates with emotional images and imaginations. For example, such material contrasts photos of orderly, nice-looking Germans with disorderly-looking people.

What is fascinating about the idea of subhumanism is its malleability and flexibility. Accordingly, anyone can be made into a subhuman if they do not act in an orderly fashion. If you are outside of the constructed norm, if you are associated with affects and imaginations outside of the normal, and if someone has the power to make this ontology a reality, with circumstances and conditions supporting that idea, then anyone can become a subhuman. Thus, the concept of the subhuman is broader than the concept of "race" and the concept of racism (Teo, 2011). My work on subhumanism is an example of the study of ontology, not only to develop a critique of psychology about implicit models in experimental or empirical research but also to develop concepts that can help us to understand current developments in a constructive way. The ontology of subhumanism allows us – while the critique is still there – to theorize contemporary problems such as migration or the COVID-19 crisis.

I have attempted to analyze the COVID-19 crisis with the concept of subhumanism, but I have realized that, although subhumanism plays a role in public and private discourses, its voice is less important than political-economic calculations. In what Mbembe (2003) has called necropolitics, meaning people in power decide who can live and who can die, or who is *dieable*, as I call it in the COVID-19 crisis, subhuman emotionality takes a backstage to economic-instrumental rationality. In the fascist being, the question of *dieability*, or affective subhumanism, is combined with social Darwinist rationalizations. Capitalism works well with fascism, authoritarian governments, and neoliberal ideologies when it concerns *dieability*.

DW: That is interesting. I was wondering about the application to the COVID-19 pandemic as I was reviewing your writing on subhumanism recently. You focus on "migrants" – a term you put in quotation marks (Teo, 2020a) – to refer to those who are in the process of migration. But you also talk about how subhumanism is not necessarily unique to migrants but extends to other populations as well. I was wondering about how that might apply to the COVID-19 pandemic. Perhaps you could say a bit more about this distinction you just mentioned between subhumanism and social Darwinism.

TT: Let me clarify. I make a distinction between fascist politics and fascist mentality or subjectivity. I believe that fascist mentality draws on (a) racism, sometimes scientific racism, a pseudoscientific intellectual stream of thought; (b) subhumanism, which allows for affective and symbolic expressions and is more malleable than racism; and (c) a pragmatic, economic Darwinism in order to justify political-economic decisions. There are other elements such as authoritarianism or nationalism, but these three elements are interesting for me because they have moved to the surface again. I have analyzed subhumanism in the context of migration and I also believe that the COVID-19 crisis shows the power of economic Darwinism. We increasingly find discourses and material practices for a fascist subjectivity.

There is a connection between social Darwinism and subhumanism, but it is not required. Social Darwinism – I like to call it, for current purposes, economic Darwinism – relies on ideology and common sense, whereas subhumanism reflects an affective-symbolic ontology. Economic Darwinism has never disappeared as an ideology in capitalist Western countries, whereas subhumanism was confined to the underground and only recently has re-emerged as a guiding ontology in politics but also in individual mental life. Neoliberal capitalism produces but does not necessarily need a subhuman ontology when Darwinist ideas are available. If you say that there are different races of people, and the White race won the historical struggle and therefore the White race can claim anything they want from colonies and subjugated other peoples, you can use a subhuman ontology, but you do not require it.

However, German fascism combined racism, subhumanism, and social Darwinism. In order to justify the extermination of people, one could use a social Darwinist, a subhuman, or a racist argument or appeal. In order to kill people with physical and mental disabilities, in the so-called T4 euthanasia program, Nazis used all of those appeals, including economic ones. They showed scientific tables and affective photos and appealed to the burden of financial costs and the impact on the German economy which would result from supporting people with disabilities. I suggest, from a psychological perspective, that many Germans were convinced by those economic, scientific, and biomedical discourses and practices in concert with the affective images and imaginations. One could turn this productively, I mean the stream of fascist appeals, depending on the circumstance and audience, when deciding which type of idea should be invoked. In scientific contexts, fascists would use pseudoscientific justifications, whereas in propaganda they could use affective images. Similarly, for educational purposes one might need to use visualizations of ragged subhumans in concert with the scientific mantle of economic Darwinism and the instrumental logic of cost–benefit analyses. Fascism provides a whole ideological, practical-political, and subjective apparatus. Subhumanism is one element in that; economic Darwinism is another.

In the context of migration, I find it fascinating that an element of fascism, the ontology of subhumanism, has re-emerged in liberal democracies. In my article (Teo, 2020a) I mention not only implicit but also explicit discourses where the terms are used against migrants in Austria, Canada, Germany, and the United States. Former President Obama needed to distance himself from the ontology when suggesting that we should not invoke the idea that certain people are subhuman. Why would he need to appeal to that? Well, there seems to be already a broad discourse in which this idea is taking hold. Yet, it is not just a matter of language but also a matter of ontology that divides humanity.

DW: Another thing I wondered about as I was reviewing your work on subhumanism is how it might pertain to the events of last week of May 2020 in the United States in terms of the acts of violence from police towards African Americans and the killing of George Floyd. I wonder how you would think about these events and these problems in terms of the interplay of subhumanism and racism.

TT: Racism can invoke subhumanism and vice versa, but subhumanism is broader than racism. In the migration debate, people who appear to be White cannot be racialized, but they can be subhumanized. Syrian refugees, who may look like Steve Jobs (who had a Syrian father), can be subhumanized even when racialization does not work. To explain the treatment of White refugees, the contempt for them, their differential treatment, we can provide an analysis based on processes of subhumanization instead of a process of racialization, which does not seem to work there. You could use religion, and suggest, from a supremacist point of view, that Islam is an inferior religion, as has been done against Muslim migrants. Again, this would not work for refugees that do not follow Islam. What is left is the subhumanization of migrants.

When it comes to the treatment of African Americans by police in the United States, you clearly find systemic racism, personal racism, combined with elements of dehumanization. The killing and mistreatment of Black citizens by police thrives primarily on racism. The mistreatment of White demonstrators, journalists, and activists cannot be explained by racism but by the *temporary subhumanization* of perceived opponents who do not need to be treated as human beings. This takes place against the background of systemic and institutional realities of police departments, their culture, and individuals with violent affordances. "Jogging while being Black" or "driving while Black" or "shopping while Black" or "birdwatching while Black" or "sleeping while Black," and their sometimes fatal consequence, are nourished by the history and actuality of racism in the United States connected with dehumanizing and subhumanizing practices. The call for Black Lives Matter, difficult for some Americans to understand, is of course perfectly reasonable because processes of racism and subhumanization have made Blackness into a category where empirically Black lives have mattered less than White lives.

Racism does not need the ontology of subhumanism, although often enough it is included, when race theories work with rankings that consider certain races below the human standard. The actual effects of racism, based on the history of racism in the United States – racism as an ideology, racism as a systemic reality, racism as an embedded practice in education, health, the legal system, the media, and the economic system – may very well produce an ontology of subhumanism that considers Black Americans below the human standard of White Americans and explains killings of African Americans, including the killing of George Floyd. The Other is not only different, representing different biological groups, if you use the language of scientific racism, but the Other is below the standards of "us" humans, a substandard, and supposedly everyone has the same feeling. That is what an ontology of subhumanism is based on, combined with actions, violent actions that can be enacted on the bodies of Black Americans.

DW: I have one other clarifying question about subhumanism. In the multiculturalism courses I teach, we talk a lot about implicit racism. Does that frame make sense for thinking about subhumanism as well? Does it make sense to think about subhumanism as an implicit set of processes that operate without one's awareness?

TT: Absolutely. That is the idea of ontologies – that they are behind one's back, so to say. They are implicit, unconscious, or we are not aware of them. I suggest that psychology operates with an implicit machine model. You ask a traditional psychologist, "Do you have a machine model in mind when you do research?" and they would say, "No, I don't think of my participants as machines." This would be an implicit ontology. It is not an explicit model, although some researchers may believe that there is no difference between machines and humans. Psychologists inherit, habituate, and socialize in the practices of doing research; one socializes into how experimental research is done. Once fully immersed in the everyday practices of research, one conducts research without realizing the actual hidden assumptions; one is not aware of how it happened that one does things a certain way and implicitly assumes that one is at the forefront of psychological science because one was trained by the best psychologists. Theoretical psychologists need to reconstruct, against a self-understanding in the discipline of objectivity, how the machine model plays out in theories by not allowing the full range of individual agency, let alone the possibility of collective agency, in overturning existing conditions. To be fair, some people implicitly operate with an ontology of subhumanism when they accept and support certain institutional or personal behaviors against migrants or Blacks, or they can be explicit in their fascist being, thinking, and doing. Subhumanism plays a role in both scenarios, but mostly implicitly.

DW: As with racism, virtually no one is going to say, "I'm a subhumanist."

TT: Exactly!

Revealing Hidden Assumptions of Psychology Within a Neoliberal Political Order

DW: Speaking of things that are implicit, it seems that a common theme in your scholarship is an elucidation of hidden assumptions or implicit practices. Your work lays bare many of the things that are somewhat hidden as part of a neoliberal political order.

TT: I would distinguish three streams. The first stream looks at implicit assumptions in the theoretical foundations of psychology pertaining to ontology, epistemology, and ethics. For instance, some of my work has focused on epistemological violence (Teo, 2008). Empirical psychologists can commit forms of violence, what I call epistemological violence, without awareness. This is not to deny that some people are aware of what they are doing. The question for me was, How does this happen? How does it happen that you find scientific racist work in psychology? Scientific racism draws on empirical research while using advanced methods and sophisticated empirical tools. Where does epistemological violence happen, now and in the past?

My argument is that there is no one-to-one relationship between results and the interpretation of results. If you choose an interpretation of results that brings harm to a group of people, then you've committed a form of epistemological violence. Let's assume that you find an empirical difference between group A and B; then you argue that it's in the nature of B to be X, and X has a negative meaning in the culture – even when there are equally viable alternative interpretations possible; and the study itself does not address nature. Then, you may have committed a form of violence once you present an interpretation of difference as knowledge (group A is by nature less intelligent than group B). Epistemological violence is often an implicit practice in psychology and does not only apply to racialized differences. One can commit epistemological violence when it comes to gender, sexual preferences, ability–disability, class – whatever social category you choose. The interpretation of differences is underdetermined, and some interpretations are not necessarily violent and do not bring harm to one group of people; but if "I" choose an interpretation that brings harm to a group of people and present this interpretation as knowledge, "I" may have committed epistemological violence. This stream of argumentation is not alien to traditional psychologists who realize that interpretations of data are not determined by the data.

The second stream of reflection and argumentation about implicit practices does not pertain to aspects of empirical psychology but to the idea that psychology itself is a neoliberal discipline. If you look at the discipline and practice of psychology as a whole, from a metatheoretical perspective, you realize that psychology has contributed to controlling and adapting people to the neoliberal status quo. From a historical point of view, the problem reaches back to the beginnings of capitalism and its consequences for mental life as well as for psychology. Theoretical psychologists like to discuss the fragmented status of psychology as something negative or positive (see Teo, 2010a). Yet, the fragmented understanding of the psychological subject matter is itself the result of the development of modern and capitalist societies and institutions. I could be interested in your subjectivity in its totality, but as a representative of an institution, I am not. Working in a modern institution, I am only interested in aspects of your mentality. In the sphere of work, "I" as a psychologist am interested in your performance, motivation, leadership, or interpersonal qualities, in your punctuality, whether you identify with a company or not; in the educational system, I am interested in your scholastic abilities; in the prison system, I am interested in whether you are going to reoffend or not; in the legal system, I am interested in the reliability of your eyewitness account; in the military, I am interested in the acuity of your senses, in your eye-hand coordination, or in your qualities as a military leader, soldier, or sniper. Modern institutions have a very specific interest in your mental life. One could make the argument that modern institutions have contributed to the subdivision of mental life. Thus, the development of modern culture and the development of capitalist society makes it very difficult to bring back the totality of subjectivity into an integrated whole. Psychologists as part of modern or capitalist institutions are interested in particular aspects of your mental life. This has been accelerated in recent developments of the capitalist economy, of what we can call neoliberal capitalism, that combines an economy with an ideology and is interested in you as an entrepreneurial being (Teo, 2018a). To what degree do you embody the entrepreneurial self? Can you sell not only goods and services but yourself? What commodities of your self can you market? Again, no psychologists would admit that they operate with a concept of *homo neoliberalus*. It is an implicit assumption that guides psychological work.

To repeat, in neoliberal ideology, the psychologist is no longer interested, let's say, in your spiritual life unless you can commodify it, make money with it, or use it. The psychologist is not interested in any particular aspect of your subjectivity unless it's part of an entrepreneurial neoliberal "form of subjectivity" (Teo, 2018a). I think we can make the historical argument that we had a differentiation of forms of life in capitalism, based on different interests in different institutions and systems, and that this differentiation has morphed into a single form, the neoliberal form of subjectivity. Thus, your aesthetic self, your spiritual self, your ethical self, and so on is only relevant to the degree that it fits into a neoliberal form of subjectivity. In neoliberalism, your artistic subjectivity counts only if you can make money with it. You have differentiation and uniformization at the same time. These processes need to be theorized and analyzed in psychology.

Finally, there is another assumption connected to neoliberalism: the idea that we need to adapt to the status quo, produce happiness through accepting existing conditions, and can change only ourselves. Psychology does not conceive of how we could change our conditions of life, collectively, in groups or in society. When people say, "You can only change yourself," I would say, "You can change yourself, but more importantly, humans can also change their shared life conditions." Although this idea is undervalued in psychology and may even be experienced as counterintuitive, it is a possibility of human life. The idea may require collective action and solidarity. That is another notion of critical psychology that is important to me: conceiving not only *what is* but also *what is possible*. Indeed, the idea has a long history that goes back to the beginnings of psychology.

DW: It seems to me that psychology is interested in what is possible within an individual's intrapsychic life insofar as it helps with productivity or happiness but not so much in terms of what is possible for societal change.

TT: I agree. For that reason, critical psychology has developed.

DW: As you were talking about the fragmentation of psychology, I was thinking about the problem in psychology of constructing humans as just the sum of a set of variables. Those variables may shift somewhat, but they are basically already determined and so constrain at the outset how we understand the human mind and behavior. And then psychology can proceed in a fragmented fashion, where one can isolate a small set of variables and conduct some statistical models on them. Would you see that playing a role as well?

TT: German critical psychology labeled mainstream psychology a *psychology of variables* (Holzkamp, 1983). This means that we can identify mainstream psychology by the requirement to transform everything into a variable, into something that varies and thus, can be quantified and analyzed by statistical means. This brings us back to what we discussed before: the need for psychology to emulate its idol of the natural sciences. Historians and theoreticians of psychology have reconstructed experimentation, operationalization, quantification, and the emergence of variables in psychology. For instance, variables, which used to be a tool for managing certain problems, became a psychological ontology (O'Doherty & Winston, 2014). All that we are is variables, and this mindset requires critical inquiry.

In an article that I am writing at the moment, I suggest that methods have an *object-intentionality* and that they try to do justice to the object. One needs to ask oneself, What kind of objects are we dealing with in psychology, and are our methods doing justice to them? We can further ask whether we are trying to do justice to persons or to an abstract concept, such as natural science. These questions require different streams of reflection. From that perspective, certain methods can do justice or injustice to certain problems. If I want to measure time, I might use, from a historical perspective, the Hipp chronoscope, an instrument that allowed psychologists to measure time. That instrument was important in the development of experimental psychology and was intended to do justice to reaction time. But the Hipp chronoscope does not allow us to measure temperature or other qualities. The question remains, Which instrument does justice towards a given object? Under what circumstance does the ontology of variables do justice to your mental life? At what point does a variable scheme no longer do justice to human subjectivity?

Community Engagement with Research

TT: At the point where variables no longer do justice to the topic, we must switch to other methods, or other methodologies – that is an important assumption of critical psychology. But it goes further: we should not decide to move to qualitative methods in a solipsistic fashion; we must involve the people who are researched. This is, of course, a principle in participatory action research and other community-based research practices. It is not "me," the researcher, who decides on the method. If I believe that I, sitting in the ivory tower in my armchair, can make all decisions about method, then I have probably failed as a critical psychologist. The decision has to be made in conversation and dialogue with community members who are impacted by the decision. This is another important element in critical psychology when it comes to methodology.

DW: Right. What I have found in some of the worlds that I work in, where I conduct research with Indigenous communities, is that there is definitely more of a shift towards some of the things that you have been talking about, such as engaging with community, working with community interests, and so forth. Yet so much of that research is still strongly guided, for example, by funding agencies, journals, and disciplinary constraints that hem in the community engagement to an extent.

TT: Indeed. A critical reflection of science has to include what has been labeled the context of discovery. In other words, what questions are asked? Why? Who is funding? What do agencies want? Who are the gatekeepers? What is power interested in and what is it not invested in? For example, Lisa Cosgrove and her colleagues' (2006) work on financial conflicts of interest in the context of the *Diagnostic and Statistical Manual* (DSM) should be considered here. That is one way of understanding science. The traditional context of justification is another stream of reflection; questions about epistemology, methodology, sample size, statistical tests, and so on come into play here. Equally important is what I call the context of interpretation, or how results are interpreted, with or about people, and then the context of application, where we make decisions about what is done with research in terms of consequences. It is a fourth stream of reflection. Critical investigations involve all four streams of reflection and address the degree to which the context of discovery influences the context of justification. Beyond granting agencies, I personally am more interested in whether psychology makes people into problems or whether we work on problems that marginalized people encounter in a given environment. Indeed, Indigenous people in Canada have been made into problems through research. Yet, critical psychology can work on the problems that Indigenous peoples encounter in Canada in collaboration with Indigenous people. Even a strategy that simply looks at empirical differences between groups can make communities into a problem. This has not only happened with Indigenous people but with all kinds of marginalized people (Teo, 2004). Again, the question is for me whether we make, for instance, LGBTQ+ communities and individuals into problems, as has been done historically, or are we working on the problems that the communities and individuals encounter in a particular country such as Canada or the United States. The focus on empirical difference has also been criticized in critical disability studies that for a long time expressed its critique of psychology because psychology, with its focus on deficits, has made disability into a problem. Again, to reiterate, from a critical perspective, work on problems that persons with disabilities encounter in Canada would be the ethical-scientific alternative.

There is another strategy that can be observed in psychology beyond making people into problems and/or working on problems that people encounter: This is where psychologists ignore people altogether and simply focus on their own career. One can easily find this form of academic subjectivity at universities. People there become a means to an end in which "I" can further my publication record and so forth. Communities, people, and persons in this strategy are not an end in and of themselves. From a critical perspective with a moral and ethical dimension, communities would be considered an end and not a means, particularly when it comes to academia. What I have learned from people who have worked in this context is that Indigenous communities are aware of this problem and have become more reluctant to participate in research in which they are just used as a means to an end or when psychologists are not really there to understand their problems and to provide possible solutions.

I'm suggesting that it might become more difficult to do research on marginalized groups should the communities refuse to participate. Hopefully, that feeds back into what you address as an issue, disciplinary requirements that hinder research with and for communities. Such disciplinary requirements and funding agencies will change when people push back against a research strategy that sees the study of marginalized communities as a means for something else. Being optimistic, I have seen improvements in research when it comes to marginalized groups in society, in my own lifetime.

DW: I was just about to say, in terms of here in Canada, the Canadian Institutes of Health Research has made genuine reforms in terms of expectations for research with Indigenous peoples in terms of emphasizing participation, community autonomy, and data sovereignty. How those changes actually happen in practice would be important to observe. Nonetheless, there truly is, I think, a real shift that is heartening to see.

Psychology's Response to Teo's Scholarship

DW: Speaking of these shifts in disciplinary practice, to the extent that you are aware, how would you say the field of psychology has responded to your work?

TT: It's difficult to say. Let me approach the problem from a different angle. If I divide my own work into historical, theoretical, and critical contributions, promoting more recently the psychological humanities (Teo, 2017), developing concepts, or what I consider counter-concepts to existing traditional concepts, then we would have to look into each of these areas.

My historical work was aimed at historians of psychology, with the history of psychology clearly being a recognized subfield within the discipline of psychology, and at teaching the history of psychology (Walsh et al., 2014). In this subfield, there is a very small group of people working, and you would get feedback from the few who have seen your work. In my current work, I have moved away from the history of psychology because history has become a tool for me for understanding current issues. Such an attitude would be a methodological problem in historiography but not in theoretical or critical psychology. I no longer do history for the sake of historiography. My work has shifted to theorizing, where I use historical knowledge to make an argument with the intent of addressing a larger psychological audience.

When it comes to my theoretical and critical work, it's difficult to say how the discipline has responded. I published in 2015 in the *American Psychologist* an article on critical psychology (Teo, 2015) with above average citations, but I'm not sure which mainstream psychologist cites the article and I don't know if it has had any impact on traditional psychology. I think that most psychologists, and this reflects the historical development of psychology into specialty areas, remain very much focused on their own specialty areas, and even general psychology has been in decline. For that reason, one cannot expect recognition and interest in areas outside of people's research, and this also applies to theoretical psychology. Nevertheless, I tried to develop concepts and ideas for a general psychological audience. For example, my concept of epistemological violence (Teo, 2008) was specifically aimed not at a critical, theoretical, or postcolonial readership but a mainstream audience. I wanted to draw attention to the possible dangers of producing harmful interpretations, based on empirical difference, against groups of people when alternative interpretations are available. At the same time, many speculative interpretations have been presented as knowledge or fact. I wanted to draw attention to the hermeneutic deficit in the discipline, that is, the tendency to *not* focus on the quality of interpretation and the quality of theorizing. We all know of psychology's focus on the technical aspects of methodology. Yet, there are no courses, manuals, or seminars on how to interpret data or theorize data. Beyond technical methodology, we do not learn how to understand research, how to reflect on our own research, how to articulate the meaning of the possibilities and limitations of studies, or how to critically assess knowledge more generally. We like to talk about distributions, scales, measures, constructs, instruments, and statistical tests, in short about technical expertise, but not about the meaning of knowledge in psychology. We do not have courses on that. When I ask students, What is psychological knowledge? – admittedly a difficult question – I usually encounter silence.

Many of my studies target a mainstream audience, but it's very difficult for me to say whether they have had any impact beyond a small group of people. Let me give you a concrete example: In *Canadian Psychology* I published an article on the term "Caucasian" (Teo, 2009). In this paper with the obscure title "Psychology without Caucasians," I made the argument that the concept of the Caucasian is a completely unscientific concept. You can go back to Blumenbach (1795), who coined the term, and you know all of his assumptions that underlie the concept have been falsified, for example, the assumption that the cradle of humanity is the Caucasus. My question then is, Why do we use a nonscientific term in psychology? My question is not about political correctness; it's about scientific correctness! The article has a few citations, but as we know, the term is still widely used in psychology; I see and hear the term used on a regular basis. That we use the term in North America and not in Germany has historical, cultural, and political roots. We do not use the equally unscientific concept of the "Aryan"; nobody would say, "My sample consisted of 150 Aryans." Yet we use the term Caucasian, which is equally nonsensical. If one really wants to be a natural scientist, then one should not use completely unscientific words in one's science! Epistemic ignorance is no longer an excuse for its usage.

DW: It is pretty remarkable. I frequently see the term Caucasian being used in manuscripts and theses I review. I pretty regularly advise the use of a different term. But it's interesting that even something so trivial and so obviously unscientific remains so entrenched in psychology. So, you can only imagine, for the deeper systemic and critical issues that you raise, how much resistance there would be. It strikes me that part of the difficulty of being a theoretical psychologist is that one's work is easily ignored. For example, I can imagine your *American Psychologist* article (Teo, 2015) is making a difference for people. People are using it, and it helps their own scholarship or their own practice. But then for everyone else, it can just be ignored. There is a proliferation of so many journals, so many voices, that it's hard to change the field. There are those moments where something really makes a splash, in the spirit of Thomas Kuhn's (1962) *Structure of Scientific Revolutions*. But it is very hard to see those changes. I have found that one of the more interesting sites to see resistances or impediments to my own work, is more on the local scene – the things that come up with colleagues in department meetings, or about curriculum, or in dissertation defenses, or whatever it might be. I wonder if you might speak to that just a little bit, about perhaps some of the resistances and impediments to your work.

TT: Using the example of the term Caucasian, I have had a variety of experiences ranging from agreement, disagreement, to ignorance. Often, psychologists say to me: "Indeed, this is a good argument.

It might be scientifically correct, what you say. But we all know what the term means." It is ironic that psychologists who commit to science are left with the argument that we all know what it means, which would confirm the position of postmodern psychologists. It is a weak argument if you commit yourself to the rhetoric of science. I think that challenging the status quo, pointing to significant deficits when it comes to concepts, ontology, epistemology, and ethics of the discipline, are not particularly welcome. I have used examples from ontology and epistemology, but when it comes to ethical deficits I would like to mention the torture scandal in the American Psychological Association and the amount of resistance in the discipline and profession when it came to addressing the scandal (Aalbers & Teo, 2017).

Interrogating Hermeneutic Deficits in Psychology

TT: Coming back to your question about resistance, we could talk about the defense against unpleasant knowledge. It is understandable that psychologists do not like it when hermeneutic deficits are pointed out, even if you do it in a nice way or when you just ask questions about research, such as, Could you interpret these results within a different framework? Would the epistemic outcome be different if you do that? Could there be different, even contradictory, conclusions? Why did you choose that framework and not another one? How did you decide what interpretation is the best interpretation of the data when the data allows for a variety of different interpretations? Such questions startle students and faculty alike. The idea that one could analyze data from a different theoretical framework, that interpretations and theories are underdetermined by results, that the meaning of results could change if you choose a different theoretical framework, are challenging. Even more, if you ask why a student is committed to a particular framework, you receive confused answers. Some students have answered honestly and have told me that the reason is that their supervisor has worked in this framework. Such observations and the literature point to the hermeneutic deficit in the discipline. Critical psychology entails pointing to those deficits.

Hermeneutic deficits also support the importance of good theorizing in psychology, which is another goal of my work. I understand that, even when you provide the best argument, holding up the mirror and asking psychologists to look into the mirror, what they see in the mirror is not necessarily the great science that they think they have engaged in. The mirror points to a problematic discipline. Pointing this out will obviously evoke resistances and complaints, or ignorance. In society more generally, if somebody challenges the status quo, many people don't really like to hear such challenges. We could address resistance to hermeneutic deficits in the discipline and profession through a history of science, philosophy of science, or sociology of science, but also through a psychology of science. Kuhn (1962) has alluded to that in reference to psychological processes involved when it comes to accepting a paradigm or a scientific revolution. Let me give you an example. If you work for 25–30 years in a paradigm, and you are very successfully advancing in this paradigm or, if you prefer, *research program* when it comes to psychology, if somebody then says this research framework has significant problems, many persons will not just give up on that research program that they have accepted, had positive experiences with, and on which their successes are based. To give up on it would be very difficult, from a psychological perspective.

When I suggest that psychology should incorporate the psychological humanities (Teo, 2017), there will be resistance for sociopolitical and psychological reasons. Psychologists know what is rewarded in science and which research is associated with power and money, to use a simplified explanation. Psychology and psychologists want to align themselves with disciplines associated with those characteristics and not with disciplines that may even experience contempt. The humanities, as we know, have been under attack for the last 20–30 years, and longer of course if you assume a historical perspective. Why would you align psychology with something that has no power? Why would you align psychology with something that increases uncertainty and that might be confusing because of its complexity? As a result, you find reactions that emphasize the idea that "We are a science!" Even psychoanalysis is believed to be a real science, a self-misunderstanding, as Habermas (1968) pointed out, because it does not understand its hermeneutic character.

Still, I make the epistemic case for the psychological humanities. The central idea is that we can learn about mental life from the humanities, from historiography, philosophy, social and political theory, anthropology, cultural studies, postcolonial thought, economic theory, and the arts. I understand that such a project is sociologically, institutionally, and politically not rewarded, but it is needed. For personal, institutional, financial, and political reasons, it will be difficult to align psychology with the humanities (Teo, 2019b). Epistemic reasons, intellectual legitimacy, and even evidence that supports incorporating these disciplines seem to be secondary.

The Challenge of Epistemic Modesty in a Discipline That Rewards Grandiosity

DW: There seems to be a kind of irony here. We have a prototype of the scientist who really wants to be proven wrong. You hear this a lot in public discourse: "As a scientist, my goal is to be proven wrong and I need to have humility." I don't doubt that there are scientists who really do their best to embody that spirit. You may see something like the epistemological modesty you have written about (Teo, 2019a) – more likely when it comes to something very narrow, perhaps pertaining to falsification in the Popperian sense. But when it comes to something that is a more substantive challenge to one's assumptions, there is a lot less modesty. I mean, we can just look at the widespread but controversial practice of null hypothesis significance testing using p-values of .05.

TT: You are right about the paths of modesty. My argument for epistemic modesty was not specifically focused on the ritual of null hypothesis testing in psychology (Gigerenzer, 2004) but on the values or virtues that scientists want to embrace more generally. We still find researchers who show epistemic modesty in certain areas, as you suggest, but we can also observe the opposite trend, what I have called epistemic grandiosity (Teo, 2019b). It can easily be observed with researchers who are experts in one area pretending to be public experts in all areas. Those public scientists, a more accurate term than public intellectuals, present themselves as experts in nature, society, and culture and are able to comment on any topic thrown at them (e.g., in media interviews).

Consider the convincing case of epistemic modesty. Most research fields have become so broad and complex that it is actually impossible to be an epistemic expert on all disciplines. Even in one field such as psychology, where you have millions of studies, and even if you commit to the project of general psychology and express an interest in the totality of mental life or the whole of subjectivity, it is impossible to be an up-to-date expert on all psychosocial issues. Given the constant contributions to knowledge in various areas and at the same time the impossibility of being an expert in all knowledge domains, the intellectual limitations of each individual, and the fact that we take theoretical shortcuts, epistemic modesty would be a necessary virtue. I ask, then, a common move in my own theoretical work, "Why is this not happening? Why is there not more epistemic modesty to be found?"

I argue that endorsing this virtue is not happening because under neoliberal capitalism you need to embody the virtues of an entrepreneurial, academic self. In consequence, researchers exaggerate their contributions, are grandiose about their findings, market and sell their ideas, and overemphasize the impact of their results when translating their research to the public. Neoliberal academia and neoliberal science, where each researcher becomes a salesperson, promote values that are the opposite of epistemic modesty. It would make you a bad salesperson if you preface your research by mentioning that you actually don't have any clear answers, that you are dealing with an extremely difficult and maybe too complex problem to give definitive answers, that you are well aware of the limitations of your own framework, which may be not only limited but even biased, that you are coming from a certain intellectual, social, and cultural background, and that what you suggest needs contextualization, which would be the appropriate way to approach research in psychology. Your audience will lose interest quickly. Contrast that with a researcher who prefaces findings by saying, "Let me tell you what's going on. I have the best answer for that problem. I can explain perfectly why this is happening," or who compares their findings to those of Darwin or Galileo.

Academic grandiosity is rewarded in the larger system of neoliberalism, whereas epistemic modesty would be an appropriate intrinsic value developing out of the reality of the growing breadth and complexity of science and knowledge. It is impossible in one discipline or even in one subdiscipline to follow the unmanageable number of books, chapters, and articles published. Epistemic modesty as a virtue also shows the economic colonization of scientific values and that extrinsic characteristics such as marketability, the entrepreneurial self, when loud, extraverted grandiosity is rewarded. Of course, if you could transform modesty into a marketable entity, it would have a neoliberal value as well.

DW: This surely has consequences in terms of the replication crisis in psychology, as well as issues of unethical data manipulation, that we see in social psychology and other branches of psychology.

TT: I have not published on this topic, but I worked with a PhD student who made a convincing argument that we need to connect some of the high-profile cases of fraud in social psychology to neoliberal thinking and doing. Again, you have a conflict between scientific core values such as academic honesty and transparency and the reality of fraud and manipulation, the latter referring to borderline activities in research that make it difficult to replicate research – not mentioning here for a moment the cultural and historical dimensions of psychological research that prevent replication. If it is the case that fraud is increasing, then we need to ask why. Academic fraudsters who have been interviewed mention the enormous pressures they experienced. They mentioned that they felt stress at often prestigious universities or institutions to publish original work. At a certain point of pressure, they moved to making data up. Such an instance is sociologically and psychologically interesting yet not surprising. What makes an academic commit research fraud? To what degree is it an internal problem of character? Do we need to understand the fraudulent person, or their character, in connection with relationships, academic life-worlds, and sociopolitical and economic-ideological contexts? In my theory of subjectivity, in a theory of academic subjectivity, this nexus between systems, relationships, and the person needs to be understood in order to understand phenomena such as academic fraud. Clearly, some of those phenomena you mention need to be analyzed within the developments of neoliberal academia.

Clinical and Educational Applications

DW: We've talked quite a bit about research and scientific production. I wonder if we might shift just a little bit to talk about psychological practice. I know that you have clinical psychology students in some of your courses. I am curious how your work has been received by practitioners or budding practitioners of psychology.

TT: Given the current problems in society, academia, and psychology, you can choose between an epistemic or an ethical-practical approach to praxis, by which I mean critical practice. You can theorize praxis problems or you can do something about praxis problems or combine both. My own academic focus has been on theorizing problems, always with an emancipatory-practical *intent*, a term I borrow from Habermas, who suggested that his philosophizing as a public intellectual has a practical intent. I am not sure if this is an excuse for not doing enough in praxis when I say that I have a practical intent in my epistemic reflections. When I develop a concept such as *epistemological violence*, it should offer a mirror to the discipline, but I also want people who are harmed through research to use it even when they are not fully aware of all the technical details in a study. When racialized students encounter in their textbooks statements about naturalized race difference in IQ, or when they are confronted with the banality of a graph on differences, they can not only say that empirical differences allow for a variety of interpretations, let alone what is meant by a Western concept, they can respond to what is presented as knowledge as a form of epistemological violence. When marginalized groups and persons encounter statements about their supposed deficits, statements they understand as harmful, they can invoke the concept of epistemological violence. In that sense, I aim at practical intent for seemingly abstract ideas.

In the process of psychologization that we go through in Western countries, I want to develop counter-psychologization, counter-concepts for and with people (Teo, 2018b). To clarify, in theoretical and historical psychology, we talk a lot about psychologization, the fact that people use more and more psychological concepts and theories to understand themselves and other people and even to comprehend the social world. Part of the success of psychology can be found in the reality that once people explain everything in the world through psychological concepts, you have a complete psychologization of the world. *Neuroplasticity* would be a more recent example for the success of neuropsychological concepts. Indeed, there are countless psychological concepts that people use to understand themselves, others, and economic life. When former President Obama identifies an empathy deficit in American society, he uses a psychological category to analyze the United States. From a critical perspective, empathy deficit might be one aspect, but American society's problems are basically due to the enormous inequalities in the political-economic system, as a starting point.

The process of psychologization represents a real trend that we can theorize. Here, my point is that instead of providing traditional psychological concepts to make sense of the world, I want critical psychologists to develop counter-concepts. I understand epistemological violence as such a counter-concept in order to make the case for understanding what is going on, let's say, in the academic literature. In current public debates, *systemic racism* would be a nonpsychological counter-concept that specifically aims at not psychologizing social issues. In order to use that concept, people do not have to study scientific data sets.

That intent of theorizing for practical purposes represents one stream. A more obvious stream is teaching, where critical work means preparing students for the conditions of the possibility and the necessity of reflexivity when it concerns psychology. I emphasize asking questions about psychology as a hermeneutic tool because psychology students are socialized in a very strict process that ends in stating that psychology is a science. They often are blind towards the problems that psychology has as a discipline and practice and to the power that it has. I hope that marginalized persons and students use critical concepts, such as epistemological violence, psychological humanities, subhumanism, epistemic modesty, hyperscience, collective agency and resistance, and critical psychology more generally, and I hope that they are skeptical of concepts such as the Caucasian or methods such as the twin method (Teo & Ball, 2009). I hope that clinical students who attend my classes on the historical and theoretical foundations of psychology consider some of the critical theorizing that we have done. I am realistic enough to know that this might not always be successful. But this is not an excuse for avoiding trying or for not continuing to develop ideas with a practical intent.

As an educator, I theorize unjust conditions, which is a limitation because it would require action. Still, I believe it is important that the fight against unjust conditions begins, at least for the privileged, with an understanding of the sources of injustice. I teach clinical students, for instance, how income and wealth inequality can lead to health and mental health problems, following Wilkinson and Pickett's (2009) work that shows that societies with higher income inequality also have more problems when it comes to mental health. Such knowledge sets the conditions for the possibility that they will take this into account when doing clinical work. The ideal solution, from a theoretical point of view, would be large-scale change, but large-scale change is difficult given the complexities of structure and power in modern societies. I accept and support small-scale change, like in community psychology, that helps homeless people, communities in distress, groups that encounter discrimination, mental health issues, and so forth. I applaud these efforts, but from a theoretical perspective helping 50 homeless people or more will not necessarily solve the problem of homelessness. This problem requires large-scale change, which at this time is difficult to envision for many people. I understand that as well.

DW: It seems to be implicit in your argument that psychology itself cannot be expected to make that change.

TT: Yes, indeed. Traditional psychology, as we know it, focuses always on the individual or, let me be more precise, on *individualization*. Research psychology, which relies on statistical methods, actually does not really care about the unique person but is rather more concerned about the aggregate. That even applies to social psychology, with streams of community psychology being exempt. Individualization means that the individual is the locus of solution. Yet, individualizing solutions means adapting and controlling individuals rather than allowing individuals to consider changing their societal life conditions. In that sense, not the individual but individualization is at the core of traditional practice. I believe this brings us back to the concept of agency and to considering not only adaptive behavior or consumer choice but also agency as a form of collective action that can change structural realities.

I follow here Holzkamp (1983) that it is in our nature, as human beings, to change our environment. Indeed, we have historical evidence that we not only adapted to our world but that we were able to change that world. It is in our ontology and in our societal nature to be able to collectively change life conditions. Despite the more pessimistic experience that it is difficult to change the lifeworld and the system, it is intellectually and practically important to emphasize a collective capability, beyond looking at agency from an individualistic perspective. Emphasizing collective agency invokes concepts such as solidarity, which is a concept lost in traditional psychology but is used in social and political theory. Not seeing the possibility of collective agency, or only seeing it in the negative, is part of epistemic ignorance, or a form of nihilism. Understanding collective agency means also that psychology connects to the psychological humanities, where we can think about those forms of activity that have brought about social change and social justice.

Hope and Change

DW: As you were talking about the potential for human change, I've thought about how it is interesting that, on the one hand, I could see some people interpreting your work as somewhat pessimistic, due to its deep criticisms of psychology and society. But what I am hearing in what you are saying actually strikes me as a deeply optimistic frame about what it means to be human and the ability of communities and societies to change, even radically.

TT: I am a dialectical pessimist and optimist at the same time. Pessimist because of the overwhelming problems in nature, society, and psychology. Optimist because, I guess, it is the only thing left when dealing with these problems and if you believe that justice remains an existential principle. I also believe that we can fight until death, as limited as this fight might be. From an existential and even ethical perspective, from the perspective of maintaining meaning in a personal life, what would be the alternative to hope? Once you have answered Camus's (1955) most serious philosophical question, the question of suicide, you need to move forward. The alternative would be nihilism. I should mention that when I use the term nihilism, I do not mean it in a religious sense but in the psychosocial meaning that we cannot change anything but ourselves. The idea that we still can change the world is the opposite of nihilism.

Hope is an important principle, as the socialist philosopher Ernst Bloch (1986) argued in his three volumes. Hope has important psychological, existential, and spiritual elements and, as his history of social utopias shows, it is part of our humanity. We envision alternatives to the status quo. If you come politically from a socialist background, and in the North American context I should emphasize that I detest any form of authoritarianism and totalitarianism, right or left, then the idea of a better and fairer future for all of humanity, and not for my privileged self that is doing fine, remains an important source to combat nihilism as well as to engender critical analyses about what is wrong and what could be done in this world.

My own oscillation between despair and hope, given our current situation, is perhaps the outcome of a negative dialectic (Adorno, 1990) combined with the principle of hope (Bloch, 1986). Critical analyses can move into despair – consider racism – but despair can move into hope – consider the current social movements against violence against Black lives supported by varieties of people. Then again, a recognition of the obstacles and calcified structures that are very difficult to change may lead to pessimism, as do some of the choices of some Americans and Canadians in the COVID-19 crisis. If you think about the global problems that we encounter with increasing wealth inequality in the social domain, the destruction of the environment in the natural domain, the reemergence of the fascist mentality, necropolitics during the pandemic, and systemic racist actions by state agents, one could fall back into pessimism. At the same time, there remain reasons for hope. The optimistic strategy is to move forward with the idea that we actually can do things about these problems until our last breath. It is part of our mental life and our nature, but it is a path that needs to be taken.

DW: When it comes to psychology as a discipline, or in its relationship to the humanities or other disciplines, what changes have you seen that give you hope for change in the future? Any emerging hopeful trends you see, such as among students or the rising generation?

TT: In psychology we have a similar dialectical process. Consider our professional organizations. I see positive change in the APA, where issues of social justice, working on behalf of the marginalized, issues of racism, and many other social issues have been addressed. At the same time, we have observed negative changes in the APA, the marketization of psychology, and even changes to the ethics code that have allowed so-called enhanced interrogation techniques, in reality, torture, to follow the law – as interpreted by lawyers with a narrow interest in fighting foreign enemies – instead of following the higher-standard ethics code. You have these dialectics, or if you use another metaphor, "One step forward and two steps back," or if you are more optimistic, "Two steps forward and one step back." The complexity of societal, institutional, or intellectual realities needs to be kept in mind when hoping for psychology.

My experience with students is very similar. I have had some students who seem to have zero interest in intellectual matters, and I have asked them why they are at university. Some students have answered this question by saying, "Well, my mother has a real estate business, and I just need a degree. Psychology seemed easy enough." You can be pessimistic about such statements, or you can analyze and theorize them. What has happened in the world of education that some, perhaps still only a few, students develop a completely instrumental, cost–benefit analysis of education as a means to an end? Indeed, the neoliberal mindset can help explain why some students have no interest in content and see only instrumental value in taking psychology or being at university. On the other hand, I also see undergraduate students who are advanced theoretically, ethically, and in terms of knowledge. When you see the positive and the negative at the same time, when you encounter dialectical processes, why not recognize the positive?

In research, my late colleague David Rennie (2012) studied the amount of qualitative research in psychology and found that the amount was marginal. We may see increasing qualitative research in psychology, published in journals and other places, and we may think that psychology is changing. Even though his original study is now nearly 20 years old, the total number of qualitative research articles in psychology has remained minuscule compared to the number of quantitative studies, based on what critics have called *positivist* or what we call *naïve empiricist* practices. This brings us back to the dialectics of despair and hope. There is hope that qualitative research may change the discipline or at least that there is a place for psychologists to publish qualitative material, aiming for a broader horizon. At the same time, when you compare the numbers of quantitative and qualitative publications, you realize that things have not changed substantially.

DW: The same can be said for research in psychology pertaining to ethnic minority groups or racialized groups. I was a coauthor of a systematic review on that literature, and there really has not been much change in recent decades (Hartmann et al., 2013). It may seem like there has been just because there are so many more publications. But, comparatively, the change is pretty minimal. I want to hope that things really are changing with the current generation of students. I guess we will see.

TT: Indeed, we will see. As mentioned before, I am impressed by some students, and disappointed by other students with no interest in the subject matter. Yet, my point was that we should not focus on disappointment and take this personally but theorize such phenomena. Why don't some students want to study? This is a fascinating question when we take the original meanings of student, education, and university into account. Clearly, meanings change, and under the realities of neoliberal capitalism, young people need to show degrees, not for the sake of the knowledge they have but to show that they can commit to something, that they can accept orders by authorities, that they have engaged in soft skills such as "communication" – the hidden curriculum, as it has been called – in order to get a job in a competitive labor market. If instrumental reasons dominate the lifeworlds of students, then it would not be unreasonable to dedicate the least amount of work and effort to knowledge and just focus on marketable skills.

Instrumental thinking, cost-benefit analyses, and utilitarian attitudes students observe from their professors as well as in teaching, research, and service reinforce instrumentality in academia. Students of psychology might wonder about future jobs and understand the marketability of degrees, with some studies showing that the financial value of a psychology degree is low. We should therefore not wonder about indifference towards learning, combined with the issue of the irrelevance of some material taught in psychology, as we discussed before. Apathy towards educational opportunities to develop traditional or critical knowledge about an area is not personally disappointing once we theorize it. What is going on in our culture and society regarding knowledge? Experiences and analyses corroborate that I should be both pessimistic and optimistic at the same time about the next generation of psychologists.

Anticipated Future Directions of Teo's Scholarship

DW: Speaking of the future, what do you imagine are the future directions of your thought, your scholarship?

TT: From a theoretical point of view, I want to advance a critical theory of subjectivity as well as work on the relationship between epistemology and ethics. From a professional point of view, I want to provide space for the psychological humanities as well as for critical psychology (Teo, 2014). For the theory of subjectivity, I start out with the idea that we need a theory of subjectivity because it is arguably an important subject matter of psychology. If you read through historical material, you can see that we have a fascination with subjectivity, which could contribute to overcoming divisions in psychology, when integrating knowledge. Strangely, we don't have a theory of subjectivity in academic psychology.

The next question is, of course, what are the elements of a theory of subjectivity? I suggest that we should make a conceptual distinction between what I call sociosubjectivity, intersubjectivity, and intrasubjectivity. Sociosubjectivity, a neologism, refers to the fact that our subjectivity is culturally, historically, and societally constituted or embedded. This sociosubjectivity is of course connected with intersubjectivity and intrasubjectivity. Using this schema, I want to challenge social deterministic theories that emphasize the external as well as purely individualistic theories that focus on internal processes; psychoanalysis would be an example of the latter. I connect these conceptual elements by suggesting that we have to understand their nexus if we want to understand subjectivity. We experience how culture, society, and history play a role in our own subjectivity, how these dimensions may be mediated for instance through personal relations, peers, friends, parents, teachers, and so forth but also by personal idiosyncrasies, self-interpretations, and activities.

The entanglement between sociosubjectivity, intersubjectivity, and intrasubjectivity makes subjectivity unique and irreplaceable, which would be a metaphysical element in a theory of subjectivity.

From a social-deterministic or sociological perspective, the problem arises as to why everyone is not the same. For instance, why do some people develop mental health issues in the context of income inequality while others do not? I do not refer to personal character or individual differences as an answer but to the fact that if you grow up in a particular economic context, culture, and time, you are to a certain degree similar, but you are also different at the same time. There will not be a perfect clone of you who is identical in their subjectivity. Even if you were able to clone a person of your age, the clone will develop in a different path and assume their own subjectivity. In that sense, neither sociological nor biological determinism can account for uniqueness or irreplaceability. What makes one unique is this nexus of personal interpretations, experiences, interpersonal relationships, and the meaning that one attributes to them, embedded in cultures and subcultures, one's position in societies, the historical stage, and institutions. I also want to emphasize that we suture ourselves into society, or immerse ourselves into culture, so that we do not experience society as something outside of us – not to deny that there might be problems in this suturing process.

Another element is, of course, that we cannot neglect *physis*. A theory of subjectivity needs to include not only mentality but also the body. When I speak of the body, I do not just mean the body as a biological entity, or psychological body images that can be measured, but the phenomenological first-person experience of the body. If you think about it, biological realities are relational realities; my height, my cognitive or athletic abilities, abstracting for the moment the sociohistorical constitution of these concepts, only make sense in relation to others. Completely by myself, I would not have language, I would not know if I am tall or short or if I am smart or not. There are also other elements that need to be included in a theory of subjectivity. For example, we need to include the the dynamics of inner life, intrasubjectivity, the fact that we should understand subjectivity in the context of everyday life, and the increasing role of technology, temporality, and power. I am working on such a project.

As mentioned, I am also working on the entanglement of epistemology and ethics, which itself is part of a larger project, not only an intellectual but also an organizational program, that is the psychological humanities. For the project on the relationship between ethics and epistemology, I begin with the intuition, but also arguments and evidence, that ethics and epistemology are closely linked. For example, I am suggesting that method itself is a way of trying to do justice to an object. If it is the case that methods are attempts to do justice to an object, then inherent in every method is a link between ethics and epistemology. I do not mean social justice here; I mean literally doing justice to an object. The idea that method tries to do justice to an object, the *object-intentionality* of method, suggests that a method is always directed towards something else, an object, and in order to understand its quality, we must analyze the degree to which a method does justice to the object.

A similar argument about the relationship between epistemology and ethics has been made by Daston and Galison (2007) in their book on *Objectivity* in which they point out that objectivity is not just an epistemic but also a moral category. Consider when someone calls you out to be more objective. It is a moral call, and you might even be outraged because you think you are objective, that you employ a moral feeling. If the issue were only scientific you would simply focus on what to do in order to achieve what was asked for. "Being objective" is a value and virtue in epistemic endeavors. I want to work more systematically on this problem, but where this project will take me, I do not know at the moment.

All of this is embedded in the program of the psychological humanities, which I hope will be a platform that people can work and identify with. When Wade Pickren and I assumed co-editorship of *The Review of General Psychology*, the APA Division 1 journal, we specifically invited people to submit papers from the perspective of the psychological humanities. We have published a few papers already within this program. Still, being interested in the history and philosophy of science, and on the background of neoliberal academic criteria, where journals are evaluated in terms of impact factor and other numeric criteria, I realize that a paper from the psychological humanities, with fewer people associated with this program, may decrease the journal's impact. But I am not worried much about it at the moment because the content of knowledge is more important to me than the impact factor of the journal. My point is to do justice to a problem, and if a psychological humanities article does justice to a problem, then there is no reason not to publish it, even if traditional psychologists may think that it is not science.

Concluding Thoughts

DW: Well, we have covered a lot of territory in this interview, and I wonder if we might just try to bring things full circle. How would you frame, through your own work, an ethics of psychology when interpreted in the context of a neoliberal political order?

TT: The ethics of psychology in a neoliberal order requires in my view critical psychology with a critique of neoliberal totalitarianism, a reconstruction of its discursive and material consequences on mental life, and the vision for a better future. This includes, from the perspective of an ethical critique, an analysis of the adaptive functions of the discipline and profession of psychology in this reality. It is an ethical competence to challenge the pathologies of psychology under neoliberal capitalism. In that sense, I understand critical psychology as an ethical project. Because ethics and epistemology are connected, we need to challenge a psychology that disconnects individual mental life from societal realities. If we do that, we can challenge pathologies not of individuals but of advanced capitalism. This critique will provide a more comprehensive understanding of human mental life. That would be a short answer to a difficult question.

DW: The ethical response for psychology within a neoliberal order is to in fact be critical about it and to mark the contours of what is taking place, how that's impacting one's own work as well as society, and then starting to imagine societal change around it.

TT: Indeed. Let me emphasize again: deconstructive, reconstructive, but also constructive work (Teo, 2020b) need to go together. We have to criticize and to understand, but we also have the ethical responsibility to develop alternative ideas, an alter-psychology, or an Alter-global psychology, at least as a project (Teo & Afsin, 2020). We must develop ideas on how things could be different, developing counterconcepts, new theories, different methodologies and practices. I think all of these things are actually happening in critical psychology, theoretical psychology, and other alternative psychologies. I also understand that there might be a season associated with phases of this work. Critique often occurs at a younger stage of career because you can identify the problems occurring in psychology early on if you pay sufficient attention. Reconstruction requires more work, more knowledge in order to understand why something happened as it did. Finally, construction, at least from an academic perspective, seems to be the most difficult task. On the other hand, everyone is invited to envision a better society and psychology. Maybe it is elitist to assume that this can only happen at an advanced stage of career. If we take the idea of a democratic science seriously, it seems that I have reverted back to a psychology *for* people, which is better than a psychology *about* people but still elitist. The critical need is a democratic psychology *with* people, an important principle found in the varieties of critical psychology around the world.

References

Aalbers, D., & Teo, T. (2017). The American Psychological Association and the torture complex: A phenomenology of the banality and workings of bureaucracy. *Journal für Psychologie, 25*(1), 179–204.

Adorno, T. W. (1990). *Negative Dialektik* [*Negative dialectics*]. Suhrkamp.

Baudrillard, J. (1988). *Selected writings* (M. Poster, Ed.). Stanford University Press.

Bloch, E. (1986). *The principle of hope* (N. Plaice, S. Plaice, & P. Knight, Trans.). MIT Press.

Blumenbach, J. F. (1795). *De generis humani varietate native* [*On the natural variety of humankind*] (3rd ed.). Vandenhoek and Ruprecht.

Camus, A. (1955). *The myth of Sisyphus and other essays*. Vintage Books.

Cosgrove, L., Krimsky, S., Vijayaraghavan, M., & Schneider, L. (2006). Financial ties between DSM-IV panel members and the pharmaceutical industry. *Psychotherapy and Psychosomatics, 75*(3), 154–160.

Daston, L., & Galison, P. (2007). *Objectivity*. Zone Books.

Gigerenzer, G. (2004). Mindless statistics. *The Journal of Socio-Economics, 33*(5), 587–606. https://doi.org/10.1016/j.socec.2004.09.033

Habermas, J. (1968). *Erkenntnis und Interesse [Knowledge and interest].* Suhrkamp.

Hartmann, W. E., Kim, E. S., Kim, J. H. J., Nguyen, T. U., Wendt, D. C., Nagata, D. K., & Gone, J. P. (2013). In search of cultural diversity, revisited: Recent publication trends in cross-cultural and ethnic minority psychology. *Review of General Psychology, 17*(3), 243–254. https://doi.org/10.1037/a0032260

Holzkamp, K. (1983). *Grundlegung der Psychologie [Laying the foundations for psychology].* Campus.

Kuhn, T. S. (1962). *The structure of scientific revolutions.* University of Chicago Press.

Mbembe, A. (2003). Necropolitics. *Public Culture, 15*(1), 11–40.

Mecheril, P., & Teo, T. (Eds.). (1997). *Psychologie und Rassismus [Psychology and racism].* Rowohlt.

O'Doherty, K. C., & Winston, A. (2014). Variable, overview. In T. Teo (Ed.), *Encyclopedia of critical psychology* (pp. 2051–2062). Springer.

Rennie, D. L. (2012). Qualitative research as methodical hermeneutics. *Psychological Methods, 17*(3), 385–398. https://doi.org/http://dx.doi.org/10.1037/a0029250

Teo, T. (2004). The historical problematization of "mixed race" in psychological and human-scientific discourses. In A. Winston (Ed.), *Defining difference: Race and racism in the history of psychology* (pp. 79–108). American Psychological Association. https://doi.org/10.1037/10625-004

Teo, T. (2005). *The critique of psychology: From Kant to postcolonial theory.* Springer.

Teo, T. (2008). From speculation to epistemological violence in psychology: A critical-hermeneutic reconstruction. *Theory & Psychology, 18*(1), 47–67. https://doi.org/10.1177/0959354307086922

Teo, T. (2009). Psychology without Caucasians. *Canadian Psychology, 50*(2), 91–97. https://doi.org/10.1037/a0014393

Teo, T. (2010a). Ontology and scientific explanation: Pluralism as an a priori condition of psychology. *New Ideas in Psychology, 28*, 235–243. https://doi.org/10.1016/j.newideapsych.2009.09.017

Teo, T. (2010b). What is epistemological violence in the empirical social sciences? *Social and Personality Psychology Compass, 4/5*, 295–303. https://doi.org/10.1111/j.1751-9004.2010.00265.x

Teo, T. (2011). Empirical race psychology and the hermeneutics of epistemological violence. *Human Studies, 34*, 237–255. https://doi.org/10.1007/s10746-011-9179-8

Teo, T. (2013). Backlash against American psychology: An indigenous reconstruction of the history of German critical psychology. *History of Psychology, 16*(1), 1–18. https://doi.org/10.1037/a0030286

Teo, T. (Ed.). (2014). *Encyclopedia of critical psychology* (4 vols.). Springer.

Teo, T. (2015). Critical psychology: A geography of intellectual engagement and resistance. *American Psychologist, 70*(3), 243–254. https://doi.org/10.1037/a0038727

Teo, T. (2017). From psychological science to the psychological humanities: Building a general theory of subjectivity. *Review of General Psychology, 21*(4), 281–291. https://doi.org/10.1037/gpr0000132

Teo, T. (2018a). Homo neoliberalus: From personality to forms of subjectivity. *Theory & Psychology, 28*(5), 581–599. https://doi.org/10.1177/0959354318794899

Teo, T. (2018b). *Outline of theoretical psychology: Critical investigations.* Palgrave Macmillan.

Teo, T. (2019a). Academic subjectivity, idols, and the vicissitudes of virtues in science: Epistemic modesty versus epistemic grandiosity. In K. O'Doherty, L. Osbeck, E. Schraube, & J. Yen (Eds.), *Psychological studies of science and technology* (pp. 31–48). Palgrave Macmillan. https://doi.org/10.1007/978-3-030-25308-0_2

Teo, T. (2019b). Beyond reflexivity in theoretical psychology: From philosophy to the psychological humanities. In T. Teo (Ed.), *Re-envisioning theoretical psychology: Diverging ideas and practices* (pp. 273–288). Palgrave Macmillan. https://doi.org/10.1007/978-3-030-16762-2_11

Teo, T. (2020a). Subhumanism: The re-emergence of an affective-symbolic ontology in the migration debate and beyond. *Journal for the Theory of Social Behaviour.* Advance online publication. https://doi.org/10.1111/jtsb.12237

Teo, T. (2020b). Theorizing in psychology: From the critique of a *hyperscience* to conceptualizing subjectivity. *Theory & Psychology, 30*(6), 759–767. https://doi.org/10.1177/0959354320930271

Teo, T., & Afsin, B. (2020). The impossible conditions of the possibility of an alter-global psychology. In L. Sundararajan, K.-K. Hwang, & K.-H. Yeh (Eds.), *Global psychology from indigenous perspectives* (pp. 159–174). Palgrave Macmillan. https://doi.org/10.1007/978-3-030-35125-0_10

Teo, T., & Ball, L. (2009). Twin research, revisionism, and metahistory. *History of the Human Sciences, 22*, 1–23. https://doi.org/10.1177/0952695109345418

Walsh, R., Teo, T., & Baydala, A. (2014). *A critical history and philosophy of psychology: Diversity of context, thought, and practice.* Cambridge University Press.

Wilkinson, R., & Pickett, K. (2009). *The spirit level: Why greater equality makes societies stronger.* Bloomsbury Press.

Woodward, W., & Ash, M. G. (Eds.). (1982). *The problematic science: Psychology in nineteenth-century thought.* Praeger.

3

Culture, Context, and Coloniality

Bhatia's Decolonizing Psychology and Kirschner's Sociocultural Subjectivities

Sunil Bhatia and Suzanne R. Kirschner interview each other
Sunil Bhatia and Suzanne R. Kirschner

Introduction

Sunil Bhatia and Suzanne R. Kirschner are cultural and critical psychologists who have been friends for two decades. Each has pursued distinctive projects, but their contributions have several key themes and sensibilities in common. Both Bhatia and Kirschner are committed to advancing a psychology that foregrounds the sociocultural nature of human development, subjectivity, sociality, and identity. Their contributions have cast light on the ethnocentric and parochial assumptions, beliefs, and values inherent in many conventional psychologies. They have challenged claims that hegemonic theories of human development and personality provide universal norms of health and measures of maturity. They have also explored the ways that such theories, and the practices they inform, have been used to rationalize or extend systemic societal and global inequities. Drawing on multiple disciplines, both Bhatia and Kirschner have developed theories and methodologies that help to reconstitute psychological inquiry. Both of them have sought to develop a psychology that can better recognize the complexities of human conditions and needs and can thereby contribute to more just and equitable social and global arrangements.

Sunil Bhatia, PhD, is an internationally known professor in psychology and H\human development. His book publications include *American Karma: Race, Culture and Identity in the Indian Diaspora* (2007, New York University Press) and *Decolonizing Psychology: Globalization, Social Justice and Indian Youth Identities* (2018, Oxford University Press), which received the 2018 William James Book Award from the American

DOI: 10.4324/9781003280033-4

Psychological Association. The book was given a runner up "honorable mention" in the 2018 Outstanding Book award by the International Congress of Qualitative Inquiry. His research focuses on understanding the development of self and identity within the contexts of racism, neoliberal globalization, and migration. His current scholarly project on decolonizing psychology attempts to provide a conceptual framework to reimagine the discipline of psychology within the context of global capitalism. The concept of decolonizing psychology questions how Euro-American scientific psychology becomes the standard bearer of psychology around the world and thereby determines whose stories get told, what knowledge is considered as legitimate, and whose lives are considered central to the future of psychology.

Dr. Bhatia is a fellow of Division 24 of APA and serves on the editorial boards of several journals. He has published over 50 articles and book chapters and has received Connecticut College's 2018 Nancy Batson Nisbet Rash Faculty Research Award; the 2005 John King Excellence in Teaching Award; the American Psychological Association's 2015 International Humanitarian Award; and the 2017 Theodore Sarbin Award for distinguished contributions to psychology. Bhatia is a professor of human development at Connecticut College and has taught at this undergraduate college for 21 years. Bhatia grew up in Pune, India, and received his undergraduate and post-graduate degrees in psychology from University of Pune. Subsequently, he received his PhD in developmental psychology from Clark University in Worcester, MA.

Suzanne R. Kirschner is an internationally recognized scholar and teacher. She has published widely on the interrelationships between psychological theories/practices and their social and cultural contexts, as well as on how human subjectivities are shaped within those contexts. She is the author of *The Religious and Romantic Origins of Psychoanalysis: Individuation and Integration in Post-Freudian Theory* (Cambridge University Press, 1996) and co-editor (with Jack Martin) of *The Sociocultural Turn in Psychology: The Contextual Emergence of Mind and Self* (Columbia University Press, 2010). A concern with metatheoretical issues runs through all of her work. She is frequently invited to serve as a commentator for collections of papers dealing with theoretical and cultural psychology and their methodologies. Building on her previous projects, Kirschner is developing an approach to the study of psychological life that acknowledges the reality and importance of conflict, tragedy, and interiority, by integrating sociocultural approaches to subjectivity with the theories and methods of psychodynamic ethnography.

Originally from New York City, Kirschner studied psychology, sociology, and literature at Swarthmore College. She received her doctorate in comparative human development and psychology from Harvard University. She taught at Harvard for several years, serving as a lecturer on social studies (a multidisciplinary social sciences concentration) and a research fellow in the Department of Social Medicine at Harvard Medical School. For over 20 years, she was a professor at the College of the Holy Cross (Worcester, MA), including several years as Director of the College Honors Program. Currently, she is Professor Emerita of Psychology at Holy Cross and a visiting scholar in Harvard's Department of the History of Science. A fellow of the American Psychological Association, Kirschner is a former president of both the Society for Theoretical and Philosophical Psychology (APA Division 24) and the Society for Qualitative Inquiry in Psychology (a section of APA's Division of Quantitative and Qualitative Methods). She serves on the editorial boards of several journals and book series. Kirschner has received awards for her scholarship, teaching, and service, including the L. Bryce Boyer Prize in Psychoanalytic Anthropology from the Society for Psychological Anthropology of the American Anthropological Association. In 2019, she received the APA's Theodore Sarbin Award for Distinguished Contributions to Narrative and Critical Psychology.

Sunil Interviews Suzanne

Sunil Bhatia (SB):   Do you think your work has any core themes? How would you describe the intellectual history of your research or scholarship? These questions are connected, so you could start with either one.

Suzanne R. Kirschner (SK):   Thank you, Sunil. There are several core themes and commitments that run through virtually everything I've written. Rather than start by listing them, I'll tell a story that I think illustrates some enduring themes in my work. That story is also a response to your second question, about my personal intellectual history.

When I was a sophomore in college, I took a course in social psychology. On the first day of class, after a short lecture on the history of the field of social psychology, the professor gave us an article from *Scientific American* on some experiments that studied the effects of overcrowding on rats. We talked about the article a little bit and then he asked us to take out a piece of paper and design an experiment in which we tested the effects of overcrowding on college students in dorms. I took out the piece of paper and I wrote something down. I crossed it out, then wrote something else down, and then crossed that out. Finally, towards the bottom of the page, I just wrote, "I don't think that using this kind of scientific method and design is appropriate for studying some kinds of questions about human beings, including this one."

I handed the paper to the professor, probably without looking him in the eye, and I thought, well, I guess that's the end of the line for me and psychology. I am going to have to major in something else, maybe French Literature. That wasn't really a brand new idea for me, because I had always been more of a humanities-and-arts type of person. I wrote poetry, I wrote songs, I did a lot of theatre. The types of psychology that I gravitated toward, even in high school, were the non-experimental kinds, especially psychoanalysis and existential psychology. By the time I took that social psychology class, I had been in college long enough to be disabused of the idea that as a psychology major, I would be able to study those more interpretive or philosophical approaches. I was also interested in the history of ideas, and I had even taken a seminar in the sociology of knowledge. So, by the time I set foot in that psychology class, I already knew I was very interested in how psychological theories, like many other forms of knowledge, were related to their historical and cultural contexts. I certainly knew I was a lot more interested in those questions than I was in what I thought of as scientistic experiments. I say "scientistic," because those kinds of research designs seemed to me to be so inadequate for studying human experience, meaningful action, and other aspects of human existence that I thought should be included in what psychologists study. When the professor started off our first class by telling us about the history of social psychology, I was intrigued. But then he asked us to design the rat experiment using humans, and I thought, well, that's it – I'm out.

But what I didn't know about this professor was – well, his name was Kenneth Gergen. Unbeknownst to me, Gergen had recently written an article titled "Social Psychology as History" (1973). As you might know, that article was very provocative and also very influential; it was one of the publications that launched the social constructionist movement in psychology. In it, he challenged psychological inquiry along the lines I've just mentioned. So, as luck would have it, I had found a teacher who would appreciate, support, and even encourage my critical stance towards academic psychology. He even was generous when it came to my disagreeing with him, and I've always disagreed with him about a number of things. But the point is, I didn't have to major in literature after all!

Jeanne Marecek, a pioneer of critical and feminist discursive psychology, was also one of my professors. She was a newly minted clinical psychology researcher from Yale, and I believe that her training had been pretty conventional and empirical. She was also influenced by the feminist movement with its critiques of psychology's androcentric and patriarchal assumptions. I remember being in her Personality course and then in her Psychology of Women class, and being the only person defending Freud – or at least defending psychoanalysis – because Freud was really persona non grata among feminists at that time. There always seemed to me to be something worth preserving in some aspects of psychodynamic approaches, in spite of all the parts that were pernicious or just wrong. That, by the way, flags another enduring theme in my work, my interest in psychoanalysis as both influenced by its cultural and social contexts *and* containing some deep truths about the human condition. It's not either/or, it's both/and.

Ken and Jeanne were both wonderful teachers and had a great impact on me. My point here is that encountering them, who are my friends to this day, made me think that perhaps I could become a psychologist after all. Perhaps there would be space for me to be the kind of psychologist who focuses on critical metatheory and also contributes to the development of alternative, mostly qualitative and meaning-centered, approaches to psychological inquiry.

After college, I worked in publishing for a couple of years, but the pull of academia was strong. Of course, I had to choose my doctoral program carefully. Human Development programs at Harvard and

Chicago were known to be more hospitable than most straight psychology programs to someone with my interests and goals – partly, I think, because they were multidisciplinary. I chose the one at Harvard, because I wanted to work with Robert LeVine, a psychological anthropologist who had incredible multidisciplinary breadth. I liked psychological anthropology because the methods they used presumed that people were meaning-making and meaning-using beings. Psychological anthropologists studied people in their social and cultural contexts; of course, this is a field that has greater awareness of cultural diversity. Psychological anthropologists in general manifested much less ethnocentrism than psychologists in, for example, the way they studied and represented human development. Also, anthropology at that time was having a big reflexive moment. There were a number of epistemological issues that were front-and-center, such as questions about knowledge and interpretation, which were core preoccupations of mine. Substantively, I was interested in exploring how psychological theories and practices were influenced by their cultural contexts. Thus, I was more interested in studying the history, sociology, and anthropology of the theories themselves than I was in using them to actually study children's development, although I did some conventional developmental research, too. This is a direct outgrowth of what I mentioned before: my interest in the sociology of knowledge and the historicity of psychological theories. LeVine, who is by no means a social constructionist, taught us a lot about how all theories of human development are in a sense "folk psychologies," because they are influenced by the culture and social structures in which they are produced. I wrote a dissertation, which then became a book, about cultural influences on post-Freudian Anglo-American psychoanalytic theories of the development of the self or ego (Kirschner, 1996). It was very influenced by some of the social theorist Max Weber's ideas. It drew on multiple disciplines, and my advisor sometimes tried to categorize it as a "cultural sociology of knowledge," which I think makes sense, as does the fact that it was published in a sociology series called "Cambridge Cultural Social Studies."

One important overlap between your work and mine, I think, is that we both want to show that supposedly universal, hegemonic psychological theories of social, emotional, and personality development are grounded in assumptions, beliefs, and values that are strongly influenced by the cultural and social contexts in which they were developed. Both you and I have wanted to explore how, in their inception and their effects, many of these theories have been used in ways that are imperialistic, colonizing, and colonializing, and in many cases are constituted through colonization. In other words, they are parasitic on the encounters with "others" and have been in a position to impose upon those "others" their own yardsticks and standards in distorting and oppressive ways. Currently, in psychology, there is a movement that goes by the name "indigenous psychology." I don't like to call North American Protestant-descended values and beliefs about personhood "indigenous," because they are secularized and transmuted versions of beliefs that were brought here by settler-colonists (Kirschner, 2019a). I mean, they are not indigenous to North America. My point here is, when I went to graduate school in the 1980s, I was primarily interested in studying the range and variety of indigenous psychologies, as well as other ethnopsychologies, and in demonstrating how both formal and laypersons' psychological ideas and practices in the US and Western Europe are, to a great extent, ethnopsychologies (Kirschner, 1990, 2000). I even taught a seminar to Harvard undergraduates in the late 1980s and early 1990s called "Person and Self in Cross-Cultural Perspective," which dealt extensively with these themes.

So, those are the main forms my critique of psychology took during those early years. My interest in studying the relationship between post-Freudian psychoanalytic psychology and its sociocultural context also led me to do field research. For example, with a team from Harvard Medical School's Department of Social Medicine, I did ethnographic research in a community mental health clinic where the directors had a predominantly psychodynamic orientation, though they were also eclectic. We looked at how the therapists were responding to the advent of managed health care, which also revealed what their assumptions were about what good care is (Kirschner & Lachicotte, 2001; Ware et al., 2000). When practitioners feel that their system of practices and values is challenged, and when we can observe what they do in response to that threat, it's a great way to illuminate what those values and assumptions are.

SB: Could you give us a snapshot of how you went from your grad school kind of understanding, and your focus on interdisciplinary frameworks to study psychoanalytic theory, to your critique of neuro-scientific identities?

SK: You asked about moving from studying one psychological way of knowing – psychodynamic theories and practices – to another, biobehavioral and neuroscientific approaches. That move had a lot to do with the fact that by the 1990s, or even before, when people said "psychology," the typical association was often, "brain." Training in psychiatry certainly had gone in that direction. I had begun teaching in a psychology department, which was by no means predominantly neuroscientific, but certainly our students often came in thinking they wanted to study psychology at a biological level. There seemed to be fewer undergraduates who entered college thinking that studying psychology would be what I had hoped it was about when I was their age. Also, I got interested in temperament theory, a biobehavioral approach to individual differences in toddlers and young children. It seemed to me that some versions of temperament theory were less problematically reductionist than, say, the neuroscience of personality, and also less inherently pathologizing. I find the neuroscience of personality really interesting, by the way. But it often seems to advance, or be used to advance, a lot of unwarranted conclusions. I didn't want to do research in temperament; I wanted to study temperament approaches from a historical and sociological point of view. I was aware that temperament had been marginalized in psychology during the heyday of learning theories and American-style psychoanalysis, both of which blamed the environment, and especially the mother, for everything "wrong" with a child. But, by the end of the 20th century, it had become more respectable for child development researchers to study the role of temperament. Temperament is seen to be a function of a toddler's constitution. Of course, this was part of a much broader turn, or re-turn, towards seeking neurobiological differences as the basis of personality and psychopathology. I was interested in how this turn towards conceiving mental and behavioral differences as rooted in neurology would play out in a democratic society. The philosopher Charles Taylor wrote that democratic societies are characterized – in ideology, though often not, alas, in practice and reality – by a "modern social imaginary," which presumes that everyone is equal, with people "standing outside of all relations of superiority and inferiority" (Taylor, 2004, p. 5). Of course, democratic visions of equality – even the unrealized ideology Taylor was referencing – don't usually imply that everyone is exactly the same in terms of abilities, talents, personality, potential, and so on. Rather, I think the imaginary that Taylor talked about has more to do with the idea that, regardless of differences, we all should be seen as having equal worth, and that there should be equality in terms of citizenship. I am deeply committed to this understanding of our relations to and with each other. I am also persuaded by the evidence across historical eras and cultures, that there may be a human tendency to hierarchicalize difference. Let me be clear: I don't endorse that tendency; my point is just that you need to recognize how it plays out in human beings' social and cultural life. I can't go into the complexities of this now. But basically, I was interested in how the renewed popularity of these biologistic ways of conceiving of personality, ability and other individual differences (both normative and atypical or "pathological") was being negotiated in a culture that, at least in principle, wants to see itself as not having permanent hierarchies justified on the basis of characteristics that are supposedly inherent and immutable. Because, when it comes to putatively biologically based differences, there is the potential for seeing them as permanent, or at least there is a stronger tendency to do so. So, I did both field research and metatheoretical work in order to explore how people are identified in neurobiological terms, how they identify themselves, and what people do with those identities (Kirschner, 2006, 2009a, 2009b, 2012a, 2012b, 2013a). One of the projects I did was long-term field research at a preschool/early elementary school, studying how they practiced "full inclusion" of children with various kinds of impairments, especially neurological differences such as autism spectrum disorders and Attention-Deficit/Hyperactivity Disorder (Kirschner, 2012a, 2015b). I think it's really important to do fieldwork when one is a critical psychologist, because you learn things you didn't expect to see, and you gain perspectives that you wouldn't necessarily assume.

SB: Maybe you could tell us a little bit about your intellectual pursuits of scholarship in the last five years on subjectivity.

SK: The study of subjectivity has been my main interest in recent years. My thinking on subjectivity has developed over the past decade, and it's still evolving (Kirschner, 2010, 2013b, 2015b, 2019b, 2020). Initially, my main goal was to advocate for subjectivity as a central focus for psychology. I wrote about how the concept of subjectivity was much more developed and routinely used in other disciplines such as anthropology, cultural sociology, cultural and political theory, and literary studies. Subjectivity is such a multi-faceted term, and I think that at least some sociocultural and critical theorists recognize its multiple dimensions. I derive my own definition of it partly from the work of the anthropologist Sherry Ortner (2005), because her overview encompasses a lot of those facets and dimensions. So I'll offer my own explication of the concept of subjectivity, which is partly a paraphrase of Ortner's, but also expands on her ideas. Subjectivity is formed within sociocultural, political-economic contexts and shared by persons who inhabit similar subject-positions. But we also need to recognize it (as Ortner did) as being individual and singular. It is enacted and embodied in the *habitus* (how you carry yourself and are disposed to act and react), but is also a set of processes that are interior, insulated and inaccessible to others. Some theories of subjectivity focus on its "transparency," by which they mean that you are aware of your own thoughts and experiences. But there are also elements of it that are not easily accessible to you; some approaches to subjectivity even recognize a dynamic-unconscious dimension. Subjectivity is produced by both constraint *and* agency, or (in the parlance of some theorists) both power *and* resistance. So, the bottom line is that when people use the term, subjectivity, it points to a lot of different aspects of human experience and embodiment, as well as their contexts. I recognize that not all those who theorize subjectivity accept all of these dimensions, and I myself might not even want to encompass all of them under the term "subjectivity." But I think it's important to spell out all the ways this term is being used, and then to systematically explore what seems to go with what, as well as which elements seem contradictory or otherwise problematic. Taking this systematic, analytical approach enables me to discern what, in the end, makes the most sense to me.

One way to talk about the development of my focus on subjectivity is to see it in terms of a kind of progression in the projects I've pursued, from graduate school onward. Initially, I saw my work as primarily about exploring how psychological ideas and practices are cultural constructs, and also about explaining why it's important, both ethically and epistemologically, for psychologists to recognize this cultural embeddedness. Then, over time, I wanted to explore not just the way that psychological theories can be cultural products, but also how psychological theories and practices influence how people think about themselves, how they think about others, and to some extent how we're kind of formed by or interpellated into our ascribed identities – how we are "made up" as "kinds of people," as Ian Hacking (2006) put it. This led me to the study of subjectivity. One thing you study when you study subjectivity is how people engage with the identities ascribed to them, or into which they are "hailed" or interpellated. Subjectivity can be studied as a shared mentality and habitus, but it can and should also be studied at the individual and singular level. How do individuals take up and make use of discourses in varying ways? How are individuals not only formed by the discourses and identities in which they are immersed, but also making use of them?

I co-edited *The Sociocultural Turn in Psychology* with Jack Martin (Kirschner & Martin, 2010), and thought about the various constitutive sociocultural approaches represented in that book. In particular, I was thinking about what they implied about the nature and dynamics of subjectivity. All of those approaches – discursive, hermeneutic, narrative, dialogical, relational, cultural historical activity theory – envision subjectivity, or what some of them call personhood, as being culturally, socially, or relationally constituted. That's why we called them "strongly constitutive sociocultural psychologies." I wanted to continue to advocate for these approaches, because I think they do add dimensions to psychological theory and inquiry that are neglected or distorted in so much conventional and hegemonic psychology. I wanted to point out that constitutive models of subjectivity were much more developed and frequently found in other disciplines, like anthropology and cultural theory. I argued that the concept of subjectivity should be more widely used in psychology, rather than just on the margins, in sociocultural and critical approaches. But at the same time, I was grappling with my own reservations about these sociocultural approaches to subjectivity. I think I always had those reservations and questions, and they are evident in my work from the very first piece I published (Kirschner, 1987). I wanted to explore them more directly and make them a centerpiece of my work. So, the work I've done on subjectivity over the past several years has involved underscoring its social-cultural nature, while also increasingly criticizing some of the assumptions that one often finds in many sociocultural and even critical-psychological approaches to subjectivity.

It's true that many sociocultural and critical theories have made space for processes associated with individuality: agency, resistance, improvisation. But I am talking about something else, something that goes beyond resistance to an always-already-constituted subject. To put it bluntly, we need a sociocultural psychology that has a psychodynamic dimension (not in some strict Freudian, Kleinian, or even Lacanian sense), in order to do justice to what I can only call the tragic nature of human existence and its impact on our individual and social being. Critical psychologists focus a lot, appropriately I think, on the suffering and constraint that are imposed on a group of people by another group or a political-economic or cultural system. Indeed, this is the kind of subjection that we want to use our work to demonstrate and help to remedy. But I am also talking about broader, unavoidable tragedies, which are simply a part of being human, living with others, and living in the world. I am talking about the gap between our desires or wishes and the limitations of reality. By "the limitations of reality," I refer to both the unavoidable vicissitudes that are truly tragic losses, and the more mundane or trivial disappointments and frustrations of everyday life. The dimension I am referring to here also involves the fact that as much as human beings are related and connected, we are also separate from each other, and that a person's desires and wishes often conflict with those of other people. It also implies that we need a social psychology that is not stunted by what the sociologist Dennis Wrong called an "oversocialized" conception of human nature (1961). I think this oversocialized element is one of the biggest limitations with sociocultural psychologies, something I first wrote about in 2010 but have been developing more recently (Kirschner, 2015a, 2019b, 2020). Our desires, wishes, and responses inevitably will sometimes bring us into conflict with each other, no matter how much we work to improve our society, and to equalize resources and opportunities – which, of course, we should do anyway. But I think it's important for a psychology to recognize that some forms of conflict and competition and envy, for example, are going to spring up anywhere, along with all of our equally strong moral proclivities and tendencies toward relationality, attunement, attachment, and empathy. People also have conflicts and ambivalences within themselves, only some of which are within awareness. I'm not even sure if subjectivity is the word I will end up using. Sometimes I think psyche might be more encompassing of these processes and their complexity. I don't know yet.

There is a kind of reflexive, automatic anti-dualism in most sociocultural psychologies, many of which draw on Wittgenstein, Ryle, Heidegger, and others. But their so-called anti-dualism is taken too far. It leads to a denial that people are separate from each other in ways that are consequential for how we live together, and for how we should understand human psychology. Any reference to a split or bifurcation (between individuals, or between the individual and society) gets lumped together with so-called Cartesian dualism and is seen as both false and bad. I think that this dogmatic lumping should be more carefully considered. Our separateness from each other is part of our finitude. That separateness is an existential reality, as are its consequences and manifestations. All this is part of the human condition. So, my work on subjectivity has moved increasingly in a direction that is more explicit about incorporating that vision. In doing that, it draws on some broadly psychodynamic elements, and also some classic themes in social theory.

SB: And that has been a foundational, epistemological question for many of us who work on contentions between the individual and the culture. You mentioned your mentor, Kenneth Gergen, whose work influenced many, including myself to think of subjectivity in terms of what you would call a relational ontology. Or maybe you wouldn't use the word, relational.

SK: Yes, I see what you mean; there is an approach that says there are no foundations, everything is constituted in relationships. I do not hold to a strongly relational ontology. I think it's problematic to say that our being is completely formed in relationship, or by our culture or society. I've never been persuaded that epistemology and ontology are one and the same (Kirschner, 1987, 2012a). Or, for that matter, that we are fully identical with what we use our ethnopsychologies to say we are (Kirschner, 2019a). Certainly we are deeply shaped by the cultural practices and understandings that form us and that are often articulated in our ethnopsychologies. Yet, I don't think that's the whole story. I've thought a lot about how that claim complicates, somewhat, my original focus on the ways that psychological theories are cultural and historical. It might lead me to assert some basic elements as inherent in human existence and social life, elements that I might want to call foundational and thus would be foundational for a social psychology. But I think that tension can be dealt with. I think some ways of dealing with it are already present in the work of several psychological anthropologists. Also, sometimes you have to sit with intellectual tensions in order to figure out what is at stake, why both sides are "alive" and need to be taken seriously.

SB: So what you are really saying here is that while power subjects you, it constructs you in a certain way that you can react to. And yesterday, we heard Jeff Sugarman say that he was disavowing that there is something internal (Freeman, this volume). So, I'm not sure whether your interiority equals internal. What does it really mean if I were to sort of push you a little bit?

SK: Well, I will go even further. I think that just saying that we can resist the discourses that produce us, or make agentic use of them, or even co-construct them, isn't the whole story either. I am asserting that there are aspects of individual "being" (by which I mean your existence as a separate, desiring and reacting entity) that in some sense "precede" our social being, even if maybe not in a literal, temporal sense. Ultimately, this is a challenge to the premise that the social completely precedes the individual. I suppose that this challenge amounts to heresy among many of my friends and colleagues. It complicates the formulations of subjectivity put forward in Jeff Sugarman's work on historical ontology and also those in discursive and positioning theories, as well as in many hermeneutic and relational psychologies. As for interiority, Jeff and I have talked about this a little, and he has pointed to Rom Harré's work. In his book, *Personal Being*, Harré referred to the inner-outer distinction as "a vivid but dangerous metaphor" (1983, p. 40). I disagree. Even if it is a metaphor, I think it's a vitally important and valuable one. Actually, I think it is far more dangerous to deny it.

I have used several different arguments for why we need to retain interiority as a concept that honors the reality of insulated and complex experience. For one thing, it deepens our sense of other people as having singular, inner lives of emotional responsiveness and desire and suffering and moral complexity. It honors the reality of insulated and complex experience, encouraging a respect for the aspects of another person that are not accessible, that can't be fully known, and thus that one can certainly get "wrong." So, it encourages humility, too. Obviously, I can't go into all of the arguments here (Kirschner, 2015b, 2019a, 2019b, 2020). I will say, though, that William James wrote that the "boundary-line of the mental" should ensure that psychology is very broad and inclusive (1981/1890). So, I find it interesting that discursive psychologists, and others who draw on Wittgenstein or on some of the continental philosophers, devise analytic frameworks for psychological inquiry that don't attend to inner life *as* interior, and that don't honor the sense that we have of ourselves and of others as having "insulated" thoughts and feelings. James, himself, wrote that an essential feature of consciousness was what he called its "absolute insulation." He said something like, no thought ever comes into contact with another person's thoughts. If I understand Harré correctly, he isn't denying conscious experience, but he wants to use the word, "private" instead of "interior," owing to the deep aversion that he and many others have to *anything* that they think might be associated with the dreaded Cartesianism.

Well, I'm not a substance dualist, not in the least. But in this disavowal of inner life, of interiority and its attributes, I think there might also be a risk of dismissing what Chalmers (1995) called the hard problem of consciousness, what other philosophers have called the explanatory gap (Levine, 1982) or the problem of qualia (Nagel, 1974). I recognize that this is exactly what discursivists and other strongly constitutive psychologists want to do: they want to eliminate the mind-body problem with all its splits and hard problems. I do think the focus on discourse and the framing of mind as "public" has been valuable for psychology in some ways. It's just that it goes too far. It limits psychology and glibly closes it off to certain genuine problems. I am also concerned that in disavowing interiority based on its association with an inner-outer split, there is a dogmatic lumping together of any- and everything that asserts any kind of split or bifurcation, even the idea that you and I are separate from each other in very consequential ways. Of course, our theories need also to recognize human relationality and attunement. But to disavow interiority on the basis that it is "Cartesian" is to deny some of the gaps and separations between individuals, and between the individual and their society or culture. As I've said, I think we need to take these gaps seriously as part of the human condition. There is a lot more I could say, most of it critical, both about certain rhetorical styles used by many philosophers, and about the affinity that many of us intellectuals and academics have for psychologies that foreground cognition (whether "private" or "public") or materiality (including behavior and embodiment), or both. The bottom line is that all of these styles and tendencies authorize psychologies that can be useful but are incomplete. I wonder if I might be a politician at this point and answer a question without completely answering it.

SB: You are in a safe space.

SK: Ok, well, I will note just one of the reasons why so many different approaches in psychology have tried to disavow inner life. I'm not just talking about the obvious examples, like behaviorism or eliminativism, which assert that conscious thought is epiphenomenal at best. I'm also talking about discursivist or historical-ontology approaches, which regard humans as culturally constituted, meaning-making beings. I'm saying that they have something in common with those material-reductionist approaches. They, too, don't want to consider interiority as relevant, or maybe even real. And, if you think of the appeal of behaviorism, or any reductive materialist approach, it does suggest something about what even those very different, sociocultural approaches might also find compelling. At the beginning of his book, *Behaviorism* (1924), Watson asked, where has the study of mind gotten us so far? In a single paragraph, he lists a group of quite disparate psychologies, starting with introspectionism, and moving on to functionalism and even James' ideas; then, he dispenses with all of them by saying that they all get you nowhere. He says, they were all trying to study this thing called mind which, as they define it, you can't see and you can't touch. What can we study, he asks, to make psychology a real science? Well, he says, forget consciousness, it's a vague concept and we can't do anything useful with it. Instead, we can study *behavior*.

If we fast forward to neuroscience: again, a big part of the draw is that you can empirically study something material. There is something seductive – if conceptually sloppy – about saying something like, "Now we can actually see anger in the brain" or denying all the other explanatory gaps. I recognize that this is exactly what discursive and other anti-Cartesian psychologies are trying to refute, or rather, transcend: this idea that the brain is the source of the mind. Yet, I think part of the allure of discursivist psychologies is, ironically, similar to the allure of behaviorism and of neuroscience. It's that, by framing mind as a public process, it's easier to study it, because you can study language, discourse, ritualized activity and interactivity, and so on. Hard-core materialists still won't accept these approaches because "discourse" is still too slippery for them. But "public mind" is a lot more accessible as something to study if what you are contrasting it to is an insulated, interior realm, not to mention any kind of dynamic unconscious. The latter is even less transparent because when it comes to unconscious processes, an experiencing subject can only presume to get at those processes indirectly. Some psychologists would say that the arts do a better job of representing inner life. It's true that interior life and its complexities are represented extremely well in modernist fiction. I think all psychologists should study more literature for its insights into human motivation and moral complexity. But you can't completely replace the study of real people with literature.

Besides artistic representation, how can one study inner life (as well as the other dimensions of subjectivity) in ways that recognize its intertwinement with culture? My answer is that there are useful interpretive and methodological tools developed by psychological anthropologists. Some approaches, like person-centered ethnography, have been around a long time (LeVine, 1982; Levy & Hollan, 2014). There are also anthropologists, like Byron Good and his colleagues, who recently have begun to say that we need to have some kind of reference to interiority and to a dynamic unconscious. Some of them use psychodynamic methodologies that are relatively "experience-near," and not too heavily invested in particular psychoanalysts' elaborate metapsychologies. Of course, there are critical psychologists who also draw on psychoanalytic theories and methods. I think Wendy Hollway (Hollway & Jefferson, 2013) has made some really important contributions.

SB: So, having set that intellectual arc, what do you have to say about how the mainstream discipline, so to speak, has engaged with this scholarship? And what has been not just their positionality, but also your positionality vis-à-vis your work in relation to this larger mainstream?

SK: I think I was fortunate that early in my career, right when I started publishing and presenting at conferences, I received some recognition that was very encouraging. The first paper I ever presented, which was published shortly thereafter, and then became a chapter in my book, received a prize in psychoanalytic anthropology from the American Anthropological Association. Even before that, I had what was basically an expanded term paper published in an anthropology journal. I find it interesting that some of my most cited work has been published in medical, psychological, and cultural anthropology journals and venues. The other subfield that has been receptive is the Society for Theoretical and Philosophical Psychology, APA's Division 24. Early on, I found a real intellectual community there, with colleagues who gravitated towards theoretical psychology for many of the same reasons that I did. We could engage with one another's work, and we could "see" each other and feel seen. To be honest, I haven't really expected that most of what I did would get much attention from so-called mainstream psychology, because I wasn't even trying to fit there.

One avenue for impact, though, has been through my job as a psychology professor. At Holy Cross, I have been able to teach courses that introduced students to cultural psychology and its methodologies, to ongoing philosophical issues in psychology, and to many of the themes and approaches I've talked about here. I've supervised scores of research projects and theses, through which students could learn about those perspectives, questions, and methods. Also, I am currently President-elect [2017–2018] of the Society for Qualitative inquiry in Psychology (SQIP), a section of APA's Division 5 (Quantitative and Qualitative Methods). SQIP, which was founded by Ken Gergen, my Holy Cross colleague Mark Freeman, and Ruthellen Josselson, has promoted greater legitimacy for qualitative inquiry within psychology, because it's part of APA. Its journal (*Qualitative Psychology*), annual conferences, and other initiatives all help to advance the visibility and validity of this kind of work.

SB: In addition to looking backward or forward to all the received recognition, acknowledgments, and formal validity that allowed you to move your work, could you also think about instances where your work wouldn't have a wider reach and why? I know you said you didn't care about that, but at the same time what does it say about the larger discipline of psychology then that is unable to take up the work that you do? Why would there be this incongruence?

SK: Well, first off, I think that when a discipline seeks to model itself on a certain image it has of conventional science, which often means seeing its own knowledge as empirically derived, there tends to be less openness to any kind of reflexivity. So, questions like, "Well, where do these models or these theories come from? How are they related to their broader contexts?" are relegated to the history of science. That is often taken to imply that such questions can be sidelined. Ironically, these days, the study of the history of science is much more interdisciplinary, is broadly constructivist, and even has a strong activist dimension. From what I've observed in those departments, there is currently a lot of overlap with Science and Technology Studies (STS). I think that for many psychologists, to scrutinize their theories and practices in terms of how they are grounded in cultural or sociopolitical conditions evokes fears that psychological knowledge, either a particular approach or the field itself, will lose legitimacy. This is perhaps even truer for psychological approaches or subfields that are already considered to be on shaky ground in terms of their own status as science or even as bona fide knowledge of any kind. That defensiveness has long characterized many advocates of psychoanalysis, too – especially during the "science wars" years.

SB: Next, I have a question that has been asked in this forum and many other forums, but I feel like I have a special privilege in asking this question, because at Clark University, I studied with Bernie Kaplan, Michael Bamberg and others, and we always talked about the *telos* question. So, what would you take to be your work's *telos*? What is the end point of it? Where would you say it is? One end is of course that we know we contribute to society, but what would you say would be its *telos*? In terms of social development, maybe?

SK: I'm not sure I would use the word *telos*, because I tend to think of my interest in doing this work in terms of motives and responses, rather than as moved by a final cause. I suppose my work *is* informed by a set of ideas and sensibilities regarding how both psychology and society *should* be. So, perhaps those are *teloi*. The goal or goals of one's intellectual work can change as one learns more, thinks more, lives longer, engages with more people, and so on. Some of the strong criticisms I had of the field when I was a student have persisted, while others have changed or softened. Some new critiques and dissatisfactions have emerged. And, some of my early sensibilities have resurfaced, or at least I've become more able to articulate them and willing to focus on them. For example, for a long time I was okay with endorsing a social psychology that was basically not different from work done by cultural sociologists, symbolic interactionists, and cognitively oriented psychological anthropologists. I love all that work, but I no longer think that is enough. I believe that as psychologists, we can recognize and study the individual as being more than wholly culturally constituted, and certainly more than just a pernicious effect of modernity and capitalism. As I've mentioned, I was never a thoroughgoing social constructionist or hermeneutic psychologist, but I have always recognized the value of those families of approaches. I try to understand and get to the heart of where a theorist or theory is coming from, what their motivation is, or maybe what their *telos* is, so to speak. I have less respect, frankly, for theoretical psychologists, or any scholars, who don't even try to do that, who are dismissive without trying to consider what the theorist or approach they disparage is trying to do. I look for, and often I see, common concerns or similar motives to mine, even in perspectives I ultimately reject. I think it's important to build reflexivity into one's work, so I favor approaches that enable one to do that. By reflexivity, I mean an awareness of what one brings to the project, at many levels. I don't think this invariably influences the end product, by the way. But it helps to foster openness and intellectual humility.

Most of the work I've done is related, at a deep level, to my commitment to democratization, by which I don't mean a particular political structure, but rather a type of society. There are many theories and definitions of democracy, but one very simple definition is Alexis de Tocqueville's (2003) characterization of democracy as an equalization of conditions. So, a democratic society is one in which people aren't born into ascribed, permanent positions in the social structure, such as in an aristocracy or a caste system. Now of course we all know that inequality in this country is still perpetuated regardless of whether in principle we're all supposed to be citizens who stand in an equal relationship to each other. Also, equalization on the surface is not enough; saying we are all equally positioned or advantaged can serve as a kind of obfuscating ideology, because clearly we are not. First off, there is so much structural inequality and oppression; these systemic forces need to be recognized and rectified. And, overlapping with this, people have different needs and capabilities. So I'm also talking about a need for greater equity when it comes to access to resources and rights. I think a lot of us are committed to using our work to help make the walk be more like the talk. I also know that it can be complicated to achieve that, even though we have to keep asking the right ethical questions and trying to live and work by them. I want to always think about my work in terms of questions such as, for example, what is at stake and for whom? At the same time, I think we need to recognize that the consequences of all kinds of language and practices can be quite different from what one might predict. For example, qualitative research in several disciplines such as medical anthropology, STS, and discursive analysis, has shown that the neurological and expansionist turns in psychiatric diagnosis haven't always affected people, or been used by them, in ways that some of us expected. For this and other reasons, I'm glad to see a stronger emphasis on including more stakeholders in many kinds of psychological research, particularly the inclusion of voices and experiences of people who have often been excluded and disempowered. All of these commitments and goals serve and are served by the legitimation of qualitative and mixed methods, and by the development of various kinds of resources for rising psychology students who want to explore topics and methods like those I've highlighted here. These resources and spaces include jobs, graduate programs, journals, funding, conferences, and the like.

Finally, and perhaps most provocatively, I think a psychology that focuses on humans as social and cultural beings needs to foreground certain existential realities inherent in individual and social life. I have always been interested in psychodynamic theories because I see in them a view of the psyche that includes, in its dynamics, the tragedies and vicissitudes of the human condition, and the fact that human beings experience suffering of various kinds. A social and cultural psychology also needs to recognize that moral complexity inheres in both individual motivation and social relations. This is in contrast to both behaviorist and cognitivist psychologies, even in quasi-cognitivist theories that disavow the interior and frame mind as a public process. Along with this, there is in psychodynamic theory a soberness that I have come to appreciate, an anti-utopianism. That doesn't mean you give up the fight for greater justice and equity, to minimize oppression of all kinds and to attenuate suffering. I think there is an ethical imperative to do those things. This tragic vision implies that even as you do that, though, you still need to be cognizant of the limitations and ambivalences that I've been alluding to. So, I guess one of my *teloi* is a psychology that contributes to a more equitable, just, and compassionate society, but that is premised on the understanding that these goals are more likely to be achieved if we can temper our fantasies about them.

References

Chalmers, D. (1995). Facing up to the problem of consciousness. *Journal of Consciousness Studies*, *2*, 200–219.

De Tocqueville, A. (2003). *Democracy in America* (G. Bower, Trans.). Penguin Classics.

Gergen, K. J. (1973). Social psychology as history. *Journal of Personality and Social Psychology*, *26*(2), 309–320. https://doi.org/10.1037/h0034436

Hacking, I. (2006, April 11). *Kinds of people: Moving targets. The tenth British Academy lecture.* https://nurs7009philosophyofinquiry.weebly.com/uploads/6/0/4/0/6040397/hacking_20071.pdf

Harré, R. (1983). *Personal being: A theory for individual psychology*. Blackwell.

Hollway, W., & Jefferson, T. (2013). *Doing qualitative research differently: A psychosocial approach* (2nd ed.). SAGE.

James, W., Burkhardt, F., Bowers, F., Skrupskelis, I. K., & James, W. (1981/1890). *The principles of psychology*. Harvard University Press.

Kirschner, S. R. (1987). "Then what have I to do with thee?": On identity, fieldwork and ethnographic knowledge. *Cultural Anthropology*, *2*(2), 211–234. https://doi.org/10.1525/can.1987.2.2.02a00030

Kirschner, S. R. (1990). The assenting echo: Anglo-American values in contemporary psychoanalytic developmental psychology. *Social Research*, *57*(4), 821–857.

Kirschner, S. R. (1996). *The religious and romantic origins of psychoanalysis: Individuation and integration in post-Freudian theory*. Cambridge University Press.

Kirschner, S. R. (2000). Autonomy and the problem of suffering: Tragedy and transcendence in psychoanalytic discourse. In K. Kopping, R. Wiehl, & M. Welker (Eds.), *Die autonome Person: Eine europaische Erfindung? [The autonomous person: A European invention?]* (pp. 201–221). Ferdinand Schoningh/ Wilhelm Fink.

Kirschner, S. R. (2006). "Good babies' or 'goodness of fit?": Normalizing and pluralizing dimensions of contemporary temperament discourse. *Culture & Psychology*, *12*(1), 5–31. https://doi.org/10.1177/1354067X06061591

Kirschner, S. R. (2009a). Commentary on R. Lester, brokering authenticity: Borderline personality disorder and the ethics of care in an American eating disorders clinic. *Current Anthropology*, *50*, 296–297.

Kirschner, S. R. (2009b). Some current cultural strategies used to mitigate the tension between American democratic values and biological approaches to personality. In T. Teo, P. Stenner, A. Rutherford, E. Park, & C. Baerveldt (Eds.), *Varieties of theoretical psychology: International, philosophical and practical concerns* (pp. 329–342). Captus Press (Toronto).

Kirschner, S. R. (2010). Sociocultural subjectivities: Progress, prospects, problems. *Theory & Psychology*, *20*(6), 765–780. https://doi.org/10.1177/0959354 310375745

Kirschner, S. R. (2012a). Do therapists really "make up" their patients? *Theory & Psychology*, *22*(6), 860–863. https://doi.org/10.1177/0959354311434072

Kirschner, S. R. (2012b). How not to other the other (and similarly impossible goals): Scenes from a psychoanalytic clinic and an inclusive classroom. *Journal of Theoretical and Philosophical Psychology*, *32*(4), 214–229. https://doi. org/10.1037/a0030158

Kirschner, S. R. (2013a). Diagnosis and its discontents: Critical perspectives on psychiatric nosology and the DSM. *Feminism & Psychology*, *23*(1), 10–28. https://doi.org/10.1177/0959353512467963

Kirschner, S. R. (2013b). The many challenges of theorizing subjectivity. *Culture & Psychology*, *19*(2), 225–236. https://doi.org/10.1177/1354067X13478985

Kirschner, S. R. (2015a). Inclusive classrooms. In G. Scarlett (Ed.), *Encyclopedia of classroom management: An A to Z guide* (pp. 404–407). SAGE.

Kirschner, S. R. (2015b). Subjectivity as socioculturally constituted experience. In J. Martin, J. Sugarman, & K. Slaney (Eds.), *The Wiley handbook of theoretical and philosophical psychology: Methods, approaches, and new directions for social sciences* (pp. 293–307). Wiley Blackwell.

Kirschner, S. R. (2019a). Indigenous psychology compared to what? Some complexities of culture, language, and social life. *Journal of Theoretical and Philosophical Psychology*, *39*(2), 98–106. https://doi.org/10.1023/A:1013068803396

Kirschner, S. R. (2019b). The indispensable subject of psychology: Theory, sub-jectivity, and the specter of inner life. In T. Teo (Ed.), *Re-envisioning theoretical psychology* (pp. 131–159). Palgrave Macmillan.

Kirschner, S. R. (2020). Beyond the oversocialized conception of the subject in psychology: Desire, conflict and the problem of social order. *Theory & Psychology, 30*(6).

Kirschner, S. R., & Lachicotte, W. S. (2001). Managing managed care: Habitus, hysteresis and the end(s) of psychotherapy. *Culture, Medicine and Psychiatry, 25*(4), 441–456. https://doi.org/10.1023/A:1013068803396

Kirschner, S. R., & Martin, J. (Eds.). (2010). *The sociocultural turn in psychology: The contextual emergence of mind and self.* Columbia University Press.

LeVine, R. A. (1982). The self in culture. In *Culture, behavior and personality: An introduction to the comparative study of psychosocial adaptation* (pp. 291–304). Aldine Publishing Company.

Levy, R. J., & Hollan, D. W. (2014). Person-centered interviewing and observa-tion. In H. R. Bernard & C. D. Gravlee (Eds.), *Handbook of methods in cultural anthropology* (pp. 333–364). Rowman & Littlefield Publishers.

Nagel, T. (1974). What is it like to be a bat? *Philosophical Review, 83*(4), 435–450.

Ortner, S. B. (2005). Subjectivity and cultural critique. *Anthropological Theory, 5*(1), 31–52. https://doi.org/10.1177/1463499605050867

Taylor, C. (2004). *Modern social imaginaries.* Duke University Press.

Ware, N. C., Lachicotte, W. S., Kirschner, S. R., Cortes, D. E., & Good, B. J. (2000). Clinician experiences of managed mental health care: A rereading of   the threat. *Medical Anthropology Quarterly, 14*(1), 3–27. https://doi.org/10.1525/maq.2000.14.1.3

Watson, J. B. (1924). *Behaviorism.* The People's Institute Publishing Company.

Wrong, D. H. (1961). The oversocialized conception of man in modern sociology. *American Sociological Review, 26*(2), 183–193.

Suzanne Interviews Sunil

SK: Sunil, I was very happy when you asked me to interview you, because I have always felt like we're fellow travelers in a lot of ways. I think I've seen you at meetings of the Society for Psychological Anthro-pology, maybe on a couple of occasions, or at least I feel like I have.

SB: Yes, that's right.

SK: I think there is a lot of overlap in our interests. We are both interested in culture, obviously, and we also share a lot of interdisciplinarity. So, I first just want to thank you for your work, which is so dynamic and brings attention to such important issues. I will start with the same question that you asked me. Does your work have any core themes, motivating interests, or if you prefer, how would you talk about your own intellectual history?

SB: I think if I were to talk about my own intellectual history it would be from a very personal standpoint. I went into psychology, like many other psychology students, to know myself, thinking that I would have some insight into myself, and the second motivation for me of going into psychology was to study the society at that time especially coming out of post-independent India. But I felt very alienated with the psychology when I was studying in India.

I would say that my entire undergraduate graduate education in psychology in India primarily consisted of reading and giving exams on British and American psychology, where theories of self and identity were studied through the lenses of behaviorism and cognitive science. My professors repeatedly emphasized that "psychology is a science of human behavior" and what was of utmost importance to them was that we study behavior, in all its varied manifestations, that is "publicly observable." All our textbooks, and the psychologists we read were American or British. While B.F. Skinner's behaviorism had been usurped by the cognitive science revolution in the United States, we were expected to study and memorize facts about learning theories formulated by the pantheon of well-known American psychologists: Skinner, Tolman, Thurstone, and Hull. We were also repeatedly told that pursuing questions of identity through the frame of culture was a meaningless pursuit unless "culture" is reduced to a variable in an experiment (Bhatia, 2010).

I have spoken about my alienation with the way psychology was taught in my new book (Bhatia, 2018). I have mentioned that in the outside, so-called real world, I felt that I was surrounded by an old society steeped in cultural meanings. When I was growing up in Poona, Indian culture was everywhere, on our streets, in our homes, in all the ritual, rites, ceremonies, superstitions, and class- and caste-based hierarchies that were enacted around us. But I realized that my meaning-making activities about culture or identity happened outside the realm of psychology in spaces that was usually reserved for banter over *chai* and samosas, on cricket grounds or while discussing Hindi movies, sharing jokes, and telling stories to each other. We were a bunch of young graduate students, full of questions about the world around us, carrying copious loads of stories about our evolving identities, yet we could not bring any of our subjective alienation and angst to the psychology classroom. This was largely a legacy of colonial knowledge and how psychology compartmentalized personal, experiential, and empirical and objective knowledge. Questions of "culture" and "subjectivity" were often dismissed as being too philosophical, anthropological or deemed to be messy variables that contaminated the experimental process. Therefore, I could never bring my somewhat raw and earnest critical interrogations of the discipline to the classroom, to my exams, or to my conversations with my professors, because the mainstream (i.e., dominant form) of scientific British and American psychology disallowed it.

It was only when I came to study as a doctoral student in psychology at Clark University that I first discovered that identity and self could be studied through narrative and the frame of culture. There, I discovered the power of "culture" and "narrative." At Clark University, I had not only found an entirely new way of doing psychology, but also a blissful escape from the grip of the dominant psychological frameworks of that time: behavioral, cognitive, and biological psychology. Looking back, I am filled with gratitude to my teachers – James Wertsch, Bernie Kaplan, Nancy Budwig, Michael Bamberg, Jaan Valsiner, Sarah Michaels, and Jim Gee for exposing me to an alternative view of psychology. I am particularly thankful to Bernie Kaplan, Nancy Budwig, and Jim Werstch who inspired me and also transformed my way of thinking about the relationship between self, culture, and language. Generally, the question of "what is development?" at Clark was something we were taught to wrestle with all the time. So, my study of psychology was fairly interdisciplinary and question of identity and development became tied with scholarship in language, philosophy, ethics, humanities, and narrative. There were insights, inspirations, but also long bouts of paralysis – as the psychology I was pursuing was not reflected in mainstream American psychology and I was not certain whether what I studied counted as psychology and if I would get hired at a university after my PhD.

There was another significant moment in my intellectual development about a year into my graduate work. I wrote about this moment in a speech I gave to first year students at Connecticut College during convocation. I left my home from Pune, India, and travelled to the US to become a graduate student at Clark University, a liberal arts school, in Worcester, Massachusetts. Like many international students from my era, I carried a suitcase with my precious belongings: photographs of my father and mother taken at a studio, farewell photos with my friends, Hindi film music, my best ever report card from sixth grade when I stood third in class, boxes of tea leaves, recipes, and small bags of turmeric, cumin, and coriander powder. My first week or rather the first year in this new world was disastrous. I was so fresh off the boat that when my American friends greeted me with, "How are you?" I poured my heart out and told them my life story. I had missed the cultural point that a greeting is just a means of making polite talk. Instead of talking about the weather, I told strangers how I missed home, my family, friends, and the smells of Indian streets.

Every week I would handwrite dozens of letters home to my friends and family telling them about my life in America. I was not fleeing a war zone or poverty, but yet I experienced a displacement that comes from being uprooted from home. Crossing borders brought pain and anxiety about the world I had left behind and the future that was yet to unfold. With time, I found a way to settle in the new world of American university life. Life at the university was fulfilling, but when I left the campus to go back to my apartment, I witnessed another America. This was an America segregated from the campus by just one street. Coming into my neighborhood in South Main in Worcester was like crossing a border or entering another country. The homes were crumbling, the schools were failing, and the old factories and mills had been abandoned. The university warned us about the dangers of South Main and we were told to avoid walking at night as it was filled with "dangerous people." These so-called dangerous people bore a resemblance to my people back home – they were mostly brown, immigrants, the invisible, and the poor.

I realized I was living in two Americas. I was studying in the affluent America of Clark University and the other America where I lived was near Clark on Gates Street. In the early 1990s, I could actually see racial segregation and other legacies of Jim Crow within my neighborhood and all over Worcester, but could not bring ideas about race directly into psychological inquiry. So in that sense I felt, to use the phrase of George Yancy, I felt pain from encountering racism, but that was nothing compared to bearing witness to how my neighbors were exposed to enduring and deeply toxic legacies of, slavery, anti-migrant laws, and other exclusions.

Later on, in graduate school at Clark University, I suppose I had a racial *awakening* and one thing became clear to me: whiteness served as a powerful norm, but its power was rarely interrogated. When I *overcame* my fear and questioned whiteness, I was often met with indifference or anger. It was only much later in life, when I encountered the term "white supremacy" that I fully understood how deeply whiteness had become integrated into everyday living and structures of American society: courts, schools, laws, medicine, media, higher education, and politics as well as much of psychology. The psychological canon had largely reinforced a narrative that people of color had a deficient humanity, and their lives or stories did not matter and were not worthy of studying. When people from marginalized communities showed up in the books I was reading, they often served as caricatured props and tokens for advancing the cause of whiteness or as victims that needed to be saved.

Bringing in radical anticolonial and antiracist critiques within psychology was still not allowed, but the Clark education had prepared me to venture out and make deeper connections between colonization, postcolonial experiences, and identity formation. It was around this time that I began to ask questions about how colonization and power and knowledge are linked and how they shape subjectivities. I was trying to articulate a framework of psychology from an anticolonial and antiracist position and doing that 20 years ago was tough, and there was a lot of emotional labor involved and resistance from many places. Numerous colleagues in Division 24 of the American Psychological Association, City University of New York graduate center, and Dialogical Self society started by Hubert Hermans, my department at Connecticut College ere very receptive to new ways of thinking about the role of theory in psychology.

SK: What research did you do after your graduate school?

SB: So from there, as soon as I finished my doctoral work, I started really looking at how immigration shapes self and identity. In 2001, I published an article in *Human Development* titled Rethinking Acculturation in Relation to Diasporic Cultures and Postcolonial Identities (Bhatia & Ram, 2001). This article provided a rigorous critique of the cross-cultural models of assimilation and formulated a new theoretical model of migrant identity and development by locating it the context of transnational diasporas and postcolonial cultures. I published another article in 2002 *in Theory and Psychology* titled, Acculturation, Dialogical Voices, and the Construction of the Diasporic Self. In this article, I tried to create a new theoretical framework that links together acculturation, voice, and diaspora communities. In that article, I coined the term "Diasporic Self" to explain the identity formation of migrants coming from postcolonial societies. I drew on Edward Said's (1999) memoir to rethink model of acculturation in terms of the dialogical and diasporic self. I specifically showed how postcolonial cultures bring a new and interesting dimension to hybridity, in particular, an acknowledgment of a constellation of power relations that has, for the most part, been lacking in psychological research. I argued that postcolonialism affords qualitative research new vistas, new questions, and new reflections. Conducting research from a postcolonial perspective will never be an easy endeavor; issues of the politics of location, the politics of representation, the politics of practice, where research is conducted, what questions are asked, how the research is conducted, and how knowledge is disseminated cannot be passed over with simple explanations.

SK: Can I interrupt you? Is that something that you took up in *American Karma?*

SB: Yes, In *American Karma: Race, Culture, and Identity in the Indian Diaspora* (Bhatia, 2007), my larger goal was to engage in theorizing about culture that moves it away from examining culture as a variable or as an apolitical and historical unit of analyses. In other words, "culture" as understood in acculturation literature was usually conflated with "nation." The diaspora literature I was reading was raising specific questions about the status of "culture" in global, transnational, diasporic societies: is there anything such as a univocal, monolithic, American, English, or Indian culture? What does it mean to have hyphenated identities such as African-American, Asian-American or Mexican-American in the larger American society? How do "Third World," postcolonial immigrants residing in "First World" societies negotiate their identities in relation to both Western/European/First World settlers and to other non-European Third World immigrants?

I was involved in the local South Asian community so understanding South Asian diaspora experiences from the lens of a long-term ethnography is something I became interested in. The participants of my study spoke about their experiences with racism in America, but they were ashamed to talk about it. They denied racism and used other discourses to issue denials. I was taken aback by the paradox. I was interested in showing how heterogenous the Indian diaspora is and I was trying to come up with a theory of self that shows agency and the fact that we are not just being made by culture, but we make culture within constraints. That is why I characterize the diasporic self as made of tensions between assignations and assertions of othernesss.

From a cultural standpoint, I wanted to examine how non-European/ non-white diasporic communities bring into sharp relief the sense of constantly negotiating between here and there, past and present, homeland and hostland and self and other. Such negotiations, I argued then, have not been adequately recognized or understood in many of the existing acculturation models in the field of human development and psychology. I was going through some of these negotiations myself. A lot of my study of postcoloniality came from trying to understand my experiences with legacy of colonization and migration.

SK: What was your ethnography about?

SB: Right, and that's where I did an extensive two-year ethnography in the Indian diaspora and the book became, *American Karma*. The book drew on anticolonial and antiracist frameworks to challenge the universality of longstanding racial and ethnic assimilation models in psychology and human development. When I was doing my research, 9/11 was a historical moment, it marked a radical turning point in my research. Immediately after 9/11, I was conducting interviews as part of the ethnographic research for the book. During an interview, a Sikh man, who worked as a high-level scientist for a local company, told me that he had not stepped outside for a week. He was afraid of being a target of a hate crime, so his wife did the groceries. When I arrived at his home, he was in the middle of a family meeting discussing whether he and his son should cut their hair, beard, and if they should stop wearing their turban because it brought unwanted attention. An important aspect of *American Karma* and other publications (Bhatia, 2002, Bhatia & Ram, 2004) that followed on the topic of migration was an examination of changing notions of cultural citizenship and racial identity formation driven in large part by Islamophobia.

I explored how the Sikh American community with their turbans, beards, and their "brown identities" had become suspect in the larger American public space. They were framed as outsiders and turned into targets of racial profiling, scrutiny, and hate speech. *American Karma* has four key findings. First, I show that any discussion about migrant identity and migrant selfhood in psychology must be situated and contextualized in historical and political terms. Second, I interrogate the conflation of nation with culture that emerges explicitly and implicitly in many theories of acculturation in cross-cultural psychology and cultural psychology. I demonstrate why nation and culture cannot be used interchangeably and that home and host cultures are not hermetically sealed or mutually exclusive spaces. Third, I show how the Indian middle-class professional community adopt a "model minority discourse" and seek proximity to whiteness in their assimilation process. I speak about the various ways in which their bodies, sarees, food, accents, cultures, and selves are highly racialized and marked as different in the US, but yet they continue to position themselves as having a race-less identity and often distance themselves from African-American and Latino groups. Fourth, I offer a model of identity in psychology that not just take into account culture but also agency, and power of othering, and how collective memory is tied to remembering specific identities. So, in *American Karma* and articles I attempt to create a different framework for understanding the concept of acculturation and identity by drawing on the concept of voice and dialogical self and race and postcoloniality (Bhatia & Ram, 2001).

Model minority thinking was dominant in the interviews I conducted; it is based on a colorblind racism. Bonnila-Silva, a sociologist, explains that colorblind racism is an ideology in which racial inequality and discrimination are explained in nonracial terms. The most common example of colorblind racism is reflected in the statement, "I don't see any color, just people." Such a statement assumes that a person's race or ethnic background does not play a role in their experiences with racism or discrimination. In my ethnographic research, I found that the Indian-American study participants invoked specific discourses to maintain their colorblind racism and thus their model minority status. What I write about in *American Karma* is that when skin color, *bindi*, sari, food, gods and goddesses, and accents of Indian migrants invite racial attacks, they deflect these racist incidents by insisting, "Every culture discriminates," or "It is human nature to marginalize others," and "Europe is even worse." Neeta, a 43-year-old woman who studied in Delhi and has lived in the US for 30 years, said, "I have come to realize that no matter what nationality you are, what color skin you are, we all have the same principles. That's the bottom line."

The professional Indian-American community I studied fully embraced the idea of American meritocracy, a system that rewards an individual based on his or her intelligence, ability, and effort. I recall Raju, a professor of biology, told me, "I firmly believe that being of Indian origin or looking different has nothing to do with the way you go about your life, your professional life, career development." Like many of the study participants, Raju was aware of his difference, but he genuinely believed individual effort, talent, hard work, and merit are the foundations of the American dream and one could overcome racism by hard work (Bhatia, 2008a 2008b, Bhatia & Ram, 2009). I was specifically struck by the fact that when the participants were told of the psychological, immoral, and societal cost of failing to confront racism, they responded by referring to "our society back home in India," where the caste system is far more oppressive. But the recent upsurge in hate crimes against Indian-Americans is a clear sign that model minority status does not immunize us from racist acts.

In my recent work on cultural psychology of migration – a project done in collaboration with Basia Ellis (Ellis & Bhatia, 2019) we argue that migration in the future cannot afford to hold on to nationally defined categories if its aim is to underscore the humanity of persons who move due to global political transformations. Transnational perspectives are needed to answer such questions as, why do migrants move? What do they seek for themselves and their families? What compels them to stay? How do the local and global intersect? Starting inquiry from the perspective of the nation-state means prioritizing bureaucratic categories (including immigration statuses, nationally defined cultures, and so on) over the perspectives of migrants who make decisions and navigate international contexts (Ellis & Bhatia, 2019). In particular, I articulate the different forms of dialogicality that are involved in the acculturation experiences of first- and second-generation migrants. My scholarship in this area has appeared in *Human Development, Theory and Psychology, Journal of Theoretical and Philosophical Psychology, Cultural Psychology*, and *Narrative Inquiry, Mind, Culture. American Karma* offered a theoretical framework for thinking about the construction of selfhood and identity in the context of immigration. I raised new questions in cultural psychology about the role of race, dialogicality, and power in understanding transnational migration.

SK: What were the questions you were asking?

SB: My questions were about mostly how to theorize about self and subjectivity within contexts of power, domination and the role memories of homeland played in migrant identities. These were big questions at the time. What occurred to me that the roots of American psychology as articulated by William James and others were constructed through the social realm, but in much of 20th-century American psychology the individual is seen as atomic, self-contained and largely separate from the sociocultural context or the social realm. The cult of quantification took over psychology and lost ground to the cultural and critical human meaning-making aspect of psychology. The power of social norms, social context, and group consensus that held sway over the individual played an important role in the rise of social psychology in the 1950s. We see that in the aftermath of World War II, social psychologists in Europe and the US became concerned with how societies and individuals, living during the peak of Western civilization's scientific and rational progress, could unleash such tremendous immoral and inhumane acts on each other. In that sense, Ken Gergen's "social psychology as history" is a critical and important piece in psychology that it shows how the production of psychological knowledge is linked with social practices, human relations, and contemporary history. But somehow, we lost the dynamic meaning of "social" in social psychology.

When I was in graduate school, the sociocultural or socially situated psychology was an important framework in psychology, but I felt it had not yet fully tackled the new postcolonial psychology that was emerging in newly decolonized states in Asian and Africa – where majority of the humanity lived. The concept of culture was still associated with Eurocentric power and practices or theorists. Those theorists were important but they could not articulate the subjectivities of the colonized or those who were racialized and oppressed. There were other African and Asian psychologists speaking to the colonial legacy of psychology and what it means to examine to colonialism and racism in subject formation and I was drawn to their work. The very idea of what constitutes "culture" becomes contested when we view it from the margins. To me, Fanon and Nandy's work was crucial in understanding the making of the colonized self. European colonialism and empire building, over two centuries, had laid a systematic program of Orientalism that not only had colonized much of Asia and Africa, but also wiped out many indigenous populations. European colonization and imperialism, as mentioned before, has radically altered the social and cultural psychology of both Europeans and the "natives" that were colonized around the globe. American psychologists had not just overlooked the varied ways in which these key social and political events shaped everyday living in colonized nations, but also, they were, knowingly or unknowingly, complicit in contributing to the project of Orientalism and "psychological imperialism" (Smith, 2012). In sum, the dominance of the scientific method, the parochial framing of research through Euro-American imaginary, the rise of biological psychology, and the proliferation of psychological inquiries that are devoid of their broader social-political implications raise essential question for me about the very legitimacy of what gets counted as psychological knowledge. It also further compelled me to think how the coloniality of psychological science limits what can be studied, how it can be studied, and where it can be studied and who can be studied (Maldonado-Torres, 2007). Thus, psychological science requires that concepts such as culture, self, and identity be stripped of their inherent polysemy, intricacies, and dynamism which eventually robs us of making spaces for identities that speak from the margins and also a chance for imagining a more inclusive psychology. Much of this work, I have presented at academic conferences but also have taken it public through Opposite the Editorials (Op-Eds) and interviews in the media and shared my work with the participants as well and in the college community.

SK: Yes, many of us want to share our work with the people we are studying. We want to give something back. So, what about the wider field or fields of psychology? What was the reception or degree of interest or ways it was read? What did you find about that?

SB: I mean in a sense, like you, I really felt mainstream psychology is both a real and imaginary place; I've never met a psychologist who says, "I am a mainstream psychologist." Everybody feels the mainstream is somewhere else and they are never located there, but I think there is a larger, conventional or traditional Eurocentric psychology that has institutional power and status.

SK: I know it's not the best word. You and I have colleagues who say, "the idea of mainstream psychology is a myth." But it's something you use to index something else, in a way that I think makes sense.

SB: That's right. Coming to that, I found very early in my career that it helps to distinguish between "Psychology as a Professional or Mainstream Institution" and then "Psychology as a Mode of Inquiry." Psychology as a mode of inquiry can be interdisciplinary, a poetic science as Mark Freeman calls it, a human science as Bernard Kaplan called it, or just a mode of study or method of meaning making without having to call it science. Once I liberated myself from a narrow vision of psychology, then I was able to really draw on postcolonial psychology, narrative inquiry, and qualitative psychology, and anthropology to answer question that kept coming up in my research. Broadening the vision of what counts as psychology has been an important intellectual pursuit and this brings me to *Decolonizing Psychology* (2018), the book that I just wrote.

SK: What is *Decolonizing Psychology* about? What made your write the book?

SB: Now let me give you some background for why I took on this project. The book is published under Mark Freeman's book series titled *Narrative Explorations in Psychology*; I am grateful for the opportunity to publish my scholarship in this series and for having Mark as an amazingly open, insightful, and wonderful editor. My main motivation for writing this book was to unsettle, interrupt, and break free from the established colonial structure of Euromerican psychological science. I first came across different manifestations of colonial psychology in my undergraduate and graduate education at the University of Pune, India. The psychology that I studied in graduate school in India and the US was largely made on colonial knowledge, universalistic principles, and Eurocentric cultural assumptions about individuality and rationality.

It was only while I was writing the paper that was published in *History of Psychology*, I discovered how deeply colonialism had shaped the "Indian" self and I had not studied any of that in my university days. The British used psychological and social science knowledge to justify their descriptions of my ancestors as animals, primitives, rude, backward, lazy, ignorant, and British Prime minister Churchill called them "a beastly people with a beastly religion." (Tharoor, 2017). Yet, my seven years of study of psychology in Indian universities drilled into me that British and European theories of people and culture and their methods of inquiry were more correct, legitimate, and superior to Indian culture and history. It was a psychology based on 5 percent of the human population but yet it had the power to speak on behalf of 95 percent of humanity (Arnett, 2008). There was something wrong with this picture. I did not find my story in the canons of psychology so I wrote this book to tell a different story of psychology and human development. *Decolonizing Psychology* challenges psychology's claims of universalism, emphasis on individualism, and its refusal to acknowledge history, culture, and politics.

SK: When you say, "our focus on individuals or individualism," that can mean a number of different things. So what are you thinking of when you say our focus on individuals takes us away from our larger problems or contexts?

SB: Yes. I wanted to go deeper in articulating how the self is shaped by what we call postcolonialism, neoliberalism, indigeneity, and globalization. There is a confusion of these terms so I wanted to articulate "Indian subjectivity" by attending to these layers of modernity, colonialism, and then globalization. I think the questions you raise about interiority, subjectivity, and how the co-constitution of the self and culture and agency are important to me as well. I wanted to clarify these terms and I wanted to articulate how Indian youth who were located in specific communities and class practices were shaped by layers of modernity, colonialism, and then globalization. In addition, I was inspired by Appadurai's (2013) concept of "capacity to aspire" and how it helps us understand the cultural spaces in which the poor and the working class navigate their world. Appadurai argues that aspirations about the "good life" in slum communities in India are closely connected to local ideas about marriage, gender, divinity, cosmology, work, leisure, respectability, health, and virtue. The stories I heard in the *basti* (working class communities) reflected individual aspirations. However, the propeller of power and material resources to transform these nascent aspirations into realistic and productive outcomes was missing thereby limiting their "navigational capacity." Building on Appadurai's ideas regarding "navigational capacity," I proposed the notion of *narrative capacity* as the ability of the poorer urban youth to create stories that matter in the larger society and the maps that are required to realize their aspirations. The narrative psychology perspective provides us with a theoretical framework to connect the individual concepts of "voice," "self-control," and "capacity" to larger collective and cultural practices (Bhatia, 2018). I draw on narrative psychology to highlight how these youth narratives are agentic and how discourses of globalization are being used by them to fashion different forms of Indianness. These ideas did not come out of the blue for me. I became more aware of the various dimensions of life of the working class and poor people when I started to collaborate with a non-profit organization called Shelter Associates. I was inspired by the work of a local activist and architect in my hometown in Pune. Her name is Pratima Joshi and she is the founder of Shelter Associates, a local non-profit organization, that works with the urban poor to provide sanitation in the slums of Pune. Comprising architects, social workers, GIS experts, and community workers, Shelter Associates works with the urban poor, particularly women in informal settlements (slums) to facilitate and provide technical support to community-managed housing, slum rehabilitation, and sanitation projects. In 2005, I read an article about her on the BBC website which called her "India's New Pioneer: Slum Architect." Growing up in India, I was used to seeing people defecating in public. However, I was not aware then of the scale and intensity of the problem. For example, millions of poor women and young girls only relieve themselves either before sunrise or after dark in order to avoid rape and sexual harassment. Nearly a thousand children around the world die every day due to inadequate water and sanitation facilities.

In 2006, I started a non-profit organization, *Friends of Shelter Associates*, that focuses on providing individual toilets in urban Indian slums and creating awareness about the physical and psychological suffering that families have to endure when they have to defecate in streets, bushes, or open gutters. What struck me most about the article was that she mentioned that 45 percent of the city I had grown up in had people who lived in slums and most did not have access to clean sanitation. She challenged those in the Indian and Western media, who were describing India's annual 8 percent growth as one of the most successful stories of modern capitalism, by asking a simple question "If you cannot give basic dignity to your fellow human beings, what kind of progress can you talk about?" In 2008, the United Nations declared sanitation as a human right. For a person living in a developed country, having access to a clean, private toilet with running water may not appear like a radical humanitarian cause or a psychologically empowering act. But for many people around the world, having a toilet and clean sanitation amenities is revolutionary. I have a specific chapter in *Decolonizing Psychology* titled, Identities Left Behind: Globalization, Social Inequality, and the search for Dignity, which examines how young men and women's identity formation is shaped by poverty and sanitation practices.

Slum dwellers are at the risk of getting innumerable diseases through contact with human excrement, such as, cholera, typhoid, meningitis, and hepatitis. In *Decolonizing Psychology*, I analyzed how lack of toilets is a daily attack on the human dignity and human rights of millions of young men and women of India. The stories of youth from Panchsheel Basti, the slum community where I gathered data, demonstrates linkages between class, caste, and new practices of globalization. An analysis of their narratives illustrates that these disadvantaged youths enact their agency and assert their will within the cultural ecology of their slums. Despite their tenacity, many find themselves struggling with conditions of poverty and without the cultural resources that are necessary to improve their lives in the future. Psychology has a tendency to reframe problems related to structural inequality as individual problems, whereas I envision a psychology in which questions of social justice and the public good could become central to its mission.

That is why I state that my vision of psychology is made up of an uneasy combination of toilets and theories, cultures and stories, and local and global practices. The capacity to aspire is not equally distributed in a given society, and the affluent and well-to-do classes often have an advantage in having a much more developed capacity to aspire. In my APA Humanitarian Award address in 2015, I said that I believe that for a very long time an unbridgeable cleavage has existed between psychology and principles of social justice. Psychology has not yet developed a meaningful theoretical vocabulary or a willingness to explore questions of social justice that are wrapped around qualitative methods and community-based practices as these are usually conducted in faraway places with marginalized populations that have had no history or recognition in American psychology or in the US (Bhatia, 2018). My work builds on many scholars, places, and from across the fields and I say very clearly that my vision of psychology is inspired by cultural psychologists, postcolonial theorists, narrative theorists, feminist, and critical psychologists. For instance, you have developed a very insightful, complex, and nuanced theoretical analysis of subjectivity and culture that I draw on in my scholarship.

Decolonizing psychology as a verb means to really examine the colonial and post-colonial legacies of European colonialism. Decolonization involves understanding how individuals, cultures, concepts, country, and knowledge production are subject to processes imperialism, colonization, and neo-colonization. I was struck by the fact that there are 356 million Indian youth in the world but their stories barely feature in American psychology and so much of what we know about adolescence and youth identity originate from the study of the modern, Euromerican subject.

I was intrigued by the concept of racial and cultural coloniality and how coloniality survives colonialism and continues to exists in our contemporary society. Coloniality not only refers to brutal colonization and genocide of indigenous people and culture in the Americas, but rather it reflects the whole colonial system of ideas, an attitude and orientation, a power structure that constructs "the hegemonic and Eurocentered matrix of knowledge" (Mignolo, 2010). One project of studying coloniality means undoing its effects and to find ways to delink from modern/colonial ways of being and creating an alternative to Western modernity, modernization and development. Decolonization has different meanings in different disciplines. Linda Tuhiwai Smith (2012) argues that decolonization means disrupting the traditional research process: making spaces for storytelling and oral histories as valid knowledge, engaging in collective remembrance for healing and transformation, stories, art, community knowledge, lived experiences, and an articulation of contested cultural practices. Decolonization means asking new and radical questions about human development from the global south such as: what if Africa was the center of knowledge production?

My ideas about decolonization have been shaped by largely growing up in India and coming here as a graduate student to the US Both Fanon and Nandy have provided some important foundational framework for thinking about the lingering psychological impact of colonialism. The postcolonial cultural and political practices in newly formed Indian and other Asian and African colonies is made up of what Nandy (1983) has described as "second colonization" (p. xi). This kind of colonialism, he argues, colonizes the mind as well as the body and "helps generalize the concept of modern West from a geographical and temporal entity to a psychological category. The West is now everywhere, within the West and outside; in structures and minds" (Nandy, 1983, p. xii). Nandy further makes the point that this second form of colonization is as dangerous as the first kind, because it is "almost always unconscious and almost always ignored . . . it creates a culture in which the ruled are constantly tempted to fight their rulers within the psychological limits set by the latter" (p. 3).

One of the main points about decolonial thinking that I think is relevant for psychology is the emphasis on how coloniality, in its many forms, shapes the foundation of psychology as discipline but also how it impacts our everyday lives. Broadly speaking in my book, I use ethnographic and interview methods to draw a nuanced narrative portrait of how urban Indian youth who belong to the transnational elite, middle, and working classes are engaging with new practices of globalization. I examine how particular class identities shape youth narratives about globalization and "Indianness" generally, as well as specific stories about self and identity, social inequality, family, work, marriage, and practices of consumption. How were concepts such as *global, western, modern,* and *traditional* being imagined and deployed in their narratives? The struggle for decolonizing psychology in the age of globalization is multi-sited, fluid, contested, and involves understanding how power shapes intersecting spaces, stories, identities, subjectivities, histories, language, and resistances. One of the goals of the book, *Decolonizing Psychology,* has been to interrupt the steady, self-important, and sedimented narrative of the discipline of psychology.

I am not advocating a psychology that "rescues" people from their plight or frames the oppressed as having no voice or agency such that they need outsiders to come and teach them how to live their lives. When I contemplate the future of psychology in the contexts of global social inequality, I believe we need to make sure that we engage in research without resorting to some type of epistemological violence that that actually harms those whose oppression we wish to understand and highlight (Teo, 2011). I want to be clear that a decolonial approach to psychology via the reflecting on the lives of urban Indian youth is not to intended to merely "add on" yet another fragment of knowledge to the formidable archive of Euro-American psychology or psychological science. The turn to understanding Indian youth stories is not based on a tourist or explorer model to studying cultural and racial others (Mohanty, 2003).

SK: Can we talk about power? Who gets to set the boundaries and who gets excluded and how does one work against that?

SB: I think there are several ways to talk about power, there is the power of advancing the colonial projects, and the ways in which new circuits of power (Fine & Ruglis, 2009) are created in postcolonial nations and how elite, upper class, and affluent people wield power in shaping a dominant material and symbolic cultures. For instance, the refashioning of Indianness in contemporary India and in Euro-American psychology reveals a preoccupation with elite, affluent and middle-class identities and a larger neglect of identities that live and form in the margin. Decolonizing psychology then means asking questions about whose narratives represent India and whose stories are visible and included in the structure of opportunity and advancement. I increasingly find myself reflecting on the power of psychological theory. Adding an analysis of power asymmetry to the hybridity of Indian youth narratives allows us to go beyond conceptualizing identity through simple explanations of cultural differences or positing homogenous national identities. It is quite another thing to theorize about how young Indian intercultural identities are shaped by labor conditions, social inequalities, neoliberal economies, and colonial legacies. Obviously, these cross-cultural experiences do tell us that we are not merely moving towards cultural homogenization or standardization. It is quite common to dismiss the position that globalization does not equate to cultural imperialism and to assert that people in the "non-western" countries do not passively accept Western or external cultural flows. I believe it is also conventional wisdom in academic circles to argue that globalization produces cultural reframing, contestation, and resistance. I would, however, argue that cultural imperialism and heterogeneity, sameness and difference, mimicry and resistance, all play an important part in shaping Indian youth narratives. I think examining heterogeneous and complex narratives of hybridity that comes into play as a result of sociocultural, material, and economic transformations is crucial. This was argued by Kraidy (2005), who writes that "hybridity as a sociocultural condition at large, disconnected from its political and economic contexts and from its constitutive processes, is conceptually untenable and ethnographically problematical" (p. 75).

SK: I want to ask you about the word, "cultural," which, obviously and very appropriately, you use a lot in your work. But at the same time, many of the forces that you're talking about as oppressive are social-structural forces or political-economic forces. Do you think this calls for a rethinking or a modification of the notion of what culture is, since you identify yourself as a cultural psychologist and you're talking about culture a lot?

SB: Today, the imperialism of cross-cultural and American psychology takes many forms. One of the forms that it takes is clearly visible in the direct circulation of Euro-American psychological knowledge and products that contribute to the ideology of a neoliberal self. I write in *Decolonizing Psychology* that the cross-cultural psychology created primarily by Western psychologists provides the language to understand "culture" in diversity and cultural sensitivity workshops and extended training seminars in corporations in India. As corporations have become global and international, Euro-American cross-cultural psychology, human development, and diversity management has particularly emerged on a world-wide scale to give meaning to complex problems of history, culture, power, identity, and conflict through uncomplicated vocabularies of collectivism vs. individualism and interdependent vs. independent selves. What is interesting to note is that when Euro-American cross-cultural psychological science merges with the neoliberal language of enterprise then structural inequality, cross-cultural racism, mental health issues, and ethnocentrism become camouflaged as simple problems of cross-cultural difference and cultural misunderstandings that can be solved through individual effort, self-help, therapy, importation of Western mental health taxonomies, and diversity training.

SK: Could you elaborate on those new discourses and how they have been connected to self-fashioning?

SB: I interviewed youth from three distinct class-based communities in Pune. Here is where power and class practices were deeply connected to having the ability to fashion and reimagine a certain kind of selfhood. I show how the college-age elite youth psychologically imagine themselves as being world-class citizens not just by going abroad, but by reimagining new forms of Indianness through their active participation in specific cultural practices of watching American media, shopping at exclusive malls and constructing emancipatory narratives of globalization. In particular, I show that that the transnational urban youth's narratives are hybrid and are organized Indianness that is mobile, multicultural, connected to consumption practices and crosses borders easily. In contrast, the working-class youth I interviewed sheds light on the dark side of neoliberal globalization, where large numbers of citizens are left out of the narrative of progress. These youth had ambition, hope, energy, and what Appadurai (2013) refers to as a "map of aspirations" (p. 189). However, the structural conditions in the slums did not provide them with the resources, opportunities, stories, or the tools to implement their hopes and desires. I also interviewed middle class youth who were in the Information Technology and Outsourcing industry and were considered as part of the emerging middle class and many of their jobs were created through international corporations in search of cheap labor.

One of the arguments I advance in *Decolonizing Psychology* is that our "global" or "local" imagination about others comes alive through narratives; the stories we tell about others are created through how we imagine the other. A typical Indian middle-class call center worker in India has hundreds of daily phone interactions with customers from the UK or the US, but this worker will never be able afford to make a trip to see the country and culture of the people who he or she is speaking to on a daily basis. However, despite the physical distance, the call center worker imagines how his customers live, what they drive, eat, watch on TV, and how they spend their weekends. Indian sociologist Vasavi (2008) writes that youth employed in call centers, BPOs and IT firms are the "new brigade of global subjects/workers" (p. 212) who are threatening the ideology of the Indian family and are reimagining what it means to be an urban Indian living in times of globalization. Rather than conceiving of globalization as solely made up of a one-directed, Western external cultural flow that writes itself on the local canvas, I look at how youth strategically deploy narratives of globalization to negotiate, reimagine, and contest their "Indianness." This is where their agency comes through. I have analyzed narratives of Indian urban youth across three classes to show how the study of these shifting class identities within specific contexts of globalization is an important undertaking for psychology and human development. This is one of the projects of *Decolonizing Psychology*.

SK: Now I'd like to ask you about your *telos*. You've talked about some of your goals already, so I'm not going to ask you the exact "telos" question you asked me. You've demonstrated the deep coloniality of psychological knowledge, and you've made it clear what many of the key elements of a re-envisioned psychology need to be. So, I'll just ask whether you have additional goals or visions for what a decolonized psychology or psychologies could be or should be. What would it look like?

SB: I have not fully thought through this question. I think that is something I want to take up in another project. The Indian writer Arundhati Roy (2003) states that "We must tell stories that are different from the ones we're brainwashed to believe. . . . Remember this: Another world is not only possible, she is on her way. On a quiet day,

I can hear her breathing" (p. 127). If we were to embrace Roy's plea that we remain open to this other world, then we need to listen to different stories that have different themes, cadences, rhythms, and breathing patterns. For now, I think the telos for me would be to lay down the foundations of an anticolonial and antiracist psychological framework. I am interested in learning from and collaborating with scholars who are working in the area of decolonization in South Africa and in Community Psychology programs and indigenous studies in the US.

References

Appadurai, A. (Ed.). (2013). *The future as a cultural fact: Essays on the global condition.* Verso Books.

Arnett, J. J. (2008). The neglected 95%: Why American psychology needs to be less American. *American Psychologist, 63*(7), 602–614. https://doi.org/10.1037/0003-066X.63.7.602

Bhatia, S. (2002). Orientalism in Euro-American and Indian psychology: Historical representation of "natives" in colonial and postcolonial contexts. *History of Psychology, 5*(4), 376–398. https://doi.org/10.1037/1093-4510.5.4.376

Bhatia, S. (2007). *American karma: Race, culture, and identity in the Indian diaspora.* New York University Press.

Bhatia, S. (2008a). Rethinking culture and identity in psychology: Towards a transnational cultural psychology. *Journal of Theoretical and Philosophical Psychology, 28*, 301–321.

Bhatia, S. (2008b). 9/11 and the Indian Diaspora: Narratives of race, place and immigrant identity. *Journal of Intercultural Studies, 29*(1), 21–39. https://doi.org/10.1080/07256860701759923

Bhatia, S. (2010). Theorizing cultural psychology in transnational contexts. In S. R. Kirschner & J. Martin (Eds.), *The sociocultural turn in psychology: Emergence of mind and self in context* (pp. 204–227). Columbia University Press.

Bhatia, S. (2018). *Decolonizing psychology: Globalization, social justice, and Indian youth identities.* Oxford University Press.

Bhatia, S., & Ram, A. (2001). Rethinking "Acculturation" in relation to diasporic cultures and postcolonial identities. *Human Development, 44*(1), 1–18. https://doi.org/10.1159/000057036

Bhatia, S., & Ram, A. (2004). Culture, hybridity and the dialogical self: Cases from the South Asian Diaspora. *Mind, Culture and Activity, 11*(3), 224–240. https://doi.org/10.1207/s15327884mca1103_4

Bhatia, S., & Ram, A. (2009). Theorizing identity in transnational and diaspora cultures: A critical approach to acculturation. *International Journal for Intercultural Relations, 33*(2), 140–149. https://doi.org/10.1016/j.ijintrel.2008.12.009

Ellis, B., & Bhatia, S. (2019). Cultural psychology for the new era of citizenship politics. *Culture and Psychology*, 25, 220–240.

Fine, M., & Ruglis, J. (2009). Circuits and consequences of dispossession: The racialized realignment of the public sphere for U.S. youth. *Transforming Anthropology*, *17*(1), 20–33. https://doi.org/10.1111/j.1548-7466.2009.01037.x

Kraidy, M. (2005). *Hybridity or the cultural logic of globalization*. Temple University Press.

Maldonado-Torres, N. (2007). On the coloniality of being: Contributions to the development of a concept. *Cultural Studies*, *21*(2–3), 240–270. https://doi.org/10.1080/09502380601162548

Mignolo, W. (2010). Cosmopolitanism and the de-colonial option. *Studies in Philosophy and Education, 29*(2), 111–127. https://doi.org/10.1007/s11217-009-9163-1

Mohanty, C. T. (2003). *Feminism without borders: Decolonizing theory, practicing solidarity*. Duke University Press.

Nandy, A. (1983). *The intimate enemy: Loss and recovery of self under colonialism*. Oxford University Press.

Roy, A. (2003). *War talk* (1st ed.). South End Press.

Said, E. (1999). *Out of place: A memoir*. Knopf.

Smith, L. T. (2012). *Decolonizing methodologies: Research and indigenous peoples* (2nd ed.). Zed Books.

Teo, T. (2011). Empirical race psychology and the hermeneutics of epistemological violence. *Human Studies, 34*(3), 237–255. https://doi.org/10.1007/s10746-011-9179-8

Tharoor, S. (2017). *Inglorious empire: What the British did to India*. London: C. Hurst &Co.

Vasavi, A. R. (2008). "Service from India:' The making of India's global youth workforce. In C. Upadhya & A. R. Vasavi (Eds.), *In an outpost of the global economy: Work and workers in India's information technology industry* (pp. 210–234). Routledge.

4

Psychology as Apparatus

An Interview with Sam Binkley

Interviewed by Derek Hook
Derek Hook and Sam Binkley

Introduction by Derek Hook

In order to introduce Sam Binkley and his work, I thought I would just offer a couple of points, just so that we've got a thematic sense of where we'll go, and then I'll ask some more specific questions. First, though, congratulations are in order. Sam is a full professor. He went up for professor maybe a year ago, and part of his dossier included four articles, which took him to the "top of his game," as such. One of them was the paper "Anti-Racism beyond Empathy," published in the journal *Subjectivity*, with the subtitle "Transformations in the Knowing and the Governing of Racial Difference" (Binkley, 2016). As it turns out, in around 2014, I had acted as a reviewer of that paper. It was a fantastic piece of work, which developed the Foucauldian notion of the *dispositif* and made the argument that empathy had become a dominant trope and a model for bypassing or avoiding racism. I was tremendously excited about it, and only subsequently did I realize that it was Sam's paper, and it was nice to have had access to it at that point because it was certainly something that I recommended to my students. I'm sure we'll come back to it. A second of Sam's papers included in his dossier when he went up for promotion was "The Government of Intimacy: Satiation, Intensification, and the Space of Emotional Reciprocity" published in *Rethinking Marxism* in 2011 (Binkley, 2011a). A third, which I heard him deliver in a talk at Birkbeck, University of London, was "Happiness in the Program of Neoliberal Governmentality." The fourth paper that he included in that dossier was "Psychological Life as Enterprise: Social Practice and the Government of Neo-Liberal Interiority" (Binkley, 2011b). So, with that as a bit of a background let's begin.

Derek Hook (DH): I suppose the first question is: how has the field of psychology responded to your work?

DOI: 10.4324/9781003280033-5

Sam Binkley (SB):   Thank you, Derek, for this flattering introduction! With regard to your question, I never set out to engage the field of psychology precisely on its own terms. Frankly, it never occurred to me that such a dialogue would develop. I consider my interest to be in how subjectivity gets produced in the contemporary context with a particular emphasis on the discursive effects. So, I have always considered ways of writing and talking about the problem of subjectivity or the problem of one's own life and how those conversations translate into actually lived forms of subjective experience. I wrote a book titled *Getting Loose* which considered the countercultural lifestyle discourse of the 1970s – basically, hippies saying, "Let us live differently. Let us interrogate ourselves for the undue self-constraint we inherit from society, for our uptightness, and let's live looser. Let's open ourselves up to the impulsive flow of experience" (Binkley, 2008). I was interested in how the project they envisioned at that time, how this program of "getting loose," in their thinking, shaped new ways of living one's humanity. To understand this, I examined a lifestyle discourse that was articulated in a genre of countercultural publications with names like *The Whole Earth Catalog, Our Bodies Ourselves, Rainbook, Getting Clear,* and many others for the way they envisioned a sort of planned reduction of self-constraint through mundane daily activities like cooking or home construction. I hoped at the time that this book would add the important notion of a cultural vanguard to our understanding of the shifting ways in which new problematizations of the self develop and disseminate.

After that book, I wrote *Happiness as Enterprise,* which turned to more contemporary forms of self-help literature to understand how people set about related projects of self-government under different social and historical conditions, this time to transform themselves into happier subjects (Binkley, 2015). What did this work of being happy entail, I wondered, what was its objective? How was that objective plotted or coded within what I considered to be a form of lifestyle literature, one that took the form of a self-help discourse in which popular psychology was an important source? The psychology in question was, of course, positive psychology, the psychology associated with Martin Seligman and others, which is a psychology of the happy life translated here into a popular self-help genre. So, in a sense both of these investigations were conducted as cultural studies, or as examinations of popular cultural conversations.

In the case of the happiness book, it hadn't occurred to me that what I was dealing with was a uniquely psychological discourse. But, actually, positive psychology is an academic research field. It's not just a self-help genre, though it dovetails well with self-help. It's a rigorously studied and very well-funded academic field. So, I was very surprised when I was contacted by David M. Goodman and Lynn Layton, who said, "This is fascinating work in the field of critical psychology. You should come meet with us, because we're all psychoanalysts and psychologists and we're doing just what you're doing." I had to Google critical psychology to find out what it was, though, Derek, I knew your work. I think I had read maybe your first book, *Foucault, Psychology and the Analytics of Power* (2007). In this book you use this phrase "critical psychology," and though I didn't know at the time what it meant, I was very interested to read your use of Foucault in the analysis of the psychological profession in South Africa. Critical psychology embodies, I came to learn, this kind of reflexive critique that fits well with my interest in lifestyle discourse as a cultural phenomenon.

A Critique of Anti-Racism

DH: My response to your work has always been an intuitive affinity precisely because, whether you call it critical psychology or not, so many of those themes that you engage are actually of crucial importance to psychology, even if you're engaging them from a Foucauldian and thus more critical vantage point. So, a couple of the terms you were using right now, I mean the whole self-help discourse, lifestyle discourse, subjectivity, happiness, these are the terms that populate psychology. So, I suppose what I'm saying is, on the one hand it may sound odd to say how has psychology responded to your work, given that you're positioned in some respects outside of psychology, but in another way to me it seems that you do tackle fairly central topics within the broader discourse of psychology. One way of giving a different articulation to that question is this. We spoke briefly just before we started about the "Beyond Empathy" paper. You did a few presentations on the paper, and you mentioned that you got an unfavorable response from some colleagues. Could you tell us a bit more about that?

SB: Like many interdisciplinary scholars, I've never had a clear answer to the question "What do you do?" since this question really means: "What are you?" – it's an existential question that I have never been able to answer. But the answer to this question that I managed to muster was that I study those discourses and the broader apparatus, apparati in the plural, by which I am governed. In "The Government of Intimacy" I wrote about the history of relationships, marriage, and the conjugal bond, from the standpoint of its government by external authorities. I became very interested in the literature on neoliberalism and neoliberal modes of governmentality as described in the works of Nikolas Rose and Mitchell Dean. From this standpoint, it was possible to speak of a certain neoliberal technology of relationships and intimate life mediated by marriage and relationship counselors, advice columns, marriage blogs, and so on. This discourse has, it seemed to me, over the course of several decades, gradually tipped in favor of a certain individualistic imperative; where once marriage was defined by a set of obligatory relations, of dependency and reciprocities premised on mutuality and sacrifice, the conjugal bond has been increasingly redefined as a kind of opportunistic field, a market, if you will, which has to be governed as a field of enterprise. It was in this way that I took up the question of happiness as a similar field of governmental intervention, which was really the point of *Happiness as Enterprise* – that emotional life could be governed neoliberally, that emotional subjects are increasingly talked about as market actors, as people seeking opportunities to maximize their emotional returns on investment. In all of these conversations, the discourse in question was actually an apparatus, in the Foucauldian sense. It was a complex set of arrangements by which people were ruled or induced to adopt a certain relation to themselves or to produce themselves in a certain way.

But the happiness book was already five years ago, and now I've struck out on a new project, turning to the question of race and racism, not as real entities but as the objects of an apparatus, as an aspect of life that gets governed through the ways it is talked about. Anti-racism, as I understand it, can be considered as an apparatus that induces people – principally but not exclusively White people – to go to work on themselves, to uncover the hidden truths of their own racism and to produce themselves as less racist people. This was the approach I took in an article titled "Anti-Racism beyond Empathy," which was published in the journal *Subjectivity* in 2016, and it seemed to make a lot of sense to me as this is an apparatus that really saturates my life (Binkley, 2016). I am frequently exhorted to mediate my racism, to come to terms with it, to confront it, to speak about it, to understand it, and to explore its movement – all toward the end of resolving and eliminating it. So I thought, I want to look at this. I want to see how the discourse of anti-racism works, and I want to see what its connections are with other formations of power. How is our current discourse on anti-racism inflected by certain neoliberal rationalities and logics?

That's a hard thing to do because most of my investigations have targeted discourses that I didn't feel any particular political affiliation with, although I have always felt tremendous empathy for my topics as a researcher. In other words, in other projects I was able to approach my subject matter and my informants with a Weberian sense of value neutrality or moral detachment, that is, a kind of non-judgmental appreciation. For example, it wasn't difficult to study the workings of positive psychology because I don't feel any particular kinship with positive psychologists. That's not completely true; in my heart, I think positive psychology is deeply flawed in its approach, but that wasn't my concern. I never set out to debunk positive psychology, only to reconstruct its thinking and to show how its operation aligned with other structural arrangements, such as that of neoliberal capitalism. At some moments, my skepticism made it necessary for me to stop interviews with positive psychology self-help coaches because of this hidden ambivalence. My deep doubts about what they were doing made it impossible for me to interview them with sincerity, and they were such wonderful people and were so very nice to me that I couldn't handle the fact that in the back of my mind I was thinking something else. So, I had to stop interviewing.

Now, when you talk about anti-racism, well, anti-racism is something that I believe in, something that I've had a political commitment to my whole life, though I have never made anti-racism the center of my scholarly work. But as my project unfolded, I discovered that I was critically examining people with whom I felt deep political kinship. I wasn't necessarily criticizing, but I was examining and looking at certain linkages that develop between a political discourse that I'm supportive of and other neoliberal logics of government. From this effort came the article on empathy and anti-racism. It considered the notion of empathy as the driver of a certain logic of anti-racism. The article responded to a lot of the campus activism that had been going on in the United States and that was happening in my own institution. It extended an interest I've held for a long time in the ways in which economic logics reshape other cultural or interpersonal processes. In this way, I felt a very strong desire to move past what I considered to be the solution of empathy as it operated within this discourse of anti-racism, where it was prescribed that one had to feel the feelings of the other in order to transform oneself. And to me, this was part of the apparatus that I wanted to examine.

It seemed to me that there was a powerful tendency among a predominantly White cohort of specialists, principally with backgrounds in psychology but also education and management, who undertook the program of cultivating empathy in other people and in themselves. You had to feel what the other was feeling in order to transform yourself. I looked at that and I considered how it worked, and it seemed to me that it implied an effort to isolate, to magnify, and to invest in the emotional state of the other in order to produce an appropriate object for which one could experience empathy. In other words, efforts to feel what the other was feeling actually turned into efforts to produce the other. You could call this a sort of empathic othering, or even a fetishization. So, the imperative to feel the other's feelings, to feel the experiences of people of color and to produce oneself as a subject capable of understanding how people of color were experiencing life in a racist society, was an operation that had a certain logic to it.

To dig a little deeper: I wanted to understand precisely how this logic operated. I hypothesized that it was something of an economic logic. The project of producing the other through empathy was fashioned on a certain logic of recompense, of payment, of remuneration. What the empathic subject owes the other is precisely empathy, and that empathy is made, like a payment, in roughly equal proportion to the amount of harm that the other has undergone. Like the discourse on happiness, this logic is implicitly neoliberal, but in a different way. In place of the neoliberal sense of enterprise, the logic of empathy inscribes an equally neoliberal sense of debt. It wants to inscribe a market relation across what might otherwise have been, for another generation and in another time, a moral or a social problem. The discourse of anti-racism extends this marketization of social morality by producing the other not as a subject to whom we are morally responsible, but as a sort of great creditor, as an object to whom payments can and must be made. And that debt is paid with empathy.

Much anti-racist discourse today, the kind we find in large organizations or practiced by professionals in human resources departments and in corporate diversity training programs, presumes that empathy is not fun. It's something that can only come as the result of a concerted effort, through "difficult conversations" and under considerable expert supervision. But it is work we are obliged to do. *Empathy must be paid, like a debt.* This to me is a very limiting way of conceiving the project of anti-racism. Moreover, there is a sense that this logic, while it is no doubt valuable and productive in many situations, also has the implied effect of reproducing precisely the kind of racism it purports to criticize. The other of the empathic project, after all, remains an object – a "thing" whose feelings must be felt. This apparatus doesn't want to resolve racism any more than psychiatry wants to eliminate madness or prisons want to prevent criminality. The apparatus always reproduces the object over which it exercises its jurisdiction as part of the process of reproducing its own legitimacy. One's racism, if by racism we mean the reduction of the other to an object, has to be sustained and cultivated as an always incomplete project of remaking.

I traced this rationality back to what I consider to be a simple inversion of the basic terms of racism itself. The basic terms of racism hold that you, the raced other, are incompatible with the basic social contract; as Charles Mills (1997) says, you can't be a citizen because you don't meet the terms of the social contract. You have a biological, hereditary attribute which prevents you from being a real citizen, and for this you are in debt. The social contract requires you to raise your kids properly, to maintain a job and to keep up your house. Through a racist lens, people of color don't do these things, and are therefore in debt. Collection on this debt can be made by those (White) signatories to the social contract (which is, in fact, a racial contract, as Mills argues) through extralegal means (such as the denial of housing, credit, education and so on, or even through more direct acts of violence). This is the classically racist view in which people of color are illicit beneficiaries of the terms of a contract to which they are unable to fully comply. Anti-racism, on the other hand, seems to accept the fundamental logic of that exclusion and of that debt, only it reverses the positions. Under racism, the raced other owes you for the civility he can't pay to you owing to his animal, less-than-human nature, and this failure to pay exposes him to forms of violence that can be legitimately committed. Under a racialized logic, Trayvon Martin, Michael Brown, and George Floyd all "owed" their lives to the police, in a sense, because they were endemically incapable of meeting the contractual terms of law-abiding citizenship. So anti-Black violence is just collection on that debt. Under anti-racism, the other remains excluded, but this time it's you who's in debt and the other who is elevated to the function of the creditor. The payment you make is not racialized violence or the "social death" that Orlando Patterson (1982) talks about, but empathy. You must pay the other surpluses of empathic responsiveness in a way that confirms the other's exclusion. The attribute that marks the other is no longer biological. It's now emotional, and that attribute is not something that is going to marginalize you; it's something that makes a claim to your own affective production. I owe you feeling, or co-feeling. I owe you the activity of co-feeling your emotions.

Now, just to be clear, it's not that I specifically object to this arrangement politically, but it seemed to me that a better, or at least a different, politics of anti-racism might result from a certain hedonistic disposition that stands outside the economic logic of this empathic debtor relation. I argued that it couldn't all be about paying debts but that there had to be a pleasure in White anti-racism, a productive and transformative pleasure, that there had to be a moment of pleasure for Whiteness in becoming anti-racist. I summoned this very Foucauldian notion of the aesthetics of the self to describe the pleasures of White anti-racism. In place of the debt relation, one had to shape oneself, one's White self, into something beautiful, into something capable of bringing new pleasures, both to oneself and to others. But it's very difficult to predict how people will read your work. After the article came out, people read this as if I were presenting a new platform for anti-racism centered exclusively on the pleasures of Whiteness, one that absolved Whites from their responsibility to empathize. I was criticized for being a bad ally, for slipping into this mode of White introspection, White fragility, et cetera, for re-inscribing the centrality of the White subject at the center of a politics of race, and so on.

DH: So, you touched a nerve with colleagues.

SB: Yes, I did.

DH: I suppose in a vein of Foucauldian scholarship that is somehow inevitable, although this sounds like it's a particularly tense example of that. You could almost say the procedural methodological move in doing a Foucauldian-inspired piece of work like that is to be able to interrogate what is a common norm or a common discourse or a form of common sense. That is also a theme, I think, that seems to run through your work. Would you agree with that characterization, with the idea that part of critical labor is being able to re-inflect a norm or a popular cultural notion such as the importance of empathy?

SB: Yes. "Anti-Racism beyond Empathy" is probably the closest that I've been to something that is contemporary and that urgently matters to people. I don't think anybody was offended by my challenges either to positive psychology or to *The Whole Earth Catalog*. No one thought that there was a high stake in that. To me, there was a high stake because I was getting at other things through those engagements. But the conversation changes when you're conducting a kind of genealogy of these political forms that people are urgently committed to. Foucault himself always struggled in his relationship with the Left, with feminism and with what was then the gay movement. He was always subject to the charge that he was insufficiently supportive of the theoretical constructions that these movements depended on. To Marxists, he said, "Look, I'm going to show that capitalism is actually not based on factories but on prisons." And, of course, to psychoanalysts he said, "Listen, the thing you call Oedipus, I'll tell you it's actually part of the same disciplinary apparatus that supports capitalism." But I think that what Foucault meant to do was not necessarily to disqualify the theoretical assumptions of movement politics but to point out the ways in which these assumptions, while great for movements, don't necessarily serve so well for other projects, such as an aesthetics of the self, for the work on the self one might undertake to make oneself beautiful, to find a pleasure in such forms of self work. Not everyone is receptive to this subtlety. There are those authors who write in that classically Marxian mode, even if they're not Marxists, who insist on a clear link between theory and practice. Intellectual work is only valid to the extent that it provides political ammunition for a struggle. I've never been one of those authors, and I would specifically discourage people from reading my work if I thought it would sidetrack them from their activism or undermine their political commitments. I accept that sometimes thinking too much can actually distract you from the task at hand. In some cases, if you're that kind of person, it might be more productive to simply accept as natural and a priori all the categories upon which anti-racist work is undertaken and not bother with the kinds of questions I am asking. My work would be more likely to relativize a more pragmatically conceived project of anti-racism, and for that reason I would not necessarily recommend it for all readers.

Neoliberalism

DH: Okay. So, you've mentioned the neoliberal order a couple of times, and I've got a few things to ask about that. It's another theme that runs through much of your work. Are we still in neoliberal times in the era of Trump?

SB: Oh, gosh, sure. I take my understanding of neoliberalism from Foucault's lectures and from the governmentality literature that grew up around his very discursively oriented, constructivist view of neoliberalism (Foucault, 2008; Dean, 1999). I mean, neoliberalism is not a thing. I think it's important not to project a certain ontology onto neoliberalism or onto any other political or historical formation. Neoliberalism is not a thing; it is a way of colonizing things, of infiltrating existing formations, technologies, and institutions and redirecting, infusing them with a different kind of a logic, a different way of carrying out their operation. When a factory or a school is privatized, it is not destroyed and replaced with another. It might remain completely intact, but its mode of operation shifts in profound ways. It adopts a different relationship with its environment and with its future. It becomes enterprising, and it does this by recognizing, dignifying, and governing the enterprising dispositions of its constituents even as this recognition advances through a certain inscription. Psychology was neoliberalized when a technology of neoliberalism infused its mode of operation and made it work in a certain way. The way that neoliberalism made psychology work was by making the subjects of psychology entrepreneurs of their own emotional lives and by encouraging them to see themselves as autonomous, as not dependent on those old psychological authorities that once provided guidance for them. The therapist under neoliberalism is reduced in stature to a coach, to an equal, but is also a resource for the subject's exploitation. In the course of this, the subject him- or herself is radically truncated, condensed to a bare set of cognitive operations. Nobody is interested in depth anymore, and that's one of the ways that psychology is neoliberalized. This is something that Jeff Sugarman writes about very well (Sugarman, 2015).

So, it's not that neoliberalism displaced psychology; it's that neoliberalism infused psychology with a new way through which subjects might understand their own agency. I'm going to take charge of my emotional life, and I'm going to run it according to certain optimizing imperatives, like a business. I'm going to make it better. I'm going to maximize its potential. Through this process, the temporality of the psychological enterprise changes. It becomes less about going back in time to repressed or forgotten experiences, stored in the depths of a great interiority, less about repressed memory and the need to recover forgotten traumas. It becomes more about projecting one's thoughts into the future, anticipating and hoping for things you are going to do: about those states of happiness one anticipates experiencing.

Trumpism and the Wandering Imperative

DH: Another question I wanted to ask . . . you mentioned nationalism, populism that is happening at the moment. I know that some of the talks that you're planning on doing in the future on your coming trip to Europe will focus a little bit on Trump. Can you give us a bit of a taste of what this is about?

SB: Sure. Trump's election, together with the Brexit vote in the UK and similar events elsewhere, shocked a lot of people and drew us into a new perspective on a lot of things. It took the conversation on race that I had already responded to and put it on a new level, one that I interpreted through a perspective that I had never taken before, one that dealt more directly with the specific affective and emotional contents of people's actions and of a national and global mood and not just the discourses, the apparati through which those emotions were governed. In many ways this was a break with the discursive focus of my previous works and with the notion of governmentality as the effect of specifically situated rationalities. In light of these events, I became very interested in the affective field of the new populism and of the racial politics of this moment, and specifically in shame, and right now I'm just completing a book on shame and its relationship to Whiteness and to race.

But to get at this, let me back up a little bit. I've been very interested in Foucault for a long time. I'm very interested in the notion that these discourses are produced, they circulate, and they colonize us in such a way that we take these discourses and we use them to produce our own selves, our own subjectivities in certain ways. So, I'm a Foucauldian, I think you might say. I buy the argument. But I'm a difficult Foucauldian in that there is a lot about the way that Foucault described things and the way Foucault gets taken up in the surrounding literature which I don't like (Foucault, 1986). This led me to my more general critique of that branch of Foucault's work that is taken up in the field that sometimes is called governmentality studies. Nikolas Rose is someone that is strongly identified with this field and is still very influential in the conversation between Foucault and psychology (Rose, 1999). I admire his work tremendously – though, as in the case with the best engagements, I have my critique. There is a tendency in Foucault and in the kind of Roseian version of Foucault to which I object. This is the tendency to posit a discursive formation in very abstract terms, to describe a range of experts and institutions that disseminate this discourse, and to consider the ways in which these experts and their institutions describe a subject in terms of a certain imperative. One *should* make oneself more efficient, more productive, more healthy, more civil, and so on. One *should* govern oneself in thus and such a way. Within this mode of analysis it is assumed that the subject herself will ultimately invest in this imperative, re-inscribe its urgency within her own habits of thought by inhabiting the discourse, by speaking the language of that particular discourse to herself.

If you read the analysis of these discourses closely, in the work of Rose but also in the work of Foucault himself, there is a stylistic quality that one comes to identify with very quickly. First, a discursive field is described and, in a sense, mimicked by the author. Foucault's famous ventriloquism implies a mode of critique which in a subtle way starts to speak in the voice of the discourse he is studying. This is how he begins *History of Sexuality Volume I*, with words to the effect of "For a long time, it has been said," and then he disappears into the discourse on repression (Foucault, 1984, 1986). Then, in a subtle way, there is a shift in the position of the speaker of this discourse, from the one who *must* do certain things to the one who feels the urgency of this imperative to do certain things, or from a "one must" to an "I must." There is an implied assumption that somehow these imperatives migrate from the level of institutions and expert conversations to the level of actual people and their private intrapsychic conversations and into the fabric of their personal lives. I call this the problem of the wandering imperative. Take, for example, the imperative "Society must be defended." Who feels this urgency? Presumably, two groups of people: experts participating in a conversation on population and security, officials, police, magistrates who describe a range of deviant infiltrators, abnormals of different stripes against whom society must be defended, but also individual members of those populations and deviants themselves, who experience a sense of urgency around, for example, the presence of racial others who pose a threat to the security of the population. It is the difference between experts and the laity. But were these two groups of people really thinking with the same mind? How did they communicate, and what sort of contact did they have with each other?

I'm very much interested in interrogating the assumed relation-ship that develops between institutional discourses and private per-sonal life, everyday life. That has really been the focus for a long time. *Happiness as Enterprise* was really about temporality, and it was really about trying to understand how we apply governmental imperatives to ourselves within the fabric of everyday temporality, within the time of our everyday conducts. Temporality was the way that I got around this kind of Roseian-Foucauldian *Voila!*, this pre-supposition that since it gets talked about on an institutional level, therefore it happens on the personal level. I took on this problem in another article that came out in between my interests in neolib-eral psychology and the role that shame plays in race, and this had to do with biopower and how it is expressed through metaphor. In an article called "Biopolitical Metaphor: Habitualized Embodiment between Discourse and Affect," this problem of translation from expert to nonexpert realms is taken up through a consideration of the everyday use of metaphor (Binkley, 2018).

So, in other words, I'm still very interested in rethinking this basic Foucauldian assumption by bringing it around to the level of the eve-ryday, but with my new interest in race and shame it's not through temporality or metaphor but though affect. Trumpism is not a ration-ality or not just a rationality. It's a new way of feeling, an emotion, and it's about shame. It is very difficult to capture Trumpism through the discursively oriented tools of governmentality theory or through the analysis of an implicit rationality. Trump is pure gut. Hitler had his intellectuals and in many ways was an intellectual. He wrote a book, although a very bad one. I'm not sure you could do the kind of intellectual study of Trumpism that people have done with Nazism. It lacks an intellectual foundation, or at least a robust one such as that possessed by Nazism. Trump's impulsiveness is so deeply anti-intellectual that it's difficult to trace to a doctrinal source. So, more recently, in an effort to say something about contemporary forms of racism, I have turned to emotion, and specifically to shame. Shame not only fits with our contemporary time, it gives an affective col-oring to many of the effects of power and subjection that Foucault described. Shame presents a kind of self-encounter that helps us to resolve the question of the link between private life and public discourse or between experts and lay people. Shame helps to ground the wandering imperative in actual relations and real moments. The prisoner under the panoptic tower, the patient in the clinic, the sinner in the confessional all seem to be experiencing some kind of shame, although Foucault, who had as little interest in emotions as he had in everyday practice, would never have used that word.

Race and Shame

DH: I am fascinated by how you utilize the concept of shame. In clinical work, and indeed in the psychoanalytic clinic, shame is often foregrounded as pointing to something very crucial about the subject, such as their fantasies, their sexuality, their particular modes of libidinal enjoyment. Could you tell us a little more about how you utilize this concept theoretically, critically, politically, in your work?

SB: I've spent the last year or so working on something, tentatively titled *Strange Whiteness*, which might become a somewhat Foucauldian book on race. It reads race in terms of shame. Race, it seems to me, is all about shame, and it is through shame that we can understand the subjectifying effects of race. Race is thoroughly saturated with feelings of shame, but it's not the kind of shame that we typically discuss in conversations about race. I am not referring to the shame of racial positions – Whiteness, Blackness, and so on. It's not the shame of violence or racial privilege, or the shame of racial subordination, although those experiences also have their own shames that are important to understand. I'm interested in how race invokes shame on an ontological level. What more shameful thing could there be than to encounter one's manifest self, the self that possesses freedom and that makes moral choices, in terms of this kind of shadow self, this other biological self which is composed of a hereditary genetic attribute? This is the shame that belongs to the very idea of race itself, not just the things that are done in the name of race. It's because of this more ontological shame that we hate talking about race, that we avoid discussions of race even while we are enticed to talk about it. This is because race brings feelings of shame to anyone who is raced, which is now everyone, not just people of color but white people as well. Race makes us feel dirty, ashamed. So, race, shame, and subjection are deeply and profoundly linked, I think. The history of this shame goes back a long way to the times when only some people were raced. Traditionally, the people who were shamed were the ones who were made the object of a shaming racialized gaze, typically people of color, who were inscribed with a sort of shame through the effects of colonial subjection. This is a point made very well by Frantz Fanon, that racism induces feelings of shame in those against whom it is brought to bear (Fanon, 1967). For this reason, it became imperative to counteract that shame through the intentional production of a compensatory pride, an affirmation of racial beauty whose effect it was to reverse the racist shaming of Black people by creating this kind of counter-affect, a defiant dignity.

But other things happen later on. Not only is race shameful, but it is bound up with the shame of exposure. It's not being able to prevent others from gazing upon your race, for seeing you as raced. The literature on shame gives a very prominent role to this function of exposure before others, not necessarily for possessing a negative attribute but simply for not having the wherewithal to conceal oneself. I recently rearranged some things in my home here in Boston, and I moved a plant that sat in front of a window, exposing the inside of my home to the gaze of people walking by on the sidewalk. I felt such shame! That I could allow people to look into my living room was such a shameful thing! In other words, it's not necessarily that you are exposed for *being* this thing or that thing, it's that you're exposed at all, that you can't control, or don't care to control, the access strangers have to your intimate life. Levinas talks about the shame of poverty as tied with the shame of not being able to conceal one's own body behind ragged clothing that allows strangers to look through (Levinas, 2003). Race is kind of like that. It's an exposure, though traditionally it has been one that White people have been able to avoid. As a White person, and particularly as a White male, I can interact with anyone and, in most situations, I am allowed to imagine that they are not thinking about my race, and am thereby allowed to not think about it myself. My race functions as a universal, a nonrace, and I don't have to undergo feelings of exposure. I do not have to feel that I've given strangers access to anything particularly sensitive about myself. For a person of color, every interaction, or a great many interactions, involve the feeling of an exposure to which no direct consent has been made. Within the frame of racism, the shame that accompanies race is a shame that says, "My God, any stranger can gaze upon my race, upon such a deep aspect of myself!" To be a raced subject, any kind of raced subject, is to suffer the shame not only of having bad things, to hide or of having done bad things, (though that is also a possibility), but of being unable to conceal from the gaze of the other a deep ontological attribute, a biography and a history, and a particular formation of racial flesh. So, there is a kernel of similarity between the racial experiences of White people and others, although this similarity is obviously quite limited – significant questions of scale and intensity distinguish the kinds of racial shame black and white people experience.

Now, in the years that Whiteness was invisible, during which it was simply the anonymous norm, White people were utter strangers to this shame. Of course, Whiteness has never been entirely invisible; people of color have always studied Whiteness and come to know its ways simply as a matter of survival. But during this time, Whiteness was at least invisible to itself, which meant that White people didn't have to confront that shame of exposure because Whiteness was presumed to be the norm. Today, things are very different. Today, White people and Whiteness itself as a racial condition has been made conspicuous not just to people of color but to other White people and to themselves as raced subjects, as White subjects, and this new visibility, as a sense of exposure, has incurred new forms of racialized shame, White shame. These new White shames have led to a variety of convulsive responses, from Trumpian rage to a new politics of White introspection.

White Shame

DH: It sounds like you're moving toward a more reflexive dimension in how you think about shame in connection to Whiteness. I suppose that shame without some or other forms of reflection, or, as you put it, introspection, is not particularly useful?

SB: No, it is useful, and it's a good thing that there has developed such a robust and general conversation on Whiteness. Calls to interrogate Whiteness have opened up new conversations on race and all those small-scale conversational violences through which racism operates – microaggressions, although there is a lot about this term that I think has to be rethought. But, like a lot of good things, it has a downside. Reflexivity pushes us to think, to make ourselves differently, but reflexivity also becomes coded and incorporated into institutional structures, and right now I see a process like this happening. One way to understand the two-sidedness of this process is to consider precisely what it is that White people experience as they discover themselves racially shamed for the first time. The answer I pose is that White people are ashamed of their own ocularity, the authority of their objectifying gaze, which is the gaze that shames others. White people have historically been the great shamers of others, and they have shamed through a way of looking, glancing at people, just as Fanon noted. White looks are shaming in so far as they make others feel their bodies, making conspicuous the very materiality of other's selves. White looks can be sham*ing* but they can also be shame*ful*, if these looks themselves are exposed. White looks pry into the private realms of others' lives. The White look is a stare, or a gawk: it is an absorbed looking that exposes Whites themselves as the servants of their own racism. And this White gawking is shameful, even when it is expressed in a looking-away. What a shameful thing to be such a shamer! The White gaze is an indecent, prying gaze, the great exposer of the races of others.

So, White shame today is the shame of shaming, or the shame of being exposed shaming, being caught shaming by being caught looking, gazing and gawking at the races of others. It is the shame of the illicit spectator who gazes salaciously and in a degraded fashion on the race of others. Shame, after all, is contagious. We are ashamed for those we shame. This makes sense when one considers that shaming has, in modern society, been so radically discredited. You're not allowed to shame people anymore, and you're certainly not allowed to stare at them for the simple pleasure of doing so. The figure of the sovereign for Foucault, the king – he could shame people. He could hang you up on a public scaffold and just torture you for his own pleasure and for the pleasure of anyone who cared to look, which is a deeply shaming experience. In fact, the theme of shame and the prohibition on shame hangs over *Discipline and Punish* (Foucault, 1979) The sovereign could inflict shame through his own gaze and take a specifically ocular pleasure in it. But that sovereign was long ago shamed, overturned and replaced by the biopolitical, which mandates that we must care for each other and cultivate each other's lives (Wüschner, 2017), The shamer, therefore, is shamed as a throwback to some obsolete form of power, and the shaming gaze that is inscribed at the heart of Whiteness has itself become a shameful thing.

So, with White people's capacity to cast shame exposed, White people have become vulnerable to a new sort of shame, an experience many of them find strange and unbearable. The vulnerability of Whiteness to this shaming is evident everywhere; read the criticism of Whiteness all over the Internet and you'll notice a strong emphasis on the transparency and exposure of Whiteness to people of color. Black critics assert that they see into the White soul, that they know what Whites will do before they do it, that they know where White people come from, they know their biographies, their dreams, and their nightmares even better than White people know them themselves. There's a Netflix series, *Dear White People*, that savors the exposure of Whiteness, and it resonates through the works of people like Ta-Nehisi Coates. At the institution that I teach, I was recently invited by someone I have never met to enter into what she described as "heart-work" to deal with structural racism. I thought: My goodness! Does this person really see into my heart? Am I really so exposed? How did this person acquire such knowledge? So, I felt tremendous shame. We could read this as a sort of Hegelianism: this is the truth of the Lord that is possessed by the Bondsman, and that the Bondsman acquires through his domination. But in Hegel the Bondsman becomes smarter than the Lord, the same Lord that raised him up and held him in bondage. Servants and slaves have always known their masters better than masters knew themselves. But the new sense of white exposure is one that has acquired a certain sense of revenge. By claiming knowledge of your heart, I'm going to savor your exposure, to make you suffer the shame that I have suffered. To the extent that you have charged me with the administration of your flailing White heart, I'm going to make the exposure of your Whiteness an insufferable shame, as unbearable as the exposure of my Blackness has been for so long. That's not really dialectical in Hegel's sense. That's something closer to Nietzschean vengeance.

So, the question becomes, How does one respond to such unbearable shame? How might Whites survive this shaming? Even, how might Whites make use of it politically, in a struggle against White supremacy? Trump voters answer that question in their own way: rage and violent retribution. Shame is met with guns and MAGA hats, or tiki torches and shields. We all know that story. But for others, for those identified with progressive White anti-racism or that social pattern we describe as "woke," the trauma of shame is countered differently. Woke embraces a sort of displacement and recuperation that comes with the nobility of shaming itself. In shame, the self is split between virtuous and reviled parts. While one half of ourselves is cast out and repudiated (the bad self about which one is ashamed), the other half, the half that condemns the bad half, is valorized and redeemed. We see among White people an effort to dignify shame, to become, in effect, technicians of their own shaming and entrepreneurs of a certain self-transparency, a shaming self-exposure, mediated, as they experience it, through their exposure before a subaltern other. An odd development occurs as this truth that the slave possesses is transformed into a kind of therapeutic authority, a subaltern expert before whom one bares one's soul. White people embrace the criticism of their Whiteness as if it were a kind of therapeutic truth, as a kind of secret of their deeper selves whose discovery brings a moment of catharsis, or awakening (Binkley, 2020). In other words, the therapeutics of White shame, like reactionary Whiteness, is all about the containment and neutralization of shame. The Lord, unable to overpower the Bondsman and the Bondsman's knowledge, gets on the couch and makes the Bondsman his therapist – an Other-presumed-to-know, as Lacan put it, though perhaps a rather cruel and vengeful one. But, in doing so, the Lord preserves his sovereignty.

Freedom, or the Ends of Resistance

DH: In a way, that is also a Foucauldian type of position, and it leads me to another question. What about psychology and the relationship to freedom? That may not be particularly easy to answer in the context of your work, but here is another way of thinking about it. It's interesting that you mentioned the shift that happens when you overlay Foucault and Rose, and I think it's particularly apparent when it comes to one question of freedom, actually, but particularly apparent when we start to see how each of them deals with the notion of ethical practices of subjectivity or ethical practices of the self.

It's odd if one reads Rose in the light of Foucault's (1979) *Discipline and Punish*, where there seems almost to be a certain kind of fatalism. It seems very difficult to escape the downward and upward permeation of power into subjectivity, but of course there is a kind of optimism, slightly odd in some respects, this political optimism, that seems to come into the later Foucault (1988a, 1988b), the idea of ethical practices of subjectivity, ethical practices of freedom. What is your take on that? How would you think of freedom via Foucault in terms of your work? Because in a way I see what you're saying, because Foucault doesn't for the vast majority – certainly in the genealogical analysis he doesn't want to say this is an answer. He is doing kind of what you're saying: this is how it seems to work, but I'm not giving you any political prescriptions. There is a kind of Nietzschean quality there of a genealogy where one sees how the thing is produced, but one doesn't then become a moralist who takes on a very explicitly or overly political position – at least within the analysis being offered.

So, how would you engage with this notion of freedom, either via Foucault or just now today between us?

SB: Well, that's a question that a lot of people working in a Foucauldian tradition get asked: Where's the way out of power? And, of course, it's a question Foucault never wants to answer directly as he prefers to work negatively, dismantling an apparatus without providing any particular indication as to the way out. Methodologically, I like the notion of abandoning the reader. I'm going to lead you somewhere; I'm going to destroy a lot of things around you and then abandon you. In my imagination, this is as traumatic an experience for the reader as it is for the author, but it's a trauma that moves the reader to conceive of their own ways out. It forces the reader to become creative, to begin to imagine new alternatives to the old forms of power. Of course, this is a generous assessment of this effect on the reader, the effect of what Foucault called an "experience book." A less generous assessment would conclude that you've written a book that is simply positivistic and not really critical or that is descriptive without a critical engagement. These are debates that have surrounded *Discipline and Punish* for a very long time.

But I am drawn to the notion of abandoning the reader. I think the critical impact of a lot of analytic work gets diminished when there is a happy conclusion or a too clear invocation of some notion of freedom. On the question of race and the moment of freedom that might occur through a project of anti-racism, I think it's an important question to raise. Anti-racism as a psychological project is not explicitly political inasmuch as it doesn't directly aspire to diminish constraint and produce freedom. Psychology is a medical science, and as such its program is curative; it wants to restore people to a state of good health, and through this restored health it is assumed people will produce more democratic societies. The therapeutic telos is meant to restore health, not to secure freedom. I can accept that in some ways these amount to the same thing or that they can at least reinforce each other, but in my view they're different enough to warrant serious and separate consideration. A more radical project of White anti-racism would not be curative, in the medical sense of the term, but generative in the sense of enabling the production of a new kind of subject, of enabling a new way of enacting White subjectivity itself. I imagine an anti-racism that creates an open horizon, and in that sense there is some kinship with the kinds of aesthetics of the self that Foucault takes as the way out of the power relations he describes.

I think programmatic empathy and the therapeutics of White anti-racism offer good ways to make important structural changes and to ensure somewhat egalitarian institutions, but I don't think they're good at enacting entirely new modes of Whiteness, at unmaking and remaking racial subjectivities. These programs are necessary but not sufficient elements of a wider project on anti-racism. In addition to this, there has to be a generative moment. In fact, I would argue, White anti-racism has to operate on two levels, one defined by responsibility and the other by inventiveness. Guilt has a bad name in the conversation on race, but there are times when one should feel guilty, when one should say "I will give to you what I owe you." There are moments in which simply being a guilty White person is the only thing that you should do. But guilt by itself is not a generative relation. Guilt is a debt relation; it dictates that we remain the same in order that we might make certain remunerations. So, in addition to guilt what is required is an aesthetic element, an artistry, a pleasure in making oneself differently, or what Foucault calls an askesis of the self.

This element, too, is regarded with skepticism in conversations around White anti-racism. To claim that one is enacting one's Whiteness differently is discredited as an effort to ignore the sedimentation of history and ultimately as another reassertion of White privilege itself. I can see that this is a valid charge, but you have to do something. It's true that every situation comes laden with history, but every situation also leaves open the possibility of interpreting that history differently. There is always an indeterminate moment within every situation, no matter how historically inscribed. This is something Marxists and Foucauldians can agree on: men make history under conditions inherited from the past, and where there is power there is resistance.

To describe Whiteness as anything other than a deep and profound responsibility, or a debt which has to be paid, is something that is radically out of step with the current conversation on Whiteness and White anti-racism, which is steeped in the therapeutic logic and in the debt relation that we touched on earlier. A political emphasis on the performativity of identity as an act of self-fashioning is something that sounds like it comes from another era – I'm thinking of the kinds of queer theories that were popular in the 1990s and the activism of ACT UP, which placed a very Butlerian emphasis on the fluidity of gender identities and so on. All of that seems quite remote at this point. If you remember the impact of post-structualist theory on social movements at that time, the objective was to counter austere-Marxisms and Feminisms with a new politics of pleasure. You had to interrogate essentialism, to make identities performative, or to acknowledge their intrinsic performativity. This would, it was believed, disarm the anxiety, the heteronormative panic and the gender essentialism that fueled so much violence. Essentialism would be replaced by a politics of hedonistic performativity. We're all basically drag queens anyway, so just acknowledge that and all these problems will go away. In that light, I wonder if it's possible to consider Whiteness through that lens as a performative enactment that might be performed differently, understanding that your Whiteness is not always a curse on the other, that actually there is a pleasure in the performance of Whiteness that can be shared, one that opens new spaces of sociability – that the other might actually take pleasure in a Whiteness you shape and that you share with them. The conversation now equates Whiteness with harm, ignorance, and arrogance, as if all White people have an inner Trump they are struggling to expunge like a petulant Christian. The project now is the delve into the concealed essence of one's Whiteness, though it is my sense that once an essence is sought after, it is inevitably produced and consolidated. A different idea is that there might be ways of shaping Whiteness as a gift, as a performance, that people of color might actually find pleasure in a Whiteness that you can perform for them and with them in ironic ways and in playful ways.

I think a good place to go with this is to Bakhtin's notion of the carnivalesque. Bakhtin's interpretation of Rabelais is noted for its reading of medieval carnivals as a form of performative reverie in which uniquely traditional roles were overturned and new relations were enacted. (Bakhtin, 1965) These were dialogical enactments; there was no spectator, no audience, no performer, just an ongoing interactiveness around the debasement of everyone's traditional identities. Bakhtin focuses on the profane character in which this dialogic is enacted. Through costumes with exaggerated genitalia, enormous mouths and buttocks, these were identities meant to subvert the solemnity of the Catholic processions and Christian liturgical ceremonies such as Lent. In the carnivalesque, as I've mentioned in the broader context of race, we are all shamed, but we are also redeemed in our shame, a shame without spectators and without objects. There is no exposure in the carnival. Our shame becomes performative, a performative offering to the other, who is also a profane spectator and a participant. The conversation on race right now looks a lot more like Lent than it does like a medieval carnival. It's a place one goes to engage in virtuous self-flagellation, to seek the truth of one's racial self and exorcise one's flesh. White people today believe that their Whiteness is inevitably and only poison for themselves and for the other. They're as afraid of their Whiteness as medieval Christians were of their sexuality and hence as eager to confess, which is fine for those that enjoy that sort of thing, though as many people of color point out, listening to all that confession can get pretty tiresome. But I think it's important to keep open another possibility, that Whiteness can be the object of a profane pleasure, a playfulness from which new pleasures are generated. So, in a sense I'm proposing the reimagining of the racial field as one of performativity and play. There has to be a moment where you can say, "Hey, I'm over here now. Oh, look at that. You didn't expect that. I'm going to throw the ball to you, and what are you going to do with it?" Of course, the equal playing field that play presumes does not exist, owing to structural reasons, and work on transforming those structures has to be done. But that doesn't mean we have to wait for those structures to be corrected before we begin to imagine what play might mean. I'm not sure if that meets the requirements for freedom as you intended the question, but I think it's a good start.

The Ambivalence of Psychologization

DH: It seems to me part of what is so vital about your work is that you could say, to risk a generalization, that much if not all of psychology is on the brink of psychological reductionism just by nature of what the discipline is, or, differently put, that it invariably risks depoliticization. And I think this is also why I feel a sense of kinship with your work – because so much of what you do in some way points to that. So, for example, if empathy becomes equated simply with anti-racism, then we see a kind of psychological procedure which is adequate; apparently, it's now sufficient to be empathetic to be anti-racist. It reminds me of arguments which say, "Why do you want to now think about the response to racism simply as more tolerance?" (Zizek, 2007). Again, you have a psychological theme which is now supposed to be adequate as a way of responding to the political. Meaningful structural change, which is to say effective political change at broader sociological and institutional levels, is thus sidelined in favor of a change at the level of psychological dispositions. Such a move, while not necessarily cynical or disingenuous – it can be genuinely meant – can impede structural change precisely because people start to feel that this is effectively the most important change that should be made. So, given that in psychology we so often see a depoliticizing move of the sort I've just suggested, it seems absolutely vital that we have that type of work – critical forms of psychology – that brings that political dimension back in again and again.

It seems to me that that is very much a part of what you do. I don't know if you had a comment on that, but another question I had was about one of the other projects that you have in mind, that you may have started by now, that links to some of the work you have already spoken about and deals with Black rage and White listening. Can you tell us a bit more about that?

SB: Thank you. I think that's a very interesting question as it goes to the heart of what we mean by a critique of the "psy apparatus." When does the psychologization of an event politicize it, and when does it depoliticize it? I've concentrated on the latter instance, on what you aptly term psychological determinism, or how a discourse of psychology suppresses the political character of something. But we've known since second-wave feminism that the personal is political, that it's politicization through therapeutic intervention that can produce powerful cultural effects. I think it's important to remember that psychologization is very ambivalent, that every instance of psychological reduction is accompanied by a simultaneous politicization, that new perspectives and new possibilities are always stirred when a problem gets psychologized.

Two years ago, I presented the first version of a paper called "Black Rage, White Listening," and it's evolved into a published piece that is included in one of the anthologies emerging from the Psychology and the Other conference series (Binkley, 2019). Against the backdrop of the broader critique of psychology for its depoliticizing effect, I wanted to flip the argument and consider how the emergence of a Black psychology in the 1960s could be read in two ways. It had the effect of crystalizing and channeling certain racial affects and giving them an intensity that aligned with the Black radicalism of the time. But it also had the effect, as the years went on, of reining in and capturing this intensity, of placing it within an institutional discourse in which the problems it posed could be applied only to certain purposes.

The book *Black Rage* by William Grier and Price Cobbs was an important book from that period (Cobbs & Grier, 1968). At a moment in which Black militants were mobilizing and the country felt very threatened by this new militancy, American society was trying to understand the source not just of Black despondency or Black suffering but the psychic causes of Black militancy. Of course this militancy was very productive not only in shaping new sensibilities and racial subjectivities, but in affecting long lasting structural change. At the time, however, there was much speculation within the psychiatric community, much of it from Black psychologists and psychiatrists, that the militant response could be traced to a specific psychic formation, a fragmented psyche or an unresolved Oedipal relation. I looked at that discussion among Black psychologists, and I tried to understand how the projection of that Black psyche continues to operate in the discourse on race today. I mentioned earlier how the subjectivity of Blackness had to be invented as a subject capable of exercising credit, as a crediting subject to which payments could be made and around which the cultivation of empathy could be organized. I also mentioned how Blackness had to be invented as a kind of therapeutic authority, a subject bearing truths that could transform White shame into a project of self-discovery. All of these developments presumed the construction of Black suffering and Black anger in a specific way. And the psychology of Blackness from this time also served this function. I felt that this psychological subject had to be excavated, particularly as the figure of the angry Black entered into a kind of relationship with another psychologized figure, the listening White. To understand how these two figures operated and the kind of economy they established, one had to grasp their relation, the relation of Black rage and White listening.

DH: Can you tell us what White listening is? What is that?

SB: I was responding directly to things that were happening at the institution at which I teach. As a consequence of a student mobilization, the anger of a group of Black students, it seemed to me, was valorized, greeted with a kind of oracular reverence by a group of faculty who were intent on listening. I viewed that listening as an active process – the notion that White people are going to learn and listen and that it's very important to listen to these angry young voices because they know something that you need to know about yourself, that Black rage becomes this voice capable of shedding light on the authentic White subject, which White people don't yet understand but they have to learn to understand. This is kind of the way Foucault talked about madness as a voice that, through its exclusion from truth and reason, actually spoke the most profound truths. So, this kind of oracular authority was projected onto Black rage. We have to listen to it because it's the truth of who we are. And of course, the students were only too willing to give the faculty the therapy session they were signing up for. This initiated a long series of events centered on calls for the self-interrogation of Whiteness amongst the faculty, and at one point I was required to undergo mandatory cultural competency training, though I decided to decline the invitation. Later, at a public discussion, I was charged with White fragility after making some critical remarks and was formally asked not to attend cultural competency training at all!

In other words, what I sensed was that the linking of these two activities, raging and listening, achieved a certain symbiosis, a managerial equilibrium within the neoliberal organization. I became interested in the history of listening and raging, on the link between the two and how this linkage is transposed from a therapeutic ethos to neoliberal managerial practices. It seemed that the apparent contention between anger and listening concealed a hidden pact, a concealed therapeutic agreement that each would benefit and neither would seriously challenge the other. Have you ever quarreled therapeutically? With the implicit understanding that the quarrel itself was a kind of exercise in the release of emotion that was never intended to upset the ecology of the relationship? That's how it felt.

DH: It's a powerful argument. A question, though. You make the case about the fetishization of Black rage within certain institutional contexts very articulately, although I am also wondering what room there is for something approaching Black rage in today's America. Presumably there is some space, limited space, maybe, in institutional settings where there is perhaps a degree of fetishization, but where else is that possible? I suppose I'm just thinking of all these NFL debates and kneeling – an act which to me doesn't seem necessarily provocative is read by Trump and associated conservatives as enormously problematic. This leads to a situation where it becomes difficult to express any opposition of that sort.

SB: So, what are the limits of my critique of the fetishization of Black rage? The Trumpian reaction to Colin Kaepernick may be fetishistic but in a very different sense. Trump looks for "enemies" to confront. His view is one of simple force against force. He owes Kaepernick nothing, and doesn't give a damn for his feelings. But Kaepernick's kneeling is not an appeal to a liberal white listener. Kaepernick's gesture is a public symbol that brilliantly draws out the violence of his opponents. Trump's racism and the racism of the NFL are publicly exposed in their response. Similarly, Black Lives Matter are angry people. They're mad because cops kill a lot of Black people in the United States, and they are transported by rage. The events following the killing of George Floyd here in America but also globally suggest that not all Black rage comes wrapped in these psychologized discourses. Not all Black rage originates with the fetishism of White listening, though White listening is a mobile and flexible means of capturing the effects of Black rage.

The attack on the police station in Minneapolis or the looting of the Macy's in Manhattan were not acts of rage that presumed White listening. These were acts of rage that were willing to risk retaliatory White violence. Like those uprisings following the beating of Rodney King or the murder of Martin Luther King, these were acts of utter self-abandonment in the name of truth. So, what precisely is the relationship of these acts of rage to the psy apparatus? Let me answer this way. In one of his best-known interviews, Foucault sat down with a group of radical French Maoists sometime in the early 1970s (Foucault, 1980). They talked about the proposal that people's courts be used to judge the actions of the French police. People's courts operate autonomously and spontaneously, outside of any constitutional jurisdiction, to bring justice directly to the oppressor. Such courts had been used during the French revolution and in the Paris Commune and were a common instrument of the Maoist movements in China. While Foucault's interviewers supported their use, Foucault was critical, arguing that the introduction of any juridical process was only part of a wider absorption of the activity of direct, popular justice into an expanded state apparatus. Foucault wanted to keep direct justice, popular justice, which he considered to be a prejuridical act of revenge, separate from the juridical incorporation by any kind of court. Foucault had in mind an episode during the French Revolution recalled as the September executions in which a Paris mob attacked and murdered jailed members of the deposed ruling class – a mob act as a direct expression of revenge against an oppressor – although it was not long before a makeshift system of people's courts was established to rein in these violent responses. For Foucault, in a sense, the people's courts were too Bourgeois! This was a reply the French Maoists were surprised by. While I'm not sure I would go as far as Foucault did on the question of popular justice, I would suggest that today the ways in which we psychologize racial protest, that we adopt a "listening" posture with regard to their underlying emotions and sentiments, stands in a similar position to that of a people's court; these acts of rage directed against police, statues, department stores, et cetera, represent a certain intensity, one which brings the possibility of a shock and of new kinds of subjectivity, new shames and new selves. But such intensities are absorbed into a new "listening," a psychologized managerialism as they are remade as problems of interiority, of biography and introspection, of the "real" feelings of the other and of coming to know one's Whiteness and coming to understand the anger of Black people. These all become discoverable truths mediated by a discourse of psychology.

DH: So much psychology seems to play the role of a radical depoliticization of political issues. This seems one way of thinking about the moment of capture that you speak about. There is also a certain mode of neoliberal subjectivity which is also active in depoliticizing politics. What I'm getting a sense of in speaking to you and thinking about your work is the sense that what you do is to trace the multiple trajectories of a type of depoliticization which affects psychology and which psychology in turn relays in response to certain problematics and understandings within society. And it seems that in some respects the space for politics of a certain sort is getting smaller and smaller via these two modes, these two interlinked modes of depoliticization. That's just a way of trying to think about some of the themes in your work.

SB: Yes. Deleuze and Guattari (1980) used the phrase "apparatus of capture" to describe the function of some set of arrangements to absorb and redirect otherwise subversive lines of flight, and the Foucauldian conversation on psychology tends to fall in line with this assessment. Psychology captures, but it also stirs. If you explode in anger at me for something and I respond, "Oh, Derek, I understand you're struggling with your memories of your childhood" and so on, I've captured your explosion and put it into categories. But at the same time, if I ask, "Derek, how are you feeling? You seem tense," this is an opening, an invocation that could only come about through the invocation of a psychological sensibility. So, it's never as simple as that. Every capture is also an enactment, a mobilization of something, and vice versa. Those are the pieces that I have to work with, though I have to confess I haven't quite figured out how to put them all together yet!

References

Bakhtin, M. (1965). *Rabelais and his world*. Indiana University Press

Binkley, S. (2008). *Getting loose: Lifestyle consumption in the 1970s*. Duke University Press.

Binkley, S. (2011a). The government of intimacy: Satiation, intensification and the space of emotional reciprocity. *Rethinking Marxism, 24*(4), 556–573.

Binkley, S. (2011b). Psychological life as enterprise: Social practice and the government of neo-liberal interiority. *Journal of the History of Human Sciences, 24*(3), 83–102.

Binkley, S. (2015). *Happiness as enterprise: An essay on neoliberal life*. State University of New York Press.

Binkley, S. (2016). Anti-racism beyond empathy: Transformations in the knowing and governing of racial difference. *Subjectivity, 9*, 181–204.

Binkley, S. (2018). Biopolitical metaphor: Habitualized embodiment between discourse and affect. *Body & Society, 24*(3), 95–124.

Binkley, S. (2019). Black rage and White listening: On the psychologization of racial emotionality. In D. M. Goodman, E. R. Severson, & H. Macdonald (Eds.), *Race, rage, and resistance: Philosophy, psychology, and the perils of individualism* (pp. 90–107). Routledge.

Binkley, S. (2020). Unlearning privilege: The therapeutic ethos and the battle within the White Self. In D. Nehring, O. J. Madsen, E. Cabanas, C. Mills, & D. Kerrigan (Eds.), *The Routledge international handbook of global therapeutic cultures*. Routledge.

Cobbs, P., & Grier, W. (1968). *Black rage*. Basic Books.

Dean, M. (1999). *Governmentality: Power and rule in modern societies*. SAGE.

Deleuze, G., & Guattari, G. (1980). *A thousand plateaus: Capitalism and schizophrenia* (B. Massumi, Trans.). University of Minnesota Press.

Fanon, F. (1967). *Black skin, White masks* (C. L. Markmann, Trans.). Grove Press.

Foucault, M. (1979). *Discipline and punish*. Vintage Books.

Foucault, M. (1980). On popular justice: A discussion with Maoists. In M. Foucault (Ed.), *Power/knowledge: Selected interviews and other writings 1972–1977* (C. Gordon, Ed. & Trans., pp. 1–36). Pantheon.

Foucault, M. (1984). *History of sexuality, volume I*. Vintage.

Foucault, M. (1986). Of other spaces. *Diacritics, 16*, 22–27.

Foucault, M. (1988a). *The care of the self*. Vintage Books.

Foucault, M. (1988b). The ethic of care for the self as a practice of freedom. In J. Bernhauer & D. Rasmussen (Eds.), *The final Foucault* (pp. 1–20). MIT Press.

Foucault, M. (2008). *The birth of biopolitics: Lectures at the College De France, 1978–1979.* Picador.

Hook, D. (2007). *Foucault, psychology and the analytics of power.* Palgrave.

Levinas, E. (2003). On evasion/De l'évasion (B. Bergo, Trans.). Stanford University Press.

Mills, C. (1997). *The racial contract.* Cornell University Press.

Patterson, O. (1982). *Slavery and social death: A comparative study.* Harvard University Press.

Rose, N. (1999). *Powers of freedom: Reframing political thought.* Cambridge University Press.

Sugarman, J. (2015). Neoliberalism and psychological ethics. *Journal of Theoretical and Philosophical Psychology, 35*(2), 103–116.

Wüschner, P. (2017). Shame, guilt, and punishment. *Foucault Studies, 23,* 86–107.

Zizek, S. (2007). Tolerance as an ideological category. *Critical Inquiry.* www.lacan.com/zizek-inquiry.html

5

Infinite Greed and Transcendental Materialism

A Conversation with Adrian Johnston

Interviewed by Heather Macdonald
Heather Macdonald and Adrian Johnston

Introduction

Adrian Johnston is one of the most widely read philosophers today, and it was a great honor to have been able to be with him in this conversation. He is a distinguished professor of Philosophy at the University of New Mexico at Albuquerque and a faculty member of the Emory Psychoanalytic Institute in Atlanta. Johnston has published numerous books that draw upon French and German thinkers of the 19th century and has also been heavily influenced by more contemporary philosophers such as Žižek. Johnston has been strongly influenced by German idealism and Karl Marx. His lines of research concern vital intersections of thought regarding Marxism, psychoanalysis, and materialism. If his philosophy could be captured under a particular banner, it might be referred to as a kind of "transcendental materialism," which in sum calls for a materialist ontology that does not reduce away the gap or figure that is human subjectivity. Johnston has also called for a revitalization of Freud and Lacan (as well as Marx) as a way to rethink global capitalism and its various structures of human desire. He argues that the consumption drives of libidinal economies are *symptoms* of the production drives of political economies (not the other way around). He further asserts that Marx's historical materialism rebuts the liberal assertion of a capitalism that is directly correlated to the self-interested egocentric consumption of goods because at root capitalism is about *surplus value* – the maintenance of which requires us to "unlink" from our own facticity in order to perform a kind of phantasmic self-sacrifice to the Big Other or the "invisible hand of the market" or the "economy as God." He is the author of *Adventures in Transcendental*

DOI: 10.4324/9781003280033-6

Materialism: Dialogues with Contemporary Thinkers (Edinburgh University Press, 2014). He is the coauthor, with Catherine Malabou, of *Self and Emotional Life: Philosophy, Psychoanalysis, and Neuroscience* (Columbia University Press, 2013). His most recent books are *Irrepressible Truth: On Lacan's 'The Freudian Thing'* (Palgrave Macmillan, 2017) and *A New German Idealism: Hegel, Žižek, and Dialectical Materialism* (Columbia University Press, 2018).

Heather Macdonald (HM):   To begin with, let's review a bit of your background. Perhaps we can start with part of your early academic story. In your case, it's interesting because you've been drawn both to philosophy and psychology, in particular psychoanalytic theory. I think in previous interviews you have talked about what drew you to philosophy, such as your family background, which would be interesting to hear.

Adrian Johnston (AJ):   Yes, and there's actually a close relationship between these two. As you alluded to, philosophy was something that my family history nudged me in the direction of. You know, being born into a family in which my paternal grandfather as well as my father both had doctorates in philosophy . . . and I picked up a taste for it, I think, starting relatively early. One of the things that's funny about this is, when I started my training in analysis, early on in that process, it was clear that my analyst was very interested in and amused by the fact that I had this clear, familial, pre-/overdetermination of my choice of career path. So, that featured quite a bit in my analysis.

Without going into too much exhibitionistic detail, in terms of both my immediate family as well as in my family history, there was quite a bit of psychopathology. I do think that oftentimes you will hear people in the clinical community, especially analysts, mention that many different people who end up going into clinical analytic work had a depressed parent. There were elements of my own experience, in terms of my immediate family, as well as my extended family and family history, where I needed to confront aspects of psychopathology that informed my interest in philosophy coupled with psychoanalysis. Very early on in my undergraduate studies, where I was a philosophy major, I also developed an interest in psychoanalysis mediated through certain figures, especially in 20th-century French and German thought. Just as my choice of philosophy as a discipline was shaped by my family background, I think my interest in psychoanalysis was too, and all these forces came together when I studied French and German thought.

HM: I want to try to outline the trajectory of your scholarship a bit. Initially, you were at the University of Texas at Austin for your undergraduate studies, correct?

AJ: Yes.

HM: Were you immediately drawn to Hegel and Freud and to continental philosophy? Because I think, if I recall correctly, your father was in the field of analytic philosophy.

AJ: Yes. What's interesting is that my paternal grandfather was actually a specialist in Aquinas and medieval scholasticism. He was trained by people at the University of Toronto, which even to this day is sort of a stronghold for medieval philosophy. My grandfather did his dissertation with Jacques Maritain and Étienne Gilson and was not only committed to Catholic philosophy but was just a highly conservative Catholic overall.

My grandfather, unsurprisingly, ended up with a faculty position at Notre Dame. My father grew up in South Bend, Indiana, with my grandfather teaching at Notre Dame. At the time at Notre Dame, children of faculty were able to attend for free. So, my father and my uncle both went there for undergraduate. As an undergraduate, my father wanted to major in biology, but my conservative Catholic grandfather said, "Over my dead body! That department is packed full of atheists. No way."

My father's revenge was to then shift gears and go into philosophy. But my grandfather already worried about what he saw, as I'm sure many did at the time – the crunch coming with the collapse of the academic job market. My father ended up going into analytic philosophy, which, given the fact that it is more of a secular, scientifically minded bent, was also considered suspect by my grandfather. But my father went ahead with that, nonetheless.

I was already in high school and discovering some of the philosophy books my father had on his shelves that were even spatially marginalized – [to] unused, bottom shelves in certain corners. There, I found things like Nietzsche, some Foucault, and Derrida. My father said, "A lot of it is just jargon-ridden, fuzzy-headed French nonsense."

I started reading some of that. Once I started my undergraduate studies, reading figures such as Heidegger, Derrida, and Foucault, I then started reading things like Deleuze and Guattari. It was from that angle that I first began taking courses at the University of Texas at Austin (UT Austin), in which I was reading Freud and company. What's funny is that, at first, I was trying to be very critical of Freud, based on having read things like Deleuze and Guattari's *Anti-Oedipus* (Deleuze & Guattari, 1972).

Instead, I found myself immediately won over, just totally seduced. You know, the material took. Then, I just really began focusing on the intersection of philosophy and psychoanalysis. My undergraduate honors thesis was an attempt to use post-Freudian psychoanalytic developments to defend psychoanalysis against Foucault's critique of it, both in Foucault's early and his late work, then exploiting Foucault's thinly veiled approval of Lacan's version of Freudianism, toward the end of 1966's *Les mots et les choses* (*The Order of Things*; Foucault, 1966). That was the project that I ended with in my undergraduate career, working feverishly on [it] for that last year. Then I took a year off and began graduate school after that.

HM: I'm really struck that you read *Anti-Oedipus*, where Deleuze and Guattari (1972) *clearly* outline a staunch critique of Freud's Oedipal theory and the restriction of unconscious desire by the Oedipal triangle, and yet you ended up aligning with Freudian theory or at least more on the structuralist side of the argument. It is also interesting because in *Anti-Oedipus* they also link Oedipal forms of desire with capitalistic flows, which did not appear to win you over entirely either.

AJ: Well, initially, it did. But, of course, I said to myself, "All right, given that I'm interested in this, I really need to get the background in what's being critiqued and to get firsthand familiarity with Freud, with Lacan, and others." So, the first exclusively psychoanalytic course I took at UT Austin was offered in the German Studies Department there, taught by this faculty member who's still at UT Austin, I believe, Katie Arens. She would periodically offer a course in German studies on Freud, with Lacan and then a little bit of Kristeva at the end.

My main mentor in the Philosophy Department at UT Austin at the time was Kelly Oliver, who did a lot of her early work on Kristeva. As soon as I actually started reading Freud himself, I found his material just so overwhelmingly powerful and persuasive that I very quickly lost a lot of the reservations I thought I would have.

With Lacan, initially, he was not my cup of tea. I was forced to work through some of it in that course, and I came back to it in my honors thesis; I realized it contains a lot that's very important for my purposes. Lacan, for me, was definitely an acquired taste. The initial exposure to him – midway through my undergraduate career – I didn't imagine, when I first started reading him, that I would end up devoting so much of my subsequent time and effort to him. By the time I was in the middle of graduate work, I felt very differently.

HM: It seems to work that way! Sometimes what is most alive for us resides in the exact same location as our resistance.

AJ: Yes. Through other things I was reading, repeatedly realizing, Lacan's teaching contains this wealth of material that so many others are drawing on that I kept getting pushed back into wrestling with him. I spent time reading him and working on his texts – even if you're dealing with him in translation into your own tongue, I mean, it is like acquiring a new language unto itself! Lacanese is something, which takes quite a bit of time to just acquire comfort with, as a vernacular. Once you become familiar with his language, even including the style, his manners of expressing himself, I found that eventually I became very, very comfortable with and invested in kind of continuing to engage with his work. At the same time, I'm very committed to saying, as are a number of others, Lacan actually can survive translation out of his own language. You can present Lacan without sacrificing nuanced complexity or richness. You can present him in the terms of other discourses. I do think that that's very important work to continue doing.

HM: I think the fact that Deleuze or Derrida was part of your starting point actually has an interesting relationship with some of Žižek's early scholarship. It is scholarship that interrogates human subjectivity and desire, and this kind of work can only be done at the intersection of philosophy and psychology.

AJ: Just in terms of Žižek's intellectual biography, his very early work has never – I don't think he wants it to be translated. In Slovene, there's evidently some material from his very early years that was clearly situated – it's during the period of his development in Yugoslavia – there's this entire sort of constellation or ethos of French post-war, structuralist, post-structuralist thought that allows you to bring together Derrida, Kristeva, Lacan, and Althusser.

The sense is, there's really a way in which Lacan stands out as quite different from many of what would seem to be these fellow travelers. Žižek, in a way, backed into Lacan through a range of French figures, including Althusser, and then developed the interest in Lacan. There is, weirdly, this kind of rough similarity, in terms of that same kind of post-war French intellectual ethos, distributed across a number of figures, that was already of interest to me.

I initially approached Lacan as just one of that set. Then, I came to appreciate that no, there's a lot here that is not assimilable to the intellectual sensibilities of many of Lacan's contemporaries and immediate successors.

HM: Yes, that makes sense. Would you also say the same about your own work? That you "backed into" Lacan? And then from that point moved towards Hegel and Marx? I also want to unpack how you think about historical materialism and how you redefine this as "transcendental materialism" in more recent publications (Johnston, 2014). I think that concept, and your work in that area, is really important for the practice of psychology.

AJ: Interesting. Yeah, there's also, evidently, a few criminologists who found it useful. I'm just kind of curious to see how – I'm not fully aware of, or certainly don't have control over how – that's disseminated itself.

In terms of the German idealism component, I ended up, after a year's break following my completion of my undergraduate degree at UT Austin, I then ended up going to Stony Brook. If you want to do a PhD in continental philosophy in the US, in a philosophy department, not in, say, comparative literature or French or German studies, your options are surprisingly limited. Stony Brook, since the late 1960s, has been this bastion for continental philosophy in the American philosophical world.

My main undergraduate advisor, Kelly Oliver, interestingly enough, had already accepted a job offer at Stony Brook, but it was frozen due to a temporary freeze imposed on the State University of New York (SUNY) system by then governor George Pataki in New York. She had recommended it in the strongest of terms to me, and I ended up getting in and going. Then, she arrived at Stony Brook when I was in my second year. So, I continued working with her there.

I began at Stony Brook, and my very first semester as a doctoral student, one of the seminars I was taking was on Hegel's *Phenomenology of Sprit* (1807/1977). I already had had some exposure to Hegel as an undergraduate. I was beginning, at that point, to appreciate just how much what is called continental philosophy from the 19th century up to the present really flows out of the twin fountainheads of Kant and Hegel.

For me, it's remained the case that, just as for the medievals, so much of what they were dealing with boiled down to the relationship between Plato and Aristotle. I think about the Germans – any kind of national pride is stigmatized by the residues of Nazism – they will still allow themselves to say sometimes that, basically, all philosophical discussions still boil down to Kant or to Hegel. I do think there's something to that. When I really was beginning to bear down on specific texts, such as Hegel's *Phenomenology of Spirit* (1807/1977), early on in graduate school, it became readily apparent to me just how influential this early 19th-century material was, especially for Freud although more indirectly.

This was before I actually discovered Slavoj Žižek's work. Soon after, I was beginning to already see all of these interconnections between my 20th-century interests and the German idealists. It was during this period where I focused on Žižek's specific texts such as *Sublime Object of Ideology* (2009), *For They Know Not What They Do: Enjoyment as a Political Factor* (2008), and *The Indivisible Remainder: On Schelling and Related Matters* (2007), all of this material that was very focused on especially Kant, Schelling, and Hegel in relation to Lacan. It was extremely validating for me to come across this and realize, yes, there are indeed so many ways to productively interface German idealism with Lacanian psychoanalysis.

Later, in my graduate studies, I met Žižek; then he agreed to be on my dissertation committee. I started periodically sitting down with him when he would come to New York, which was usually several times a year, and the rest via email. So, all of that kind of came together in graduate school. During my graduate studies, I was very much focused on the German idealism and psychoanalysis intersection. I felt already like I had more than enough on my plate to deal with, with just the German idealism and psychoanalysis material. It was a few years after finishing up my doctoral work, and while I was doing my post-doc in clinical training at Emory, that I then began spending more time with political theory, and especially Marxism and its variants.

HM: Your work on your dissertation during that same time period was eventually published as the book *Time Driven: Metapsychology and the Splitting of the Drive* (2005). This work came out of that intersection between German idealism and psychoanalytic theory. Can you explain a bit more of your process in synthesizing Hegel or Kant into the structural mechanics of the Freudian drives?

AJ: Well, here, there's a perfect question in that there's a very precise answer. What's funny is, the longest single chapter in that book is actually the one devoted to Kant. That chapter on Kant really was informed by work I had done in one of my seminars on the *Critique of Pure Reason* (1781/1996) with the resident Kantian at Stony Brook. It focuses on the key place in Kant's corpus, where you see this most clearly. There are other places.

In a portion of the first critique, the *Critique of Pure Reason*, under the general heading of what Kant calls "Transcendental Dialectic," there are his paralogisms of pure reason. This involved his critique of what was then called rational psychology – so, nonempirical psychology, the philosophical, a priori foundations of the study of the mind.

HM: Such as Kant's distinctions between the noumena and phenomena.

AJ: Yes. It was, in particular, the Cartesian strains of rational psychology that were in Kant's crosshairs, and the notion that the soul is the seat of our mindedness. It's a special metaphysical object that we somehow or other have epistemological access to [so] that we can make a series of metaphysical claims about its nature, just like we can of other objects that we study.

This is one of many proto-psychoanalytic moments for Kant himself. He argues that the Cartesian strain of rationality in fact ignores an ineliminable, structurally insurmountable self-opacity that afflicts us as the kinds of subjects that we are. For Kant, I can appear to myself as an object of my own self-consciousness, but that is still an appearance. The idea of what I am in and of myself, that makes that appearance possible or that lies beyond, beneath, or behind that appearance, is not something that I can lay a claim to as an object of knowledge. This divide between – whether we think of it as transcendental versus empirical subjectivity or noumenal and phenomenal selves – the very internal dynamics of subjectivity are such that it splits itself into these two irreducible dimensions.

To make a long story short, I wanted to argue for a kind of internally predetermined self-division or dimension similar to what psychoanalysis refers to as drives. Kant purported to demonstrate something analogous with regard to our subjectivity. One could make the case for splitting each of the drives from within instead of drives being like we often would tend to think of them – as just homogeneous, undifferentiated quotas of "libidinal oomph." These ideas focused within Freud and then furthermore in Lacan in the same way that we used to think atoms were indivisible, but no! You can actually find that what we previously thought of as an indivisible unity is itself merely a kind of secondary manifestation of an underlying division or multitude. Likewise, with the drive, it is splitting the drive, in terms of each and every drive being internally divided into these antagonistic dimensions. For me, there was this real parallel between what Kant did, in terms of the structure of subjectivity, and what I wanted to do, in terms of the structure of drive.

HM: You mean that the drives themselves are divisible into internally differentiated mechanisms?

AJ: Yeah. Looking at how Freud, in the single encapsulation of what he means by drive – mainly the 1915 metapsychology paper *Drives and Their Vicissitudes* or, as it's in the Strachey version, *Instincts and Their Vicissitudes* (1915) – that Freud makes very clear by definition, each and every drive is composed of four elements: source, pressure, aim, and object.

Taking that, and then putting it into conversation with what the later Freud has to say, apropos the admittedly rather nebulous notion of the death drive and his post-1920 work (Freud, 1927/1989), and then some of what Lacan offers, making the argument that source, pressure, aim, and object don't fit together neatly and don't rub along well together. Yes, they are forced to come together, or drive is that which holds these things together. It's an uneasy, tension-ridden marriage of elements that, as Lacan puts it in *Seminar XI: The Four Fundamental Concepts of Psychoanalysis* (1964/1977), you should think of this more like these strange machines, these kluge-like contraptions, involving slapping together all of these disparate elements. It functions, perhaps, well enough, but it's not some sort of well-oiled, internally well-organized machine.

HM: From there, it seems to me, there was a real pivot point because Marx does not figure very strongly in *Time Driven: Metapsychology and the Splitting of the Drive* (2005). So, it was after *Time Driven* where you really moved into the Freudo-Marxist conversation.

AJ: Yes. There are a few gestures that I make in that direction, especially of classical mid-20th century Frankfurt School Freudo-Marxism. So, some passing criticisms of the Marcuse-style project of libidinal liberation, the fact that, if this theory of a split drive has anything to it, this creates new problems for the sort of Freudian model that a figure like Marcuse was using in terms of how he was interfacing this with Marxism.

I don't really develop it any more than that in the dissertation. Again, part of it was just for space reasons. The dissertation ended up being in the form in which it was actually printed out and submitted. This was still in the old days, where you had to march the hard copies over to the Office of Graduate Studies. You know, it was a little over 600 pages. This was even after my committee had told me to not add certain other things that I had been thinking of adding! Some of it was that.

In order to work on German idealism and psychoanalysis in tandem, I just had to set aside a lot of other interests, especially during the second half of my stay in graduate school. When I was younger, in high school, one of the big formative activities for me was policy debate. That involves a lot of social scientific sort of research. I had been thinking in high school, and then at the start of undergraduate, that I wanted to major in political science. Then I found that the philosophy courses at UT were proving to be more satisfactory to me than other humanities and social sciences courses I was taking.

It was not until after the PhD, and once I was settled in at Emory for my clinical training, that I found myself. I think in part this was due to the pull of events; bear in mind, while I was in graduate school, it was this strange American holiday from history, the interim between the collapse of really existing socialism and the abrupt rude wakeup call of 9/11. It was almost as though it was easy for me to take a certain holiday from political theory during the Clinton '90s. While I was at Emory doing my clinical training, the period in which you have the Bush administration, the wars in Afghanistan and Iraq, it was – for me – this feeling of not only did I have the interest in Marxism already, but feeling pulled in that direction by what was happening. By the end of my clinical work at Emory, I was beginning to get asked to contribute to volumes, where often what people were interested in was the political dimension of psychoanalysis. It was through various events that kind of conspired to pull me back in that direction; that's how things began to unfold in that way.

I also felt like I just needed more time; I mean, the Marxist tradition, like with German idealism, like with psychoanalysis, you know, these are huge bodies of literature. I don't feel comfortable really sticking my neck out in print until I feel like I've had a chance to do a certain amount of homework.

HM: Yes, but this has been the main thrust of your argument, which is that if we are going to respond to psychopolitical questions, you need both psychoanalysis and Marxism. Psychoanalytic theory alone is insufficient in attending to historical materialism, and Marxism is unable to account for libidinal drives. We need both of these discourses in conversation, but they have proven difficult to marry.

AJ: Yeah, absolutely. For me currently, this summer, assuming that the kids stay in camp because there's always the threat that another COVID-19 outbreak could close everything down, but assuming no emergency situation arrives, I'll probably be able to finish this new book that is very much at the intersection of Marxism and psychoanalysis. It is tentatively entitled *Infinite Greed*. It's been coming together slowly. I still have just a couple more pieces to finish for it to be complete.

Part of what I'm motivated to do here, and that I hope gives my work some distinctiveness, is to forge some sort of marriage between Marxism and psychoanalysis. There is a whole tradition of literature, going back to authors like Reich and Marcuse from the Frankfurt School, that attempts to bridge the two. One of the big problems with traditional versions of this is that there is an influence of specifically Western Marxism, which colors how this is done. There's been a real neglect in this interfacing, looking specifically at Marx's critique of political economy and looking at the more economic dimensions of Marx's mature work rather than other aspects of Marx's work, which, at first glance, seem a little more amenable to psychoanalytic appropriation.

I'm hoping that what I will be able to do is to draw attention to Marx's economics for those interested in the Marxist/psychoanalytic relationship and remind them of the importance of economics for Marx himself. For those who read him, including psychoanalytically, really seeing how central his historical materialist critique of political economy is to his perspective on capitalism, and not just look at the more superstructural cultural, socio-symbolic dimensions of his work. Instead, really look at the nitty-gritty of the economic core and what it offers to those of us who also are invested in psychoanalysis.

HM: As I recall from reading sections of *Infinite Greed (2017a)*, you suggest that (1) psychoanalysis and the analytic drive would not have been possible without capitalism, (2) Marx's theory of historical materialism (his formulas for capital itself) anticipate Freudian drive theory, and (3) "[t]he consumption drives of libidinal economies are *symptoms* of the production drives of the political economies (and not the other way around)" (p. 18).

AJ: Yes, Marx's formulas for capital, I mean, they're just amazingly rich, despite their apparent simplicity, once we take seriously the idea that we are indeed, and this is something which psychoanalysis shares with Marxism, at least in part very much creatures of our surroundings. We are political animals, as Marx suggested following Aristotle.

If we take that seriously and look at the manner in which political economy mediates libidinal economy, which it cannot but do, we're thrown, at birth, into what Marx called modes of production. How do we rework things like psychoanalytic drive theory on the basis of an appreciation of that? I think that that requires looking at the interaction between the economics in the Marxist sense and what is happening on the libidinal drive side, psychoanalytically.

HM: I think that brings us to an important question. How has psychology (philosophy, too) been complicit in the neoliberal late-stage capitalist drives? How have we deployed Freud's drive theory to "capture" individual identities? Not necessarily because of the structure of the drives themselves. Does your argument, in a way, call out how psychology as a discipline has been complicit?

AJ: I think, yes. Now, of course, my hesitancy just comes given the diversity of orientations, approaches, traditions, and so forth. When we think of the psy-constellation, we've got this enormously rich kind of panorama of different approaches. Here, I could begin by starting close to home, in terms of what I feel more qualified to speak about. A few years ago, I felt a little bit kind of lured into working on something I didn't intend to devote as much time as I ended up devoting to it.

These three fellows who you may know from the Lacanian world, Derek Hook, Calum Neill, and Stijn Vanheule, decided to embark on this project of a complete commentary on Lacan's unabridged *Écrits* (1966). They approached various Lacan scholars and asked each of us to focus on one chapter in the *Écrits*. We gave them our preferences, and they divvied out the assignments. I ended up being assigned Lacan's 1955 essay, "The Freudian Thing." What we were instructed to do was provide a paragraph-by-paragraph, even sentence-by-sentence, exegetical unpacking of the text. In hindsight, I cannot but describe myself as idiotic; I just took them at their word and started about doing it. As I was working through it, I realized, "Oh, my God, the ratio of the number of pages I have to write to, you know, the number of pages of Lacan's *écrit*, it turned out to be 10 to one!"

This is like a 25-page text, and, indeed, I ended up with 250 pages (Johnston, 2017b). As I was doing it, I was emailing the editors, saying, "This is insane. There's no way Routledge will allow you to publish a volume in which each chapter is a book unto itself." But they reassured me, "No, no, we have the go-ahead. Keep going." Stupidly, I kept doing it; my spouse was even like, "Why are you doing this to yourself?" It was painful because literally unpacking every sentence of one of his texts was just maddening. It ended up being a book unto itself. So, I published it separately as a book and then an abridged version as a chapter for their volume.

I bring it up because that 1955 text is one of the key places in which Lacan elaborates in excruciating detail – and I can say it was excruciating, because I did. . . . I painfully went through all of it. His critique of Anglo-American ego psychology, much of that was subtly proximate to Marxist concerns – even though the Lacan of this period merely, we could say, "coquetted" with Marxism. He got much more active in terms of playfully referring to it, especially in the aftermath of May 1968 in Paris.

But this was in the mid-1950s. Although Lacan's not heavily drawing on Marxism, nonetheless, it's very clear that one of his biggest objections to Anglo-American ego psychology is that it has both a theoretical and clinical emphasis on the adaptation to reality as the gold standard of nonneurotic mental health, which was nothing but essentially turning the consulting room into a factory manufacturing conformity. The idea is that you identify with the person of the analyst, representing a kind of comfortable bourgeois, heterosexually married, you know, x number of children, white picket fence, two cars in the garage sort of figure and lifestyle. This was to make psychoanalysis into nothing but the guarantor of libidinal conformity to a certain stereotyped American dream.

It's not that Lacan was saying that the alternative to this, what we should push for, is a form of clinical practice where we indoctrinate our patients with just good left-wing ideology, where we turn it into, all right, you're going to learn your Marxist lessons here on the couch. No. It already takes an enormous amount of effort for any practice, especially any practitioner in the psy-fields, to really be constantly and continually vigilant and self-critical in terms of repeatedly questioning how might I, even if inadvertently, be complicit in holding up, even if only implicitly, a certain normative model or ideal that itself is insufficiently critical of the surrounding status quo reality that we're in. How much of the patient's desire is initially a desire to just allow me to better conform to, or to return [to] conforming to, reality as it is in an uncritical fashion?

I think, for instance, with regards to psychoanalysis, the idea is that it's a place to question your desires and to see whether you desire what you think you desire. Even just trying to hold open a space like that, that does not involve contamination and compromise by a very pervasive surrounding ideology, is already a lot of work.

HM: If not impossible.

AJ: In a way, yes. Part of why it's an impossible profession, as Freud already warned us.

HM: Yes.

AJ: But in terms of interdisciplinarity, part of what Lacan also pushed for, and this was another part of his campaign against the ego psychology dominating the International Psychoanalytic Association (IPA) in that era, is that this also went hand in hand with the drive towards the medicalization of psychoanalysis and turning it into a profession where only those who have a MD in psychiatry are allowed to join the ranks of analysts. The legacy of that continues to linger in at least, for instance, in the American Psychoanalytic Association. I mean, getting trained as a PhD rather than an MD, I had to jump through a whole series of additional hoops to reassure a medically dominated community that yeah, I passed muster.

Freud warned about medicalization, and the question of lay analysis; both Freud and Lacan really envisaged proper psychoanalytic training as requiring the familiarity with a whole range of disciplines and with, really, kind of a broad swath of the wealth of human knowledge, and cultural tradition. I think that, along with this, the kind of critical awareness of ideology in its various forms is something that [one] would be more likely to get through that sort of intellectual training or formation. I think that in many psy-disciplines, the pressure to specialize, including in certain currents of psychoanalysis the modeling along the lines of medical training mitigates against that.

HM: It also mitigates any kind of opening for considering psychotherapy as a practice of ethics, for example.

AJ: Yes.

HM: Or maybe disruptive ethics would be a better term?

AJ: Right, exactly. The sort of medical-style application of a predetermined diagnostic framework and the sense that these are the treatment modalities that the framework itself dictates. These are the dangers that come along with, for instance, approaches that rely too heavily on whatever the current version of the *Diagnostic and Statistical Manual of Mental Disorders* (American Psychiatric

Association, 2013) lays out. Of course, turning it into that idea, that it's just about a certain kind of highly specialized expert knowledge, then closes off the ability or tends to lead people not to think in terms of ethics, politics, what we might call . . . all [of] which involve an abyss of judgment, that can't be guaranteed or vouched for by some sort of body of authoritative knowledge that predetermines the right decision in advance.

HM: This is really the question I've wanted to ask the most: Is there a direction psychoanalysis should take? Is there a revolutionary practice that psychoanalysis should engage, especially at this point in time?

AJ: Yeah. I mean, here I'm going to be a little more, I don't want to say conservative, but there's a certain cautiousness for me, which is that in terms of the actual clinical experience of analysis, and on both sides of that equation, for both analyst and analysand, I do think that there's something about it in terms of it being this unique opening for questioning and confronting things in a way that I can't think of any other particular relationship or space that operates in quite the same way. I think that there is something incredibly valuable about it. When you think about the encroachment on psychoanalysis, such as the economics of healthcare and insurance that require one to deliver results within a certain window, for a certain cost, and so forth, that even to try and protect the space of psychoanalysis becomes almost impossible. But psychoanalysis is a revolutionary gesture in resisting the demand that everything be sped up, everything be done faster and more efficiently.

As I indicated a few minutes ago, apropos Lacan, I certainly would not want to recommend that analysts in any way impose certain alternate political perspectives or push anything directly in that way. But I do think that being aware of how much all of us, analysts and analysands alike, how much of our own intrapsychical and libidinal dynamics are mediated and shaped by a historically transient socio-economic framework, is very important. I think that allowing for the possibility of analysands to go so far as to question whether they really desire the desires that have been foisted on them by external forces. . . .

This eternal vigilance on the part of analysts in terms of really being on their guard for not allowing themselves complacently to fall into certain forms of theory and practice, such as the ego psychology Lacan was critical of in the mid-20th century, I think does end up being very much complicit. Psychoanalysis was complicit in seeking to mold patients into good capitalist subjects in a way that is not necessarily beneficial to them and certainly reflects a series of at least tacit judgments approving of the status quo; for me, this is really hard to approve of, then as well as now.

I do think that a struggle to move away from the models of education and training that are aligned with a kind of capitalist-style division of labor, reflected even in the academic or intellectual spheres in which we're all sorted into categories and subcategories, is needed. Often, we just focus on our given specialization, so that if I'm training to be an analyst, it's best if I have a MD in psychiatry, which involves not taking very many courses at the liberal arts level, for example. Or, I'm just going to focus on this one particular modality of clinical treatment, you know, whether I'm a cognitive behavioral therapy (CBT) specialist or otherwise.

Lacan was well aware that, already, psychoanalytic institutes were becoming very narrow-minded in this way. Instead of trying to create, at the level of our educational institutions and practices, we all pay lip service to interdisciplinarity work; I think it is mostly hollow lip service. We have yet to really follow through on what interdisciplinary would look like. That's where you would have the greatest chance of aspiring analysts to be exposed to traditions like Marxism, if they were taking more courses involving people in the humanities and social sciences, for example.

That might sound much more modest. I think that those would be some nonutopian practices – even though just getting those would be, it would seem, almost miraculous. I also think that this holds for philosophy, too. I mean, one thing for me that I feel like I have to work against, too, is as a discipline it tends to become very insular and windowless. Really pushing my students and saying, "You shouldn't just be reading philosophy. You should be reading in other fields, and if you want to make headway on any of these problems, as Marx would put it, only recourse to the general intellect beyond narrow disciplinary specialization is going to give you any hope of getting anywhere."

HM: I think Nietzsche also warned us against this.

AJ: Oh, yes. I spend more and more time in the 19th century, intellectually. I mean, you might even say that part of what has made, for instance, certain 19th-century figures, and especially Marx in this case, so contemporarily timely is that we weirdly regressed in a way back to a form of capitalism that's much closer to the rapacious unregulated variety that flourished right up through the first World War and the Great Depression. I think that that weird kind of regression, collectively, that we have undergone has allowed us to have a renewed appreciation of figures like Marx and Nietzsche.

HM: I think that's so interesting and true. I also think that's why you're now writing about atheism and religion and this resurgence, really, of these forms of belief as well as Christianity. Speak to that a little bit, because I think it relates to what you were just talking about, how these 19th-century thinkers describe tensions between the secular and the religious.

AJ: This is where I think, in particular, the Marx-Lacan coupling is especially powerful, Lacan apropos atheism, and you've come across this I'm sure, since I referenced it in a number of places in my own work, where he says in *Seminar XI*, "The true formula of atheism is not God is dead, but rather God is unconscious" (1964, p. 59). When you unpack what he means by that, it's very rich. I experienced one version of this firsthand in my clinical training. I did not find religion in general, and more specifically Catholicism (despite attending a Catholic elementary school), to be appealing or plausible. I was able to talk my parents out of making me go to church. I've left it behind. I washed my hands of it. You discover that the residues of that stay with you, and the less you consciously believe yourself to believe, the more you're likely to just complacently remain in the grip of the, in a sense, spectral cobwebs – old beliefs that continue to persist unconsciously.

Alternatively, I remember this happened on a couple of occasions where I was in one of the seminars at the Psychoanalytic Institute. I recall, on occasions when it happened, nothing explicitly religious was part of the discussion. For instance, we'd be talking about Freud's metapsychology in what would seem to be a way that didn't have any direct link to anything overtly religious. I remember the training analysts who were presiding over these seminar sessions at one point pointed at me and said, "Catholic, aren't you?" and it was just very jarring. But it's like, all right, what were the tells!? It's almost like that experience of that game you play where you put a card on your forehead and you ask questions, you have to guess what it is. I mean, feeling like that, like it's on my forehead and they can see it. I can't see it. I'm not sure how they're figuring it out and reading it.

HM: This is what Lacan means when he says desire is always the desire of the Other.

AJ: Yes. Lacan came to psychoanalysis, too, out of a heavily French Catholic background. He, of course, from an early age onward, was left to the tender mercies of the Jesuits for his education. Likewise, when he was a teenager, [he] decided he didn't believe in it. Nonetheless, it was very clear that there was a lifelong influence of the sort of Catholic cultural milieu that he was raised in that he learned to channel in certain ways. For instance, his brother ended up being a Benedictine monk, or Lacan's symptomatic things, like his taste for Yves Saint Laurent dress shirts with clerical-style collars. There's all of this, so Lacan had his own way of playing with his lingering Catholic symptoms.

One thing about the notion that God is unconscious, [and] I think I take this from Lacan to also be a warning applicable to Marxism, is that even when you think you're dealing with what appears to be secular, be on your guard, because there is this weird way in which there can be this kind of secret theology that's underpinning what you're dealing with. Reading Marx with this kind of Lacanian hindsight, you see Marx himself indicate as much.

The best example is perhaps the single most famous part of *Capital: Volume One*, the subsection of the first chapter entitled "The Fetishism of the Commodity and Its Secret" (Marx, 1867). As people like Étienne Balibar and Žižek have pointed out, when you look at the first paragraph of that famous stretch on commodity fetishism, what Marx indicates is that it's not that people wander around in their daily lives, beguiled by these fantasies about supernatural entities and events. They have this whole mysticism or supernaturalism that they have to be disabused of. You use critique to make the scales fall from their eyes so they can see everything as the nitty-gritty, nonmystified worldly reality that it is. What Marx suggests in the opening paragraph of the section on commodity fetishism, in *Capital:*

Volume One, that's the inverse. If, for instance, I'm at the grocery store, and I'm just trying to choose which cans of soup I'm going to put in my cart, I think that, "Oh, this is a very banal, ordinary, this-worldly, unremarkable, straightforward, dull experience." But Marx proposes that, no, it's . . . in our daily behavior, and the apparently secular sphere of the marketplace, [that] we implicitly subscribe, or our actions testify to, a not fully avowed or even a totally unconscious belief in some very strange things. As Marx (1887) described, theological niceties and metaphysical subtleties.

In a way, the first step of ideology critique here is convincing us that we're not the hardnosed realistic pragmatists we take ourselves to be; rather, we subscribe to this unconscious theology of the market that is as strange and otherworldly as anything we've come up with at the level of theology, religion, and metaphysics. For me, in applying this to Marxism, to cut a long story short, is that today we tend to be religious where we believe ourselves to be secular and to be secular where we believe ourselves to be religious. With fundamentalisms, and the resurgence of things like evangelical Christianity in this country or certain fundamentalisms elsewhere, I think much of that is actually relating to religion, already as someone like Feuerbach, and I think before him Hegel, indicated, which is that our god or gods, and the whole framework of religion, is really just a kind of reflection of these worldly concerns. As Feuerbach (1841) put it, anthropology is the secret of theology.

What we're really concerned with, and I think it's very clear in things like evangelical Christianity, is all about markers of this worldly cultural identity. I mean, in their churches it's no accident that the American flag is put side by side with the cross. This is really about secular identity politics. Yet, that's supposedly where we're religious. You could call it a profanation of religion. It is turning religion into the vehicle of secular cultural struggles or identity politics. Even if you are an atheist, in capitalism you're forced to participate in an economic system. As Marx already discerned, in things like his treatment of commodity fetishism, you have to have a very strange set of beliefs, and a kind of metaphysical theological framework, that you're not necessarily aware of subscribing to but that structures how you relate as a supposedly rational agent, calculating your transactions in the economic sphere. The idea that we subscribe to this hidden theology or metaphysics at the level of the economy is where we're religious where we think we're secular. So, to me, that's the strangeness of our circumstances.

HM: I know you've written about it, and I hope you keep writing about this, because I think it is so important.

AJ: Well, I wish I had the expertise, frankly, in religion. I have to draw on what knowledge I do have, but coming back to the inherent inter-disciplinarity of all of this, it's overwhelming. It sometimes feels almost paralyzing because I feel like I really would need to spend time reading literature on contemporary religious phenomena as well as the history of religion, even more Marxist economic litera-ture, and so on.

My hope is that there are people with those bodies of expertise who can run with some of this, too, and do interesting work. Again, the only way I can do it is trying to think in terms of . . . just as Marx talks about the socialization of production in general, the production of knowledge, likewise, has become so socialized that I can throw my two cents in and hope that it proves resonant and useful to others who can likewise contribute.

HM: When you were talking, I was also thinking of the term described to me earlier from your more recent writing, the return of the repressed sometimes is the most effective repression.

AJ: Yes, yes, yes. I was interested in using it because a lot of readers of Marx, of course, when they talk about commodity fetishism, obvi-ously they gravitate towards the section in *Volume One* on "The Fetishism of the Commodity and Its Secret" (1867). But what some-times is neglected is that, for Marx, he argues that we don't get capi-talist commodity fetishism in the most fully realized form until we have the development of the way in which interest and money capi-tal functions under capitalism that you don't have until you arrive at volume 3 of *Capital*.

What I found when I was looking at volumes 2 (Marx, 1885/1992) and 3 (1894) of *Capital*, specifically at the discussions of fetishism in volume 3, where we have its supposed apotheosis in the guise of what Marx called "interest-bearing capital" under capitalism, there are ways in which the very notion of fetishism in Marx gets fur-ther refined. It offers points of contact for psychoanalysis and espe-cially how psychoanalysis thinks about the manner in which defense mechanisms operate so as to keep things unconscious or nullify them from having any effect if they become conscious. It struck me that there was a lot that could be done with Marx's own further refinement of the notion of fetishism à la volume 3 of *Capital*, which thus far it seems hardly any psychoanalytic work has focused on. . . . Lacan himself, periodically in the seminars starting in the 1950s, looks at the cross-resonance between Marx's account of commodity fetishism and Freud's notion of fetishism. But I don't think Lacan had read volume 3 of *Capital*, and he certainly doesn't draw on it, even if he had. There's a lot that you can do in terms of this interfacing that requires looking at those subsequent volumes of *Capital* after volume 1 to really pull [it] off.

HM: I'm thinking of Freud and *Civilization and Its Discontents* (1930) here.

AJ: That's right. But drive, too, it was especially present in certain stretches of the *Grundrisse* (Marx, 1939) . . . the manner in which he talks about it. Freud even uses the German *Trieb*, and what's amazing is you find an incredible amount of unexpected anticipation of more ingredients of psychoanalytic drive theory already in Marx. If you go back, and you really check the German, too, I mean, it's quite striking. There's this amazing kind of prescience in Marx's work. In terms of talking about drive, in terms of talking about defense mechanisms and so forth, you can find an enormous amount in the *Grundrisse* and the volumes of *Capital*. And my work is about highlighting that prescience.

References

American Psychiatric Association. (2013). *Diagnostic and statistical manual of mental disorders* (5th ed.). Author.
Deleuze, G., & Guattari, G. (1972). *Anti-Oedipus*. Penguin Classics.
Feuerbach. (1841). *The essence of Christianity*. Published by C. Blanchard of New York.
Foucault, M. (1966). *Les mots et les choses: Une archéologie des sciences humaines* [*The order of things: An archeology of the human sciences*]. Gallimard.
Freud, S. (1915). Instincts and their vicissitudes. In J. Strachey (Ed.), *The standard edition of the complete psychological works of Sigmund Freud* (Vol. 7, pp. 109–140). Hogarth Press.
Freud, S. (1930). *Das Unbehagen in der Kultur* [*Civilization and its discontents*]. Internationaler Psychoanalytischer.

Freud, S. (1989). The future of an illusion. W. W. Norton. (Original work published 1927)

Hegel, G. W. F. (1977). *Phenomenology of spirit* (A. V. Miller, Trans.). Oxford University Press. (Original work published 1807)

Johnston, A. (2005). *Time driven: Metapsychology and the splitting of the drive – Studies in phenomenology and existential philosophy.* Northwestern University Press.

Johnston, A. (2014). *Adventures in transcendental materialism: Dialogues with contemporary thinkers.* Edinburgh University Press.

Johnston, A. (2017a). From closed need to infinite greed: Marx's drive theory. *Continental Thought & Theory, 1*(4), 270–346.

Johnston, A. (2017b). *Irrepressible truth: On Lacan's 'The Freudian Thing.'* Palgrave Macmillan.

Kant, I. (1996). *Critique of pure reason* (W. Pluhar, Trans.). Hackett Publishing. (Original work published 1781)

Lacan, J. (1956). The Freudian thing. *Évolution Psychiatrique, 21*(1), 225–252.

Lacan, J. (1966). *Écrits.* Éditions du Seuil.

Lacan, J. (1977). *The seminar of Jacques Lacan, Book XI: The four fundamental concepts of psychoanalysis* (J.-A. Miller, Ed., A Sheridan, Trans.). W. W. Norton. (Original work published 1964)

Marx, K. (1867). The fetishism of the commodity and its secret. *Capital: Volume One.* Progress Publishers.

Marx, K. (1887). *Capital: A critique of political economy: Volume I.* Progress Publishers.

Marx, K. (1894). *Capital: A critique of political economy: Volume III.* International Publishers.

Marx, K. (1939). *Grundrisse der Kritik der politischen Ökonomie.* Rohentwurf.

Marx, K. (1992). *Capital: A critique of political economy: Volume II* (D. Fernbach, Trans.). Penguin. (Original work published 1885)

Žižek, S. (2007). *The indivisible remainder: On Schelling and related matters – Radical thinkers.* Verso.

Žižek, S. (2008). *For they know not what they do: Enjoyment as a political factor – Radical thinkers.* Verso.

Žižek, S. (2009). *Sublime object of ideology – Essential Žižek.* Verso.

6

On Destructiveness

A Conversation with Sue Grand

Interviewed by Jill Salberg
Sue Grand and Jill Salberg

Jill Salberg (JS): Sue Grand has been thinking about, working with patients, and writing in the area of personal, collective, and cultural trauma for nearly four decades. She engages with politics, history, literature, ethics, trauma theory, and psychoanalysis. Throughout all of this clinical and academic work, Sue pursues her mission: the healing of our wounded selves and our wounded world. In particular, Sue has focused on personal and collective re-enactments of violence and on the meanings and functions of those re-enactments. These enactments occur in people on the level of the body in terms of physical ailments and pain as well as in the emotional and psychic registration of hurt and anguish. As an expert in trauma, she has a gentle, down-to-earth approach with her patients and in her written work which reduces shame, heals self-esteem, and repairs relationship trouble. Sue encourages her patients to listen to their own story and to tell their own story. Sue believes in the healing qualities of compassion and attachment. She facilitates self-love and the capacity to empathize with the Other.
Sue's writings, which are drawn from her years of clinical work and teaching, reveal her willingness to push herself and the field of psychoanalysis to rethink how we understand and react to violence. In her first book, *The Reproduction of Evil* (2002), she worked to unpack why it is that victims of abuse so

DOI: 10.4324/9781003280033-7

often become perpetrators, and she queried what psychoanalysis can offer to these survivors-perpetrators, whose criminal conduct seems to transcend the possibilities of empathic psychoanalytic inquiry. Her goal was to elucidate the link between traumatic memory and the perpetration of evil. To this end, she presented an interdisciplinary analysis, scholarly and passionate, of the ways in which families and cultures transform victims of malignant trauma into perpetrators of these very traumas on others. Through intensive case studies, Sue drew us into the world of the survivors-perpetrators who committed acts of child abuse, of incest, of racial persecution, even of homicide and genocide. By infusing psychoanalytic inquiry with cultural analysis and by supplementing clinical vignettes with well-chosen literary illustrations, such as Frederik Douglass's *Narrative of the Life of Frederick Douglass, An American Slave* (1849) or Mary Shelley's *Frankenstein* (1818). Sue was able to convey the survivor-perpetrator's immediacy of experience in a manner that readers may find unsettling, even uncanny. It is her ability to empathically enter the mind and world of the Other that makes her work feel so immediate and important.

By interweaving psychoanalytic, sociohistorical, and literary perspectives, Sue fills a critical lacuna in the literature about trauma and its intergenerational transmission. Her analysis of the psychodynamic processes and cultural tensions that bind perpetrators, victims, and bystanders provides trenchant insights into the violence and fragmentation that beset our society. This work led Sue, in her book, *The Hero in the Mirror* (2009), to deconstruct the myth of the hero and argue for the "ordinary hero," a more realistic figure with the same limitations, concerns, and fears as the rest of us but one who nonetheless stands up for the greater good in the face of danger, despair, and villainy. From the foundation of relational psychoanalysis, Grand incorporated cultural and ethical considerations in her examination of what this ordinary hero might look like. In times of stress, trauma, and crisis – whether on a personal or global scale – it can be all too easy for us to externalize a larger-than-life figure who can assuage our suffering, a hero who comes to the fore even as we recede into the background. Sue demonstrated that the best place to ultimately find the ordinary hero is within each other; the hero is us.

Although Sue and I had met during psychoanalytic training at New York University's (NYU) Postdoctoral Program in Psychotherapy and Psychoanalysis, it wasn't till over a decade ago that we added to our friendship a collegial work relationship. She contributed a chapter for my book on *Good Enough Endings* (2010), and over lunch in 2011 she wanted to ponder with me why understanding the transgenerational antecedents to traumatic and painful experiences would matter. That discussion led us to co-chair a conference sponsored by NYU's Postdoctoral Program in March 2013 titled The Wounds of History: Repair and Resilience in the Trans-Generational Transmission of Trauma. This well attended and highly valued conference became the basis for our two 2018 Gradiva Award-winning edited books: *The Wounds of History: Repair and Resilience in the Trans-Generational Transmission of Trauma* (2017) and *Trans-Generational Trauma and the Other: Dialogues across History and Difference* (2017).

Sue, given your body of work, how has psychoanalysis responded, particularly to your talking about evil, something that is traditionally a concept of theology, of religion? It's not one that usually gets any traction in psychoanalysis.

Sue Grand (SG): Well, I just want to say, times have changed, and I think it's because of what's going on in the world. There were never any books on evil at a psychoanalytic conference. I went to the book display at the Psychology and the Other Conference in 2019 and saw about ten of them, which is unfortunate because it's a testament to the fact that we are in such a chaotic and destructive time.

I want to speak to why I needed to use the term "evil." I also want to address the controversy that emerged about that language when my first book was published. Evil had always been a presence in my own transgenerational legacy. My father was an American Jewish soldier during World War II, and he was stationed at the Dachau concentration camp right after its liberation. I grew up during the civil rights movement, in the shadow of my father's memories, always cognizant of the parallels between Nazism, Jim Crow, and African American slavery. I began my work as a young clinician with patients who had suffered child rape and severe physical abuse. These contexts are interwoven for me, and in thinking about culture and psyche I felt it was important to mark certain *acts, such as torture and genocide*, as *beyond* our ordinary human "badness."

Certainly, we are all capable of ordinary human transgressions – the exploitative use of another, the collapse of care for the Other, an inability to recognize their wounds or their humanity. In times of anxiety, insecurity, deprivation, rage, greed, or competition, we can trespass on each other. We should all be aware of these capacities within ourselves. But to me, there are acts (and people) whose insensate cruelties are beyond our ordinary human badness. I wanted language for it, and I wanted to mark it, and I wanted to really take a look at it.

When I published my book, there were ripples of criticism and discomfort because I chose this language. At NYU Postdoc, where I have had the gift of training, thinking, and teaching, there was burgeoning work on social and cultural critique. In an effort to examine, and dismantle, these problematic structures, myself and my colleagues were trying to *own* our place in these structures. In particular, we were trying to understand how oppressive cultural assumptions were recycled in psychoanalytic theory and practice. From the perspective of a social justice psychoanalysis, we were increasingly concerned with the problem of splitting, projecting, and Othering. In examining violence, for example, there was an important turn towards *owning* the human affects and self-states that inspire aggression. Instead of claiming our "innocence" and projecting *our* "badness" onto others who were *enacting* these self-states, there was an effort to recognize the shared human condition that led to these enactments. From this perspective, describing some people (or their actions) as *evil* put this entire project (*The Reproduction of Evil*) at risk. The denotation as evil could recycle the very splitting and projection that social justice analysts were trying to deconstruct. It might allow us to claim "our" purity and innocence.

I was always in some agreement with this perspective; if we psychoanalysts don't recognize these affects and urges within ourselves, we cannot stop contributing to the conditions which evoke, and permit, this violence in others. We will keep finding a category of "them" to carry our darkest urges. It is certainly true that we can never know what we, ourselves, would do in extremis. In genocidal conditions, we all like to imagine ourselves as resistors, as rescuers. Unfortunately, history demonstrates that most of us would become passive bystanders, collaborators, or worse. So, here was an important turn in psychoanalysis; we were trying to own that and not split it off into the Other and extrude them as nonhuman. I'm coming along and saying, no, there really are things that surpass the human order. It doesn't mean that people who commit these acts can never be recognized as human or embraced back into a human community. But there are acts that require a more distinct ethical marker that marks something beyond ordinary human badness.

I personally feel those acts and/or people who are beyond conversation need to be contained, not dialogued with. I think we've got one in the White House. I don't think dialogue is where it's at. I think that containment is where it's at and that you have to work the system around certain people. I think there are people who were neo-Nazis for all kinds of reasons who could change – there are programs and dialogues in which there is real transformation and awakening. Then there are people who just want to kill you; they're not going to ever want anything else. If those apparently unreachable people do get to the point where they have remorse or concern or they've made a shift and they want to work their way back into dialogue, I'm all for it. It's not all about dialogue. It's also about mobilizing around people and creating firm structures of containment so that they can't be so destructive. Sometimes this containment involves a communal recognition of this "evil," a wholesale refusal to collude or enable this destructiveness. Perhaps we can also think of containment as humane forms of incarceration, operating according to reparative justice, sequestering this destructiveness while creating conditions that can evoke reparative guilt in those who have been remorseless. There was another reason I embraced the ethical marker "evil." In maelstroms of violence, there are always some people who *refuse that violence*. They are rescuers, resistors, at great risk to themselves. In the midst of hell, they *don't engage in violence nor do they enable it*. If we are too busy claiming that we all have the same basic interior as the *genocidaire*, how do we honor and recognize those who *do not?* I felt we needed an ethical register for those heroes and for the torturers.

JS: A moral judgment.

SG: A moral judgment, right. So, that was another problematic element. I was injecting language that irreligious psychoanalysis splits off into theology and religion. How could we embrace a category of "evil?" This resistance created a problematic reception. Now we have a whole issue of *Contemporary Psychoanalysis* that's devoted to evil.

JS: It's funny because I always thought there were two things that were controversial in the title of that book and I love the book. One was the use of evil, which you've just been talking about. The other was the word "reproduction." Up until that point, the only title in psychoanalysis that I knew of that had used that word was Nancy Chodorow's 1978 *The Reproduction of Mothering*, which was a feminist statement, but it's a sort of benign-sounding thing. However, *The Reproduction of Evil* suggests that we're all stained in a certain way and we're all culpable. Yet, it seemed important for you that that was out there in the title. So, maybe you can speak to that, too.

SG: First of all, I have to thank Nancy Chodorow because she did inspire me, and I always felt like I really should write to her and tell her that I felt a little bit like I stole part of her concept. But if I ever see her, I'll thank her.

But the reason why that spoke to me, actually, was precisely because when I was first treating severe childhood trauma – and that was in the days when there was no literature on trauma – people thought incest occurred once in a million, and so if you had a patient reveal this to you, there was nowhere to go to read anything, to get supervision. If it was accepted as true (a big if), it was considered extremely rare. Now we know that this isn't true. Incest and childhood sexual abuse are all too common. The other thing that inspired this perspective was that some of my early patients revealed undetected murders to me. I was in graduate school and doing therapy with adults who had been victimized as children. I began to think about the transformation from victim to perpetrator. No one was talking about this at all. Later, when we began to really understand the prevalence of childhood trauma, we naturally focused on caring for those who had been victimized. Were there no perpetrators among them? After my own early clinical experiences, this seemed highly improbable.

When I first started working in the trauma field, of course, that was when the research was happening to show that neuroplasticity means that therapeutic intervention actually resets the neurochemistry of someone who's been traumatized, which gives me great comfort. When I consider what may happen in the future with trauma research especially with neuropsychology, I can only hope that it doesn't feed into a more and more mechanistic kind of intervention that just involves more pills or more behavioral evidence based brief treatments. I'm not against them. People need to live their lives and feel better. So, I'm not against any of these things. But I worry that psychotherapy will become more mechanistic and omit the deep relational interactions, which are the most healing. On the other hand, I think that there's more awareness that people actually need to talk to a human being to be well.

JS: Why do you think things have changed in terms of our conceptualizations of evil being more acceptable? Ten books on evil. Is it only the social context? Is there a political dimension to this now?

SG: Well, I was thinking of that when I went into the book exhibit. So, what's changed? Remember that insular, sheltered, purely psychic universe that we were supposed to be treating in the analytic hour? That enclosure was always imaginary; in recent years it seems more and more penetrated by the world. And clinicians are thinking more about the effects of politics and culture on people's psychic wounds. So, the sacred shelter and insularity of the analytic process has become both more porous, open, *and* more broken into.

The result, which I think is wonderful, is this kind of conference (i.e., Psychology and the Other). The magnitude of human suffering is calling us to abandon our own limited silos of thought. All of us in our individual disciplines have to have interdisciplinary discussion for the kinds of questions that we're asking in regards to trauma, social justice and healing. Even with integrative conversation, the human condition perpetually exceeds what we can even think together. Certainly, our interdisciplinary focus has permitted ethical philosophy to enter psychoanalysis. At the same time, we are refining our critique of moral bias in psychoanalysis. We are better at acknowledging our moral biases and how they have defined "pathology." We have a better understanding of how normative cultural assumptions have imposed on, and damaged, our patients. We have a better capacity to query our implicit image of the good and the good life. For example, we no longer think of the "good life" as requiring a heterosexual marriage. Just in the domain of gender and sexuality alone, we have radically re-written what a "good life" is.

Along with recognizing the imposition of moralisms, we also have been reclaiming what David M. Goodman (2016) and Lynne Layton (2020) talk about as the social-ethical turn. There has always been an ethic in psychoanalysis: "to love and to work." Well, what does "to love" mean? To love, for Freud, was a "genital" achievement, an exit from insular narcissism, an ability to love and desire an imperfect Other while having your own imperfect self. To me, there is an I/thou ethic in psychoanalysis from its inception. Recent discussions of Buber and Levinas (Goodman, 2012; Orange, 2010) have been more explicitly engaged with ethical philosophy and theology in the realms of social justice and psychoanalysis. All of these shifts seem to have changed our attitude towards speaking of evil.

JS: You're reminding me that in the era when we were both trained as psychologists in the 70s – in New York, I was at NYU, you were at the New School – at NYU there was a PhD program called Community Psychology. I took some classes in that. I always thought community psychologists were my, to use your word, heroes because they were on the political forefront. The community psychologists and social workers were activists. They were going into communities, and that was where they saw the traction. The focus was not having somebody come into a private office, or even dutiful work in the clinic, but in the collective.

SG: Out in the streets, as it were.

JS: Right, right. And so, that got lost. That program eventually closed. It got lost to psychology and psychoanalysis, and it feels to me like it's slowly reemerging in some transformed way. Do you have some thoughts about why it got lost? It was a program that certainly came out of Fromm's (1941, 1980, 1997) work and a lot of other people's work that also fell out of favor. So, thoughts about why that was and what the reemergence might be about.

SG: I'm glad you mentioned the context. Sometimes, life is fate. I went to the New School, and the New School was founded by refugees from Nazi Germany. So, gee, how did I wind up there? I guess the unconscious really *is* unconscious. Anyway, for me at the time, social activism permeated New York. It was the women's movement, it was the civil rights movement, it was the Vietnam war, it was everything.

Judith Herman (1992), when she wrote her wonderful, masterful text on trauma, stated that the history of studying trauma in psychology is one of "episodic amnesia," where it comes into the foreground and then is foreclosed. I'm just wondering if there's some kind of parallel that in the 70s our social milieu would link to the work of Fromm.

JS: And the countercultural movement.

SG: Yes, the countercultural movement, which echoed with the edict to question authority. After the Nazis, with Jim Crow and White supremacy and President Johnson lying about the war in Vietnam, we were passionate about questioning authority. So, I think that there was a milieu at that time. The Vietnam War ended; some civil rights legislation passed; and at the same time, our social justice heroes were murdered. I think too many White people got oblivious and complacent. And, I don't know, analysts got rich. It may be hard to recall but at the time this was a very elite, rich profession.

JS: It's interesting you're saying that because the analysts who got rich were the MDs.

SG: Right, that's true. White male psychiatrists.

JS: As well as PhDs, and we were amongst them. A lot of our training and work were in local clinics. During my internship experience at a hospital in Brooklyn, I brought families in as part of the treatment model. I needed to be part of and reach out to whoever I could in the community. That was the only way you understood making a difference because you could see that the economics, the community, there were so many factors that affected the person in your office.

SG: Right. My first work was in a clinic for about seven years, which is where I encountered some of the most painful cases that I wrote about in my first book, *The Reproduction of Evil: A Clinical and Cultural Perspective* (Grand, 2000). The impact of class was very clear. So, why mass social activism faded, I'm not sure. But the thread of social justice and social critique has always been there in psychoanalysis. It was there in Freud (see Danto, 2005). It was there in Fromm.

There's a wonderful new edited collection on community psychoanalysis that just came out six months ago, edited by Alpert and Goren (2017). There are community psychoanalytic projects. They're not nonexistent. There are clinics and programs that are purposely trying to use psychoanalytic premises and kind of thinking in community settings.

JS: And there is activist stuff, like the Theatre of the Oppressed or group work aimed at teaching people how to advocate for themselves. Now the splits are even bigger between the haves and the have-nots and the political arena is so bifurcated. How do you imagine psychoanalysis is now taking this up, the diseases, for lack of a better word, the sufferings and problems of society, political life, cultural life? And, what role could we have?

SG: Well, there's a big question. Even today, generally speaking with regard to psychotherapeutic intervention, particularly with the insurance predicament, the only people who are going to have psychoanalysis are people with lots of disposable income. The culture is generally moving towards these much more mechanistic ways of treating mental health problems, but it's not entirely outside the reach of people of different classes and cultures.

The other thing is that there are many other transformative healing practices in different cultures that we could learn something from and integrate with, and lots of cultures in which going into psychotherapy is not the way to go.

JS: I just want to say as an aside. I know Sue thinks about this a lot because we'll plan to get together and the next thing I know, she'll

say, "We're going to a protest." Or she'll say, "We're not going to do
any more work on our books, we're going to go to the movies." And
we end up seeing *Twelve Years a Slave*.

SG: Everybody teases me. My time off is seeing a light genocide film.
Or reading a "light" war novel. One of the things that – it's not quite
an answer because I don't really have an answer, but one of the
things that I struggle with, that I think a lot of people struggle with,
is that the problems that we're having are so vast, especially with
this administration (i.e., Trump's Presidency), everything is being
destroyed. Too many of us feel hopeless and impotent.

Perhaps part of psychoanalysis' role within the political and cultural arena is to offer empathy across difference to try to engage
with those we see as enemies. People have struggles, and when-
ever there's a lock in a personal conversation, in a therapeutic
situation, where there's a lock of hostility and misunderstanding,
offering empathy – accurate empathy, not false empathy, but real,
genuine empathy – I find goes a long way. Appreciating the person
we are communicating with is also very important. Where are their
strengths? Where have they shown resiliency? We need to see and
affirm that in order for them to feel recognized as an equal human
being, whom we are genuinely interested in knowing. In that sense,
I think there's a very legitimate critique of liberals – our tendency to
shame, degrade, and disdain less educated people in the US – this is
a big problem that evokes hostility. Psychoanalysts should be able to
conceptualize this problem and open it up.

So, I think that that's something to offer politicians and to help politicians. It's like Jessica Benjamin's (2004) moral third – how do you
keep hold of your own position about certain fundamental concerns
and still empathize across so much hostility and difference? I think
that it's really essential to help politicians do that. Without betraying
their important positions.

I think another thing, which is one of my pet peeves – pardon me – is
that I don't like to make an assumption in a group that we're all on
the same political page. But the Republicans are brilliant at the language that they use for the narratives – for example, pro-life or tax
reform. No matter what progressive media you watch, we use their
language – tax reform. Well, tax reform could mean anything. It
could mean a redistribution of wealth. But we know what it means,

right? Still we become captive to their language. This is brilliant, and it's been a huge problem for us in the opposition.

This is related thing that psychoanalysis has to help people do. I think Drew Westen's (2007) research is brilliant in this way. He really looks at how many people would agree with a particular position if it was framed differently. The percentage of, say, Republicans who will agree with a Democratic position if the language is reframed, it's not like a minor difference, it's a huge difference. Why do we get locked in like that?

JS: We have to change the conversation in our country and maybe the larger world to change that to a new understanding, which is, if you lose, I lose and we can only get better if we all get better. Some may get better sooner and with more, but that doesn't matter. What matters is the ethic of concern and connection, that our lives are actually connected. Part of the way of the super-wealthy getting wealthy while others get poor is that they have an impoverished life, too. They may have a lot of money, but something's wrong internally. We have to change the whole conception.

SG: It's been hard to convince people that climate change is going to affect them, too, because they think they're in their remote private bunker. But there's another thing about this, which is that many activist efforts evoke shame instead of guilt. Shame, of course, can mobilize compliance with recycling, for example. But reparative guilt is a more powerful, more sustained form of motivation. We need to make a study of how we shift political discourse from shaming towards the evocation of reparative guilt. Healthy guilt allows us to feel concern; it's not the neurotic, paralytic, self-referential looping guilt where we just endlessly beat ourselves up.

The other thing – I'm going to say something radical, but why not? What would it be like, instead of just – which I do all the time – vilifying these infinitely wealthy people who, for example, only want to put more money back in their pocket and are willing to starve 3.5 million people in Puerto Rico – what if we started to think about their psychic interior? What is going on inside of these billionaires that makes it impossible for them to share some of their money? Is there a way to get at what this anxiety really is? What is this greed, after all? What is going on in there? What can psychoanalysts offer about what's going on that might allow us to start using different language, addressing this differently? Talk about human-izing the Other, right? If you've got billions of dollars and it's never enough, and you want your taxes and your estate tax lifted because you don't have enough money . . . that really suggests some deep fear of deprivation and annihilation. Your children can't possibly spend it before they die and neither can you. Meanwhile you are starving the 3.5 million homeless people in Puerto Rico – excuse my French – what the hell is that? What is going on in that?

A huge problem for me personally is the vast sense of what is being destroyed. I feel helpless, overwhelmed, small, and paralyzed. And I do a lot of thinking about my position within this context.

JS: I think your theories about the small hero are relevant here. Maybe you can pick that up.

SG: So, I try to keep reminding myself that I could be a small – very small – hero. In one of my books, which is *The Hero in the Mirror* (Grand, 2010), I discuss the many subtle ways that we resist and sur-vive destructiveness. In some ways, this was inspired by my studies of African American slavery. Here is a group that has been relent-lessly enslaved, persecuted, incarcerated, tortured, killed, raped, and they are not committing mass genocide when they are freed. Instead, freed slaves are pursuing education, land, paid work, stable commu-nity, family bonds. In the short years of Reconstruction, people who were forbidden to read become lawyers, doctors, judges, teachers, politicians. There are obviously many determinants for this absence of mass violence upon liberation. This dignity, bravery, resource-fulness: it built in hundreds of years of small heroes caring for one another, finding modes of resistance. So I think we need to ask: What can we learn about this? Because one of the reasons I wrote the sec-ond book is that evil, call it what you will, violence, the dark side, is very intriguing to psychoanalysts. But really, the more you look at extreme conditions, the more we need to flip our inquiry over. Instead of trying to understand contagions of violence, perhaps we need to study those that maintain their ethical core, their capacity to love, their compassion. What can these "small heroes" teach us? Is there something that we can enhance about that? That seems like a really good role for psychoanalysis. Because that's really the miracle, right? I think that is something to be very curious about. Where did that come from? How do we learn from that to end cycles of violence?

Of course there is also another look at this lack of retaliation – that the master had sufficiently terrorized the slave, breaking his/her will, that the liberated lacked that violent agency.

JS: Actually, I thought it was more complicated. At least, it struck me in another way. I talked about the power of hope, the hope for kindness in that the master who broke the slave also broke him with kindness and care – he took him into his bed, he took him into his house, he fed him, took care of him. And so, it's a perversion to break with love and kindness. Yet, it spoke to the human need for hope – hope that there's somebody to trust, that there's some place that might be safe. And that's both perverse and wonderful simultaneously.

SG: One of the things that I think about is that I really believe very deeply, and I think I always have, that to achieve mental health one has to achieve a capacity for kindness. To me, kindness is the most important human attribute that there is. There are a lot of other ones that I like and cherish, but that is my top priority. I don't think there has been a "successful treatment" unless I help my patients develop human kindness – towards themselves and towards others. I'm not a Pollyanna! They can hate people and want to kill them; they can want to do all kinds of things; they will still hurt others. But I would hope that they are basically situated in that capacity for concern.

I feel, whether we talk about political and cultural issues explicitly or not in their treatment, that every time I help another human being to go out in the world with the capacity for concern, and I know that they're going to touch all the people in their lives, that I feel that I have made a daily contribution to moving this vast system in the right direction. That holds me together because what's going on in the world enters my body, and it's making me sick. My reflux is horrible; I mean, it's just awful.

How do we sustain our own reverence for the earth, our commitment to redressing poverty, racism, classism . . . while speaking respectfully with someone who likes Trump? It's easy to do what we are doing right now – speak to the "converted." How do we actually converse across difference? Can we hope to effect change without that conversation? How do we recalibrate our approach and our attitude so that this is possible? Psychoanalysis holds some promise here – when you want to hate and just completely disqualify and attack whoever you feel is tearing your world down, there is inner work that can allow us to try again.

JS: In a way, it feels to me that you're saying that psychoanalysis should have – should is a funny word – but needs to have and needs to constantly have it more elaborated, a scaffolding of ethics.

SG: Yes – but in particular we need to embrace our I-thou ethic (Buber, 1970).

JS: Without that as the framework that we build upon, we're in a misguided, misaligned place.

SG: I think, first of all, that the ethics have always been there in psychoanalysis. But because Freud did help us liberate ourselves from some oppressive moralisms (while recycling others), we tended to conflate ethical conversation with those moralisms. Then, we threw ethics out with the bathwater. So, we've been retrieving that. I think it's very important that we explicitly retrieve *both* our social justice origins *and* that I-thou ethic.

JS: Or maybe rebuild it again.

SG: And rebuild it. Not to be ashamed of it or in denial about it.

JS: But the other thing that's interesting is when you talked about kindness, I thought how much you've absorbed Jewish values, the Jewish value of *chesed*, loving-kindness, and acts of loving-kindness. This idea that we are commanded to perform this, that this is our mandate as humans.

SG: It is certainly true that many of my passions are from my socialist Jewish ancestors. I am very wary of claiming these ethics as uniquely Jewish, which can imply that non-Jews don't have the same access. That's very problematic. If all peoples actually lived by their highest, most ethical religious precepts, we would have a very compassionate world. But it's certainly in my bones, yes.

JS: What do you feel the role of mentors has been in your life?

SG: That's a really interesting question. Well, I had none until very, very late. And I think I wasn't even aware that there were mentors available. We all go to school, and sometimes there's a professor or teacher that we resonate with. Or not. It's a funny thing because I used to be even more introverted and quiet and interior. So, the idea that I would have a mentor was not a concept. I went through all of college and half of graduate school not speaking in class. The idea that you would go and talk with a professor after class or form a mentoring bond – it was just not a concept. So, I came to this very late. What was a real gift to me were people who offered to mentor me when I didn't know that could exist. So, Judy Alpert has been an incredible mentor to me and to generations of people from NYU. She just has an extraordinary generosity in facilitating people's own nascent gifts. She encouraged me to write my very first piece for an edited book. So, that was lovely. Then Marylou Lionells from the William Alanson White Institute was a supervisor who became more of a terrific mentor.

I had to really have a big shift in my interior to even have a place for mentoring to enter my life.

JS: Were there theorists or people that you never got to know personally but their work was instructive? We can feel mentored in lots of ways.

SG: Well, yes. One of the things that first pulled me into awareness of the Other and ethics was reading literature. So, that's where I experienced my resonance all through my childhood and growing up. So, I loved Winnicott; everybody loves him, right? I loved Searles. I loved R. D. Laing. I loved Guntrip. I loved the first narratives that I read, like *I Never Promised You a Rose Garden* (Greenberg, 1964) – remember that one? The sense that there were certain psychoanalysts who really got it. Then I found Dori Laub, whose work spoke to everything my patients were trying to tell me. Basically, I was having a dialogue about all the issues that I care about, but I was having it in my head, with literature. When I began to realize that I was interested in psychology and starting to read psychology, what I hungered for were those writers who really spoke to human pain. I don't have much use for very abstract, theoretical acrobatics in writing. I get very frustrated. I need to be close in to what the human struggle is.

JS: Given that, is it ever a hope that your writing will be a kind of mentoring for other people? Or for the field? And how much do you feel that should be an ethic that we promote in psychoanalysis, to nurture and provide mentorship to people?

SG: I hadn't thought about it that way. It's an interesting question. Mostly, what inspires me to write is the pain that I'm absorbing, first from some of these trauma cases and these collective problems, so that I need a space where I can go inwards to process what I'm struggling with. I always start my writing from inside a particular person's story and how they've spoken to me and how I've struggled to discover something or learn something very new or different from being with them. The thinking that I do is always in response to that.

I'm always hoping that my work will find that place in somebody else that literature found within me. I hope that my work brings light or comfort or meaning to someone who is lost or suffering. When I'm supervising someone about treatment, and I want to help them to grow, the important ambience is curiosity. Instead of being reactive to their patients, or to someone who seems like our Other, the point is to have genuine curiosity. The tone follows from that. If you're really wanting to know how did you get to voting for Trump, etc., then tell me about that. Because you're curious. You could be curious about something that is so completely where you would never be. But you are inquiring from a position of basic respect. You have to really be open to dialogue in a genuine way, expecting to discover something you didn't know before, and then somebody will talk to you.

JS: And to feel like you're going to learn something.

JS: What might we in psychoanalysis be able to offer to social, cultural, political domains?

SG: One of the things that I think psychoanalysis has to offer profoundly, and we have been offering – I don't know whether anybody is receiving –

JS: Receiving the message?

SG: Yeah . . . it's the whole paranoid/schizoid understanding of annihilation anxiety, shame about dependency, the extrusion and assault on the dependency that we've evoked and deposited in the other person or group to put it outside of ourselves and then kill it and degrade it because of this shame and repudiation. The formulation around shame, the work around shame is so critical. The kinds of violence and retribution and vengeance that follow from people feeling humiliated – this is critical to understanding social systems and contexts. In the context of Gilligan's work, the way we arrange paranoid-schizoid systems so that there is always a transfer of shame from the dominant to the oppressed. I think we need to think about what I have called "creative shame" – which the dominant need to be willing to feel within themselves *without* transferring it to those we have oppressed. I think we need to wonder why we haven't created social systems that operate more around depressive guilt, the capacity for concern and remorse, and the need to make reparation. Instead, you see this continuous recycling of shame and attack.

When you study the history of this country, the book *White Trash* (Isenberg, 2016) was enormously helpful to me in understanding how we got where we are and why some White working class people are so much more willing to identify with a New York billionaire than with a Black president who actually, if given the opportunity, would support their economic interests so much better.

It gave me a lot more empathy for the centuries of dehumanization and shaming. We all know this, what was offered as a sop to this kind of White trash shame was, "Well, you're superior to Black people." So, the identification with the vastly wealthy White overlord, who's stealing your wallet, is much stronger than it ought to be in this country. I think those concepts are profound and profoundly helpful in understanding what's going on in our destructive world. Whether there is an opening for that and where that opening is with all this being constantly recycled, I don't know. I'm not feeling real optimistic – we are increasingly devolving into hostile opponents.

JS: It's frightening.

SG: Yeah, it's really terrible. Well, we've solved the world situation. We know all about good and evil, no problem.

JS: We've contained it.

SG: Well, that would be nice.

JS: Thank you.

SG: Thanks for having me.

References

Alpert, J., & Goren, E. R. (Eds.). (2017). *Psychoanalysis, trauma, and community: History and contemporary reappraisals*. Routledge Press.

Benjamin, J. (2004). Beyond doer and done to: An intersubjective view of thirdness. *Psychoanalytic Quarterly, 73*, 5–46.

Buber, M. (1970). *I and thou* (W. Kaufman, Trans). Scribner.

Chodorow, N. (1978). *The reproduction of mothering*. University of California Press.

Danto, E. A. (2005). *Freud's free clinics: Psychoanalysis and social justice, 1918–1938*. Columbia University Press.

Douglass, F., & Garrison, W. L. (1849). *Narrative of the life of Frederick Douglass, an American slave*. Anti-Slavery Office.

Fromm, E. (1941). *Escape from freedom*. Rinehart & Co.

Fromm, E. (1980). *Beyond the chains of illusion: My encounter with Marx and Freud.* Sphere Books.

Fromm, E. (1997). *On being human.* Continuum International.

Goodman, D. M. (2012). *The demanded self: Levinasian ethics and identity in psychology.* Duquesne University Press.

Goodman, D. M., & Severson, E. R. (2016). *The ethical turn: Otherness and subjectivity in contemporary psychoanalysis.* Routledge.

Grand, S. (2000). *The reproduction of evil: A clinical and cultural perspective.* Analytic Press.

Grand, S. (2002). *The reproduction of evil: A clinical and cultural perspective.* Routledge.

Grand, S. (2009). *The hero in the mirror: From fear to fortitude.* Routledge.

Grand, S. (2010). *The hero in the mirror: From fear to fortitude.* Routledge.

Grand, S., & Salberg, J. (2017). *Trans-generational trauma and the other: Dialogues across history and difference.* Routledge.

Greenberg, J. (1964). *I never promised you a rose garden: A novel.* Holt, Rinehart, and Winston.

Herman, J. (1992). *Trauma and recovery: The aftermath of violence – From domestic abuse to political terror.* Basic Books.

Isenberg, N. (2016). *White Trash: The 400 year untold history of class in America.* Viking Press.

Layton, L. (2020). *Toward a social psychoanalysis: Culture, character and normative unconscious processes* (M. Leavy-Sperounis, Ed.). Routledge.

Orange, D. M. (2010). *Thinking for clinicians: Philosophical resources for contemporary psychoanalysis and humanistic psychotherapies.* Routledge.

Salberg, J. (Ed.). (2010). *Good enough endings: Breaks, interruptions and terminations from contemporary relational perspectives.* Routledge.

Salberg, J., & Grand, S. (Eds.). (2017). *The wounds of history: Repair and resilience in the trans-generational transmission of trauma.* Routledge.

Shelley, M. (1818). *Frankenstein, or the modern Prometheus.* Lackington, Hughes, Harding, Mavor, and Jones.

Westen, D. (2007). *The political brain: The role of emotion in deciding the fate of the nation.* Public Affairs.

7

Taking Persons Seriously

A Conversation with Jack Martin

Interviewed by Jeff Sugarman
Jack Martin and Jeff Sugarman

Introduction

It is a privilege to have known Jack Martin for the past 30 years. He was my doctoral supervisor, after which we became close colleagues and good friends. Jack is undoubtedly among the most accomplished and respected scholars in theoretical and philosophical psychology today. He is widely recognized as an erudite, clear-minded, insightful, innovative, and prolific thinker. Recently retired, he continues to be highly productive and, at the time of this interview, is on the verge of completing two new book manuscripts.

Jack received his doctorate in educational and social psychology from the University of Alberta in 1973 at age 23 and accepted an academic appointment at Simon Fraser University in British Columbia in 1975. By the time the ink dries on most bachelor's degrees, Jack was already a professor. He moved to the University of Western Ontario in 1983 and remained there until 1991, when he returned to Simon Fraser, holding positions in the Faculty of Education and, subsequently, Department of Psychology until his retirement in 2018. In an academic career spanning more than 40 years, he has published over a dozen books and more than 200 chapters and articles comprising an impressive, important, and, in many cases, ground-breaking corpus of work brought to print by such prestigious publishers as Oxford University Press, Cambridge University Press, Teachers College Press, Columbia University Press, SUNY Press, Springer, Routledge, and Wiley. His articles have appeared in such notable journals as *American Psychologist*, *Review of General Psychology*, the *Journal of Theoretical and Philosophical Psychology*, *New Ideas in Psychology*, *Theory & Psychology*, *Philosophical Psychology*, *History of Psychology*, *Integrative Psychological and Behavioral Science*, *Journal of*

DOI: 10.4324/9781003280033-8

Humanistic Psychology, Journal for the Theory of Social Behavior, Journal of Mind and Behavior, Journal of Constructivist Psychology, Journal of Counseling Psychology, Journal of Consulting and Clinical Psychology, Educational Psychologist, Educational Researcher, and *Human Development*, to name but a few. The topics and issues to which Jack has applied his capacious and incisive intellect, meticulous approach to investigation, and skilled powers of expression are too numerous to mention. However, I want to sketch a few of the major programs of inquiry that have given shape to his scholarly journey in theoretical and philosophical psychology.

Over the course of a decade beginning in 1995, Jack initiated a program of work (in which I had the good fortune to be involved), the aim of which was to articulate the proper subject matter of psychology and its distinctive and irreducible features. The import of this project resides in the fact, that unless the features of human psychology can be shown to be ontologically exceptional (i.e., not fully reducible to material, organic, or sociocultural determinants), then psychology has no subject matter genuinely its own, which puts its status as a distinct discipline in question. At the center of the project is the thesis that the proper subject matter of psychology is persons, a thesis that Jack has defended vigorously and that has informed all his succeeding work. Elements of the thesis include an original argument (by elimination) for an irreducible, self-determining, psychologically capable human agency; a distinctive theory of emergence that accounts for the ontology of psychological phenomena; a socioculturally founded developmental theory; detailed conceptions of selfhood and identity; and a hermeneutically inspired and historically oriented epistemology based on the extensive critique of the "received view" of psychological science. This program of work generated three books (Martin & Sugarman, 1999; Martin et al., 2003, 2010) and a spate of chapters and articles.

In further pursuit of clarifying personhood and its development, Jack became immersed in the ideas of George Herbert Mead. Among the fruits of his study and extension of Mead's contributions were two innovations, one theoretical and the other methodological. The first, position exchange theory, comprehends the development of self-consciousness, self-understanding, and identity as issuing from the physical, relational, societal, and cultural positionings of individuals and their exchange of positions and perspectives within the contexts and conventions of social life (see Gillespie & Martin, 2014; Martin & Gillespie, 2013). The second, life positioning analysis, is an approach to the study of persons by tracing how and in what ways individuals have been positioned through their experiences with particular significant others and the consequences for the unfolding of their psychological lives and the persons they become (see Martin, 2013, 2015). Not only has Jack produced a series of papers elaborating on these innovations in developmental theorizing and psychobiography, but he also has provided a number of vivid case illustrations through life positioning analyses of famous athletes Jim Thorpe (Martin, 2013) and Steve Nash (Martin & Cox, 2016); noted Canadian author Mordecai Richler (Martin, 2015); Pulitzer-winning social theorist Ernest Becker (Martin, 2014); and psychologists B. F. Skinner (Martin, 2017), Carl Rogers (Martin, 2017), and Stanley Milgram (Martin, 2016).

Jack also turned his seasoned critical eye toward educational psychology. The result was several papers and a book, *The Education of Selves: How Psychology Transformed Students* (Martin & McLellan, 2013). Building on ideas explored in the papers, the book provides a trenchant analysis and critique of the contemporary ideal of the "enterprising, "expressive," and "entitled" student promoted by educational psychologists. In response to difficulties with this ideal, such as the individualism, psychologism, and rampant conceptual and definitional confusions that attend it, the book presents an alternative vision of the student as "communal agent" and the psychological theorizing required to support it.

Jack has been coeditor of four volumes that assemble and showcase the work of leading scholars in theoretical and philosophical psychology (Kirschner & Martin, 2010; Martin & Bickhard, 2013; Martin et al., 2015; Sugarman & Martin, 2020). As initiator and lead editor of *The Wiley Handbook of Theoretical and Philosophical Psychology*, 37 authors contributed essays that exemplify what theoretical and philosophical psychologists do and why they do it. Kurt Danziger described the book as "a volume of vast scope that provides an indispensable resource for anyone undertaking a serious study of almost any field of psychological inquiry" (Martin et al., 2015, back cover), and Kirk Schneider wrote, "I highly recommend this volume to all those who seek to illuminate – in vivid and concrete detail – the array of philosophical contexts in psychology, and by implication, the very edges of our inquiry" (Martin et al., 2015, back cover).

There is much, much more. Jack has a restless, inquiring, and fertile mind. But what I would also wish to say is that Jack is not just a first-rate scholar. He is also a first-rate person. He is intellectually and personally generous. He has given altruistically of his time and energies to mentor countless students and young scholars. He has been a model for pursing ideas vigorously but always respectfully, holding himself to the highest standards and encouraging, by example, others to develop high standards for themselves. Jack is an inspiring and cohesive influence, admired by many. As I know him well, let me say also that Jack is exceedingly modest. He would be the first to point out his imperfections and, no doubt, will blanch at my effusive characterization of him. But, in fitting words penned by the 18th century playwright Oliver Goldsmith (1917), "Modesty seldom resides in a breast that is not enriched with nobler virtues" (p. 35).

Jeff Sugarman (JS):	It's my great pleasure to be conducting this interview with Jack Martin, although usually at this time on Wednesdays we would have retired to the pub after a game of tennis and be conversing over cold pints. But, as we find ourselves in the midst of a pandemic and respecting social distancing, we are communicating electronically. So, let's begin. How has the field of psychology responded to your work?
Jack Martin (JM):	Well, overall, I think quite positively, which sometimes worries me. But, I need to clarify this a bit. For the first 18 years of my 45-year career as an academic psychologist, I was a mostly conventional applied research psychologist in counseling and educational psychology. After that, I turned to theoretical psychology and, more recently, to the history of psychology and the use of methods of life writing, such as biography and psychobiography. This later work pulls as much from the humanities as from the social sciences and attempts to focus directly on particular people and their lives.
	Getting back to your question of how the field of psychology has responded to my work, most of those who liked and supported my work as a purportedly scientifically oriented counseling and educational psychologist are different people with different orientations from those who have supported my work in the theory and history of psychology. I suspect many of the first group would be disappointed in my later

work and most of the second group would be happy to dismiss my earlier career offerings.

But this merely reflects the fact that psychology, as Sigmund Koch (1993) noted, encompasses very different kinds of study. Almost anyone with some degree of seriousness and industry can find a supportive group somewhere in the ever-expanding subdisciplinary structure of psychology. The problems of psychology do not hinge on my or anyone else's receipt of support for our particular work. They stem from mainstream psychology's long-standing and continuing disregard for what ought to be its primary subject matter – i.e., people and our lives as actually lived – and from its equally long-standing and continuing embrace of pseudoscientific methods and orientations.

JS: What have been the resistances and impediments to your work being received in the contemporary discipline of psychology?

JM: Well, as I say, I think different groups have received my work in different ways but that it's usually possible to find some group of psychologists who will be supportive of what one tries to do. It's just that some of these groups are more marginal than others and, for the most part, are dismissed by the more mainstream groups. But, moving away from my own work, the main resistance and impediment I see to a bona fide psychology of the person is the institutional culture that supports conventional psychological research as providing an adequate scientific base for its professional practices.

Ironically, it is the complacency induced by the scientist-practitioner model that I think prevents psychology from adequately investing in what I believe ought to be its subject matter – persons as self-interpreting moral and rational agents. In its zeal to be scientific in the manner of natural sciences, psychology has mostly overlooked, diminished, and reduced people to things that can be manipulated and controlled and has undervalued or ignored important resources for understanding persons and our lives – resources that are readily available in the vast and long-standing literature of the humanities and other areas of human creativity and accomplishment, failure and suffering, and existential and moral concern. In consequence, I think psychology is more scientistic than scientific.

Psychological scientism manifests theoretically in its reductive individualism and reductive psychologism. It manifests methodologically in its pseudoscientific and reductive statisticism. It manifests ethically in its self-serving instrumentalism. Reductive individualism treats people as isolated silos in the immediate and impoverished "heres and nows" of quasi-laboratory research settings or the clinical settings typically favored by professional psychologists. The inquiry methods and findings of scientific research in psychology almost completely ignore, and are largely irrelevant to, the lived realities of persons as historically and socioculturally embedded and dynamically constituted within the normative interactions, conventions, practices, traditions, and ways of life of their families and communities, as well as their broader societies and cultures.

We are social beings. We are constantly in coordination and relationship with others within our everyday life contexts. The objects of physics are mostly unaffected by alterations and sociocultural contexts and can be studied in ideal laboratory settings. The same hardly can be said for persons, our actions and our experiences. When we are removed from the communal sociocultural contexts within which we have developed as psychological beings in interaction with others, we are differently and unfamiliarly situated. What you see and what you get from psychologists' experimental manipulations and measures are not who we are and how we function in our everyday lives.

Matters are only made worse by the reductive psychologism so prevalent in contemporary cognitive and neuroscience that treats inner psychic and brain processes, structures, and mechanisms as primary causes of our actions and experiences. Is it really sensible to treat physical/chemical patterns of cerebral activity, cognitive schemata, or computational information-processing modules as independently operating entities that make the decisions, determine the actions, and create the aesthetic preferences of persons?

Who even knows what or where such schemata, structures, or modules are? By comparison, at least the blood flowing in our brains is not fictional. But why and how it could be a specific cause of who we love and what our political attitudes are, I don't know. I think all of this is very mysterious and unspecified, unless one believes in the highly unlikely possibility that everything from our loves to our politics is nothing more than physiochemical cerebral stirrings.

I think this situation is rather embarrassing in what is thought, by many psychologists, to be the most rigorously scientific of psychology's many areas of study.

Whereas individualism removes persons from our constitutive sociocultural context, from our lives and formative experiences, psychologism leaves us at the mercy of mysterious interior entities over which we have no control. The former removes us from the world. The latter removes us from ourselves (i.e., the people we are).

Much has been said about methodological statisticism and psychology, so I won't belabor the matter here. But the simple fact is that being a member of a group in a psychological experiment that benefits, on average, from a psychological intervention tells us nothing about whether or not any particular individual in that group is benefiting. In my days as a researcher in applied psychology, I used to marvel at, and was constantly surprised by, how many individuals did not benefit from, or even reacted negatively to, educational or psychotherapeutic interventions that demonstrated statistically significant higher average scores (indicative of positive change) in comparison with other groups.

Marty Byrde, protagonist of the Netflix series *Ozark*, puts the matter well and succinctly. To paraphrase one of his observations, "Casinos can bet the house on the law of large numbers. But this law is useless in predicting how any particular player might fare on any given night." The problem for psychology's scientist-practitioner model is that psychological interventions typically are targeted at individuals, not at large groups.

To complete my litany of reductive practices in psychology, I believe there is an ethically compromising instrumentalism of convenience in the institutional culture of psychology that ties together reductive individualism, psychologism, and statisticism in the service of psychology and psychologists at the expense of the persons they claim to understand, value, and help. Simply and bluntly put, it is much easier and more efficient for psychologists to conduct research in their laboratories down the hall, using instruments that can be filled in by research participants and yield data that can be converted easily to quantitative scores, and then to run such data through statistical packages from their laptops, than it is to grapple directly with the realities of actual people in their everyday life contexts.

JS: These seem to be pretty serious and pressing problems. But, given the context of the neoliberal, neocapitalist order, what would the field need to do to right its course?

JM: I would say that it's mostly the same kinds of "isms," the same kinds of difficulty that I've just alluded to in psychology, that also define much of the attitudes and methods of neoliberalism and neocapitalism. How many times do we hear psychologists urging government agencies and the public to base policies and practices of governance and living on psychological science of the sort I have just critiqued? If it is to avoid being increasingly implicated in the neoliberal, neocapitalist order, I think psychology needs to be clear and honest about what it can and cannot do. As it stands, in its conventional practice, so-called psychological science is not capable of undergirding the much-vaunted scientist-practitioner model; nor is it capable of offering scientific evidence in support of the framing and implementation of public policy. Again, the basic problem is that psychology as currently conducted is not about people. There is a huge gap between the typically reductive mechanistic and psychologistic research of psychologists, which assumes persons are highly determined by what psychologists assume to be our inner workings, and the reality of our lives as situated, lived, experienced, and interpreted by us in interaction with those around us.

Persons are self-interpreting, rational, and moral agents with developmental trajectories that unfold within sociocultural contexts saturated with social and moral concern. It is *persons* who discuss, debate, and decide, not our brains, our cognitive structures, or our psychic interiors. It is us, the persons we are, within our life contexts, who act individually and collectively with purpose and concern.

Throughout its history, scientific psychology has taken as its focal subject matter (in roughly chronological order) consciousness, behavior, cognition, and cerebral activity, often tossing in hypothesized mechanisms and processes of psychologists' own invention (e.g., psychic and computational architectures and schemata). The most important thing the field can do now is find a way to focus its attention on persons in actual life situations, with full recognition and respect for our diversity and our common existential condition, in ways that sanction our individual and collective right to meaningful participation in our lives.

Neoliberalism and neocapitalism benefit from reducing and devaluing us as persons, even when they advertise lavishly to the contrary. By offering up a picture of persons as less than whole, agentive only when assisted by psychological experts, and decontextualized from their quotidian engagements, purposes, and concerns, psychology, whether it intends to or not, inevitably fuels these "neo-isms." It is time for psychology to take persons seriously and to help us understand ourselves and our capabilities as socioculturally situated, culture-capable agents of possibility and change.

Of course, most humanistic psychologists would agree with what I am saying here. In many ways, I think they would be right to do so. However, a close look at the history of humanistic psychology also indicates a strong psychologistic focus on our inner psyches and processes as exerting a kind of causal force that somehow can overcome most of the situational problems and circumstances that many of the world's people endure. Nonetheless, there is no denying humanistic psychology's emphasis on the uniqueness and dignity of persons whose experiences and lives matter deeply to them and others close to them. Existential humanism in psychology is a rich and deep vein of life study and writing. When I say this, I think of the rich philosophical and psychological anthropology of G. Marian Kinget. Kinget is unknown to most psychologists, overlooked and unappreciated. Yet her major life work, published in 1975, *On Being Human*, is, in my opinion, a clarion call to psychologists to take people seriously.

Mentioning Kinget's work in humanistic psychology reminds me that there are theoretical and philosophical psychologists who also have said much of what I'm saying here and more eloquently, individuals like Sigmund Koch (1993), Liam Hudson (1975), David Bakan (1966), and several of my colleagues in the Society for Theoretical and Philosophical Psychology and the International Society for Theoretical Psychology. The history of psychology is liberally sprinkled with calls for a nonscientistic psychology that matters to persons and the lives we lead. Surely, it is finally time that psychology takes note of such expressions of concern or at least attempts to respond robustly to them. When I was in graduate school, I recall a few older psychologists sitting around a common room table agreeing that psychology might be defined as "the discipline that never quite manages to study what it should be studying." Yet, 50 years later, it continues mostly to neglect its subject matter even as it triumphantly trumpets simulacra of personhood that it has constructed for its own scientific and professional purposes (e.g., self-concepts, cognitive schemata, executive functions, and many others).

JS: What have been the crucial changes to your way of thinking or approach to the discipline over time?

JM: As I mentioned earlier, I spent the first 18 years of my 45-year career as an applied psychological researcher in educational and counseling psychology, steeped in exactly the kinds of views I've just been criticizing. By midcareer, I became increasingly concerned that the kind of psychology in which I was engaged was not getting me any closer to understanding what initially had drawn me to psychology and caused me to switch my undergraduate major from physics to psychology. After my first stint at Simon Fraser University, I spent 9 years at the University of Western Ontario, where I and my colleagues conducted an extensive program of research aimed at understanding the nature of psychotherapeutic change, work that we described in several articles in the *Journal of Counseling Psychology*, the *Journal of Consulting and Clinical Psychology*, and others. When I eventually pulled together and interpreted all this empirical work in my book *The Construction and Understanding of Psychotherapeutic Change* (Martin, 1994), I was struck by the amazing fact that, despite learning a great deal about how to ask and pursue what I regarded as interesting questions within the strictures imposed by the operational definitions, methodological constraints, and subpersonal theories of scientific psychology, I knew surprisingly little about most of the people who had participated in this research as therapists and clients and their lives as actually lived. Startled by this realization, I turned to the theory and philosophy of psychology in an attempt to understand better exactly why I found myself in this befuddled condition. The critical results of my immersion in this literature, and my attendance and interactions at meetings of the Society of Theoretical and Philosophical Psychology and the International Society for Theoretical Psychology, are evident in much of what I have said thus far in our conversation.

For many years after abandoning traditional statistical empiricism, I committed myself to the development of a philosophical and psychological anthropology that might contribute to and assist the study of persons and their lives. Much of this work was done in collaboration with you, Jeff, and resulted in what I think of as our "trilogy of the person" books: *The Psychology of Human Impossibility and Constraint, Psychology and the Question of Agency*, and *Persons: Understanding Psychological Selfhood and Agency*.

I subsequently completed this stage of my work by coediting three other volumes: *The Sociocultural Turn in Psychology* with Suzanne R. Kirschner, *The Psychology of Personhood* with Mark Bickhard, and *The Wiley Handbook of Theoretical and Philosophical Psychology* with you and Kate Slaney. Working on these various volumes was tremendously enjoyable and satisfying. I learned a great deal about human existence and personhood in the process.

Since I have given up on traditional statistical research, I have nonetheless wanted, especially toward the end of my career, to say something in response to the constant stream of students who ask me, What kind of empirical psychology is possible? Or, more pragmatically, What can I do for my thesis? In these situations, I often have found myself saying that there is much useful empirical work that can be done in psychology that avoids many of the difficulties that I and many others have talked about in our theoretical writings.

But it's only recently that I have experimented seriously with what Margaretta Jolly (2017), in a mammoth two-volume work, has called "life writing." By this term, she refers in particular to biography and psychobiography but also to the wide array of means by which human individuals have monitored, written about, talked about, filmed, and documented their lives and learned from the lives of others.

In the last 10 years, I've spent considerable time and energy conducting and developing my own approach to life writing (life positioning analysis, or LPA) and applying it to the lives of particular people – social scientists and psychologists like Ernest Becker, Stanley Milgram, Carl Rogers, and B. F. Skinner; athletes like Jim Thorpe and Steve Nash; writers like Mordecai Richler; and, currently in progress, former Canadian Prime Minister Pierre Trudeau. I think of LPA as a flexible, pragmatic, and hermeneutic tool to explore particular lives as lived in coordination with others within their immediate communities and broader sociocultural contexts.

JS: Can you elaborate life positioning analysis as a methodology and the kinds of psychological explanations, understandings, and insights it's capable of providing, in light of those you've studied?

JM: LPA uses ideas developed originally by George Herbert Mead. I always find it amazing how many ideas were developed by early psychologists that can be used in what I now see as a "new" way of doing psychology. Of course, such ideas always have been embedded here and there in various, somewhat hidden, niches within the history of psychology. Yet, how many psychologists, outside of the theory and history of psychology, know that Wilhelm Wundt spent the last 10 years of his life developing a sociocultural psychology for understanding people and human life in ways that he didn't think his laboratory work could come anywhere close to disclosing? How many know that William Stern, who coined the term "intelligence quotient," advocated biography as the best way to understand particular persons?

But, back to Mead. What I've taken from Mead are parts of his social developmental theory. Alex Gillespie, who's at the London School of Economics and Political Science in the Department of Psychological and Behavioral Science, has worked with me to adopt and adapt Mead's ideas in the context of contemporary theorizing in social developmental psychology (e.g., Martin & Gillespie, 2010, 2020).

A social developmental process central to life positioning analysis is the exchange of social positions. Think, as Mead was fond of doing, of children's games like hide-and-seek. As young children participate in this game, initially with the assistance of caregivers and older peers, they gradually are able to recall and imagine their experiences in the position of hider while actually in the position of seeker and vice versa. When this happens, they are able to be in two positions at once – one in actuality, the other in recollection and imagination. This double positioning allows them to anticipate the perspective of the seeker when they are hiding and the perspective of the hider when they are seeking. By taking the perspective of the other, they become more adept at playing the game but also, in general, at taking the attitudes of others towards themselves – it is this ability that

Mead held to be essential for the development of self and other understanding and awareness.

LPA looks for position exchanges that are repeated and develop across the course of a person's life. These exchanges occur with particular others close to the focal person within the context and against the background of more general sociocultural practices, understandings, customs, and ways of life – what Mead referred to as "generalized others."

Sometimes these life positionings are symmetrical. Sometimes they are asymmetrical. Sometimes they change from asymmetrical to symmetrical or vice versa. They play out in ways that become central to the personal development of the focal person as a socially spawned rational and moral agent. They function as central themes, challenges, and strategies in her or his life.

A good example of asymmetrical positioning is found in the life of Carl Rogers, who grew up in a highly religious family in which he often felt judged and found wanting by his deeply religious parents and older siblings. In consequence, he grew comfortable in, even if increasingly frustrated by, occupying the position of listener and much less comfortable in the role of speaker. Learning to become at ease with intimate self-expression proved to be a lifelong challenge for Rogers, one that he began to overcome more fully only after his late-career move to California and his work in the encounter group movement. Freedom of self-expression became deeply engrained as a goal in Rogers's personal and professional life.

In contrast, and illustrative of a more symmetrical and reversible life positioning, Fred Skinner showed an early aptitude for "engineering" his way out of interpersonal conflicts by controlling his own behavior through purposeful environmental manipulations. For example, as a young adolescent, he hung a sign that hovered at eye level near his bedroom door and was attached to a pulley system he constructed to move the sign out of sight when he hung up his pajamas, a source of frequent scolding from his mother if left unhung. Throughout his life, Skinner was able to engineer his way out of social positions of being controlled and reposition himself as in control.

The identification and documentation of a number of prototypic scenarios involving position exchange, such as those drawn from the lives of Rogers and Skinner, are part of what occurs in the early stages of LPA. Later phases look for patterns of positioning across the life course and attempt to link them to more general themes, practices, and ways of living embedded in relevant sociocultural practices, conventions, and ways of life.

For example, more general sociocultural orientations in American social life are on full display in debates between Rogers and Skinner held in 1956 and 1962. Here, it is possible to witness Rogers's life-long search for and commitment to personal freedom pitted against Skinner's lifelong search for and commitment to personal control – two sides of what many understand as essential to achieving "the American dream."

JS: You devoted a considerable amount of time and energy to studying Ernest Becker. Can you talk about that work, why you became interested in Becker, and what you gained from studying him?

JM: Yes, I'd be happy to do that. It was my interest in Becker, from the time I was a graduate student at the University of Alberta and first read his *Denial of Death* (Becker, 1973), that initially got me thinking about doing some biographical work sometime in the future. This interest was heightened when I arrived at Simon Fraser in 1975 to take up my first full-time academic position. Becker had spent his final years at Simon Fraser. He was there from 1969 until his death at the age of 49 (of cancer in Vancouver General Hospital) in 1974, the year before I arrived in 1975.

The reason Becker's writings fascinated me was that I suffered greatly from night terrors and death anxiety as a child and young adult but found something helpful in Becker's admonishment to face inevitable facts concerning life and death. I was very disappointed when I arrived at Simon Fraser to discover that almost nothing had been done to commemorate Becker's passing or his previous presence. At that point, I vowed to do something to right that particular wrong at some future time.

So, when I returned to Simon Fraser after my period of working as a professor of counseling and psychotherapy researcher at the University of Western Ontario (from 1983 to 1991), I began to research Becker's life and work, with the help of his widow, Marie, and the occasional visit to the Becker Papers archived at Columbia University. The papers had been put there for two reasons: first, because

Ernest and Marie had grown up in the Atlantic Northeast and secondly because the papers of Otto Rank, whose work exerted enormous influence on Becker's later thought, are housed in the archival holdings of Columbia's Sterling Library.

I've spent many enjoyable hours in the archive reading room of the Sterling Library going through those papers. It was a wonderful experience. My eventual study of Becker's life was published in the *Journal of Humanistic Psychology* in 2014. In answer to the last part of your question, Jeff, I think I've gained many things from working on Becker. I learned a good deal about his thought and life, including several things that I have applied to my own life and subsequent work. Two very important things were to discover how hard he worked (the meticulous notes he made on the many books he studied were just one indication of the hours upon hours he devoted to studying carefully the works of others) and to appreciate the generosity of spirit he frequently displayed in crediting his great appreciation for the insights he gained from those authors and texts that most affected him and his thought. Even, and perhaps especially, in facing his own death, he never stopped studying and trying to order and improve his thinking. I believe he felt it his duty to continue to do all he could to expand and refine the ideas that most occupied him, up to the very moment of his death.

Biographical work has a way of getting you thinking about your own life and the human condition you share with others. I grew very fond of Becker. His deathbed interview with Sam Kean still breaks me up every time I read it. His ideas and beliefs never stopped developing. I was continually impressed by how hard he worked. I also learned a great deal from the copious notes he made and inserted on and within the covers of the books he studied, all carefully crafted in his meticulous hand.

Working on Becker brought me into contact with some wonderful folks associated with the Ernest Becker Foundation in Seattle, individuals like physician Dr. Neil Elgee, who passed away earlier this year. Neil headed the Ernest Becker Foundation, located in Seattle, for many years. For me, he always will be a charming reminder of what it is to be classy.

JS: Jack, I know that you're a lover of good fiction, music, and film. I was wondering if your appetite and interest for the arts influences your work in psychology. If it does, how so?

JM: It's taken me a long time to appreciate fully how my lifelong interests in literature, film, and music can be integrated with my work
in psychology. When I first attended the University of Alberta as
an undergraduate, I majored in physics and later went into behavioral psychology. Skinner kept his musicianship and love of poetry
separate from his psychological research, and I did the same. Only
in the last few decades have I more openly connected my love of art
and the humanities with my work as a psychologist. Perhaps this,
more than almost anything else I can think of, testifies directly to the
pernicious hegemony exercised by the institutional culture of scientific psychology.
Art, in all its forms, constitutes a large part of the vast historical and
contemporary resources of life study and writing concerning what
matters to us most. It amazes me that with so much directly available, objective evidence concerning persons and their lives right in
front of us, we psychologists have felt it necessary to invent simu-
lations and construct demonstrations, like the Milgram studies of
obedience or the Stanford prison study, to gain what we think of as
objective scientific evidence about persons and our tendencies.

JS: I know that you've recently completed a book on the psychiatric
institution in the town you grew up in. Can you tell me about that
project, what kindled it, and the process of researching and writing
it?

JM: Well, I'm pleased and just a touch annoyed that you ask about this
book. The annoyance isn't at you. It reflects some of my frustration
with this whole project, which is a local history and memoir, entitled
Hometown Asylum. On the one hand, it's been a wonderful opportunity to revisit some of my early life experiences. My father worked
at the hospital as a baker, and I worked there as an institutional atten-
dant in the summers when I was doing my undergraduate degree. It
also has allowed me to reconnect with people from my hometown
of Ponoka, Alberta, many of whom I haven't seen or spoken to for a
long time.
However, on the other hand, this is intended to be a nonfiction trade
book for a nonacademic audience, and I'm finding it frustratingly
difficult, and extremely humbling, to learn to write in a way that
communicates easily to a general audience. However, various editors who have seen one or another version of the manuscript have

provided extremely helpful feedback, and the learning process continues.

Having said this, one aspect of this project that has held my attention perhaps more than any other connects to some of the themes we've touched on earlier in this conversation. When you look at what happened in the history of psychiatric institutions like the Alberta Hospital Ponoka, you get a powerful sense of the human tendency to dehumanize those judged to be different. The history of institutional psychiatry and psychology is disturbingly littered with a terrible array of professionally sanctioned physical assaults on those suffering from mental illness. The fact that many of these were conducted in what seem to have been genuine attempts to help speaks loudly to me about the dangers of "scientific" dehumanization.

I felt a similar gut-wrenching disquiet watching the recently released film *The Report*, which concerns the psychologist-assisted tortures at various inquisition and incarceration facilities like Abu Ghraib, Bagram, Guantanamo Bay, and elsewhere. It's difficult to imagine a more important rationale for a psychology that insists upon taking persons seriously and respectfully than such demonstrations of what can happen when personhood is denied and inexcusable scientistic excess and moral absence are tolerated.

JS: I want to turn again to psychology and the sociopolitical context. How should psychology take up the issue of civic obligation and the freedom to make choices when current living conditions in our society are so inequitable and unjust? And how should psychology promote psychological freedom within both personal and political domains, given that we would think freedom is an important thing?

JM: That's a great question. You might be disappointed in my response. I certainly think psychology has a civic and moral responsibility not to contribute to societal inequality and injustice. And, as I've already indicated, unfortunately, I believe psychology often has done so and continues to do so, even if mostly unintentionally and unwittingly. I think it does so by producing practices, procedures, and technologies that support a strong form of solely individual responsibility for problems of poverty, addiction, and what are seen as "life failures." As I mentioned earlier, some of the central beliefs, values, and orientations of neoliberalism and neocapitalism bear striking resemblance to the tenets of individualism, psychologism, procedural technicism, and instrumentalism that are evident in much psychological literature and practice.

I think there can be little doubt that psychology is an integral part of contemporary aspirational and enterprise culture (see Moore, 2019; Sugarman, 2015). I think we certainly can do better in facing directly our likely contributions to neoliberal and neocapitalist trends. However, I don't think psychology has a particular mandate to determine how best to create a more equitable and just society. It might even be presumptuous and misleading for us to suggest that we have such a mandate beyond what all of us share as concerned, involved citizens. Even if I'm wrong about this, I do not believe we have the knowledge and understanding that such a mandate requires. I'm not sure who, if anyone, does. But, in general, I think psychology and psychologists sometimes have been guilty of overreach. We should not forget that with respect to matters of social justice, equity, and reform, we are people and citizens first and psychologists second. As psychologists, what we can do is get our own house in order – insist in our research, professional practice, teaching, and writing, that we take people seriously as self-interpreting moral and rational agents.

Perhaps psychology ought to do more, as Carl Rogers attempted to do in his later life projects for world peace. Maybe he was right. But perhaps he, with the very best of intentions, indulged in the hubris of assuming expertise in the lives and life contexts of others similar to and yet different from himself. I think it is our fundamental, ethical priority as psychologists not to overestimate our discipline or ourselves. We always must strive to do no harm, perhaps especially when we want so desperately to help.

In saying this, I want to emphasize that, as citizens, I think we all have and need to shoulder responsibility for the state of our commonwealth and must do whatever we can to secure its health and beneficence.

JS: I know you're retired and looking to other things with which to occupy yourself. But what do you imagine as the future directions of your thought?

JM: It's nice to have a chance to talk a little bit about this. I hope to spend as much time as I can promoting and demonstrating possibilities for a psychology of persons that draws from the arts and humanities as well as from the social sciences and sciences. In my retirement thus far, I have been delighted to work with you to produce our recent edited volume that does exactly this (Sugarman & Martin, 2020). In addition to my ongoing studies of life positioning, I think there is tremendous value in work that examines, in critical, theoretical, historical, and biographical detail, some of the classic studies in the history of psychology – how and why these were conceived and conducted, how they've been interpreted, how they've traveled across time and context, and how they've been presented by psychologists to themselves, to students of psychology, and to the general public.

I have become fascinated by why psychology and most psychologists choose to ignore, rather than take seriously, numerous intellectually powerful expressions of critical concern raised about psychology presented as if it were a natural science, concerns dating back at least to the mid-1800s. In this historical context, I think it might prove tremendously worthwhile to conduct detailed studies of major research programs and their legacies, to document exactly how such enterprises have persisted and fended off all of these well-constructed critiques. Such studies might take on particular importance in light of the current debate raging about the failure of psychological research to replicate.

For the vast majority of psychological research that reports only aggregated statistical outcomes, I see no reason why we should even expect such studies to replicate or take seriously the idea of replication (as developed in natural science) as a possibility. There are no specific, real-world "point predictions" made in the vast majority of psychological research. There are only much more liberal thresholds of statistical prediction levels, intervals, and "significance" that can be stepped over with relative ease, without much in the way of what is meant by precisely mathematized replication in natural science.

To take a classic example, in the 1930s and 1940s Clark Hall attempted to mathematize his behavioral psychology using algebraic formulae. His efforts met with spectacular failure. Yet, Hull was trying to do something roughly comparable to what physicists actually do (but without differential geometry or calculus, which are mostly impossible to employ in psychological research as currently conducted) and should be given full marks for his efforts. Unfortunately, psychologists seem to have learned little from Hull's failure other than not to make the mistake of attempting such an exercise again. Of course, to me, the bigger methodological problem faced by psychology is the seemingly inevitable reduction of personhood that quantification entails. Having said this, I should add that even qualitative research in psychology does not necessarily or by itself ensure against the reduction of persons as moral and rational agents. At any rate, in answer to your question about future directions, I think detailed critical, historical, theoretical, and biographical work in psychology can help not only to expose what is wrong with psychology but also to demonstrate what psychology can do. I look forward to engaging in work of this kind for as long as I can – an inquiry that can help us better understand what psychology currently can and cannot do and how it might reconfigure itself, a goal I share with you and several others who work in theoretical psychology.

JS: Thank you very much, Jack. We'll conclude the interview on that note.

JM: Thanks Jeff. Much appreciated. In closing, I'd like to add that working with you, Kate Slaney, Ann-Marie McLellan, and others at Simon Fraser University, during my second tour of duty here, has provided some of the most satisfying moments in my career as a psychologist. It is extremely gratifying to watch your careers develop, sometimes in tandem and sometimes diverging from my own interests and positions, which is as it should be. As Hannah Arendt said toward the end of her life, "Each time you write something and you send it out into the world and it becomes public . . . you should not try to hold your hand on whatever may happen to what you have been thinking. . . . You should rather try to learn from what other people do with it" (Arendt, 1973 cited in Canovan, 2018, p. xxxii). Of course, some of the work I have most enjoyed doing has been done with you, Jeff. I feel very fortunate to have had the good fortune to work with a number of talented and conscientious colleagues throughout all phases of my academic life.

References

Arendt, H. (1973). *The origins of totalitarianism*. Harcourt.

Bakan, D. (1966). *The duality of human existence*. Rand McNally.

Becker, E. (1973). *The denial of death*. Free Press.

Canovan, M. (2018). Introduction. In H. Arendt (Ed.), *The human condition* (2nd ed., pp. xix–xxxii). University of Chicago Press.

Gillespie, A., & Martin, J. (2014). Position exchange theory: A socio-material basis for discursive and psychological positioning. *New Ideas in Psychology, 32,* 73–79.

Goldsmith, O. (1917). *She stoops to conquer.* Ginn and Company. (Original work published 1773)

Hudson, L. (1975). *Human beings: The psychology of human experience.* Anchor Books.

Jolly, M. (Ed.). (2017). *Encyclopedia of life writing: Autobiographical and biographical forms* (2 vols.). Routledge.

Kirschner, S., & Martin, J. (Eds.). (2010). *The sociocultural turn in psychology: The contextual emergence of mind and self.* Columbia University Press.

Kinget, G. M. (1975). *On being human.* Harcourt Brace Jovanovitch.

Koch, S. (1993). "Psychology" or the "psychological studies"? *American Psychologist, 48,* 902–904.

Martin, J. (1994). *The construction and understanding of psychotherapeutic change: Conversations, memories, and theories.* Teachers College Press.

Martin, J. (2013). Life positioning analysis: An analytic framework for the study of lives and life narratives. *Journal of Theoretical and Philosophical Psychology, 33,* 1–17.

Martin, J. (2014). Ernest Becker at Simon Fraser University (1969–1974). *Journal of Humanistic Psychology, 54,* 66–112.

Martin, J. (2015). Life positioning analysis. In J. Martin, J. Sugarman, & K. L. Slaney (Eds.), *The Wiley handbook of theoretical and philosophical psychology: Methods, approaches, and new directions for social sciences.* Wiley Blackwell.

Martin, J. (2016). Ernest Becker and Stanley Milgram: Twentieth-century students of evil. *History of Psychology, 19,* 3–21.

Martin, J. (2017). Carl Rogers' and B. F. Skinner's approaches to personal and societal improvement: A study in the psychological humanities. *Journal of Theoretical and Philosophical Psychology, 37,* 214–229.

Martin, J., & Bickhard, M. H. (Eds.). (2013). *The psychology of personhood: Philosophical, historical, social-developmental, and narrative perspectives.* Cambridge University Press.

Martin, J., & Cox, D. (2016). Positioning Steve Nash: A theory-driven, social psychological, and biographical case study of creativity in sport. *The Sport Psychologist, 30,* 388–398.

Martin, J., & Gillespie, A. (2010). A neo-Meadian approach to human agency: Relating the social and the psychological in the ontogenesis of perspective coordinating persons. *Integrating Psychological and Behavioral Science, 44,* 252–272.

Martin, J., & Gillespie, A. (2020). Position exchange. In V. Glaveanu (Ed.), *Palgrave encyclopedia of the possible.* Palgrave Macmillan.

Martin, J., & Gillespie, A. (2013). Position exchange theory and personhood. In J. Martin & M. H. Bickhard (Eds.), *The psychology of personhood: Philosophical, historical, social-developmental, and narrative perspectives* (pp. 147–164). Cambridge University Press.

Martin, J., & McLellan, A. (2013). *The education of selves: How psychology transformed students.* Oxford University Press.

Martin, J., & Sugarman, J. (1999). *The psychology of human possibility and constraint.* State University of New York Press.

Martin, J., Sugarman, J., & Hickinbottom, S. (2010). *Persons: Understanding psychological selfhood and agency.* Springer.

Martin, J., Sugarman, J., & Slaney, K. L. (Eds.). (2015). *Wiley handbook of theoretical and philosophical psychology: Methods, approaches, and new directions for social sciences.* Wiley Blackwell.

Martin, J., Sugarman, J., & Thompson, J. (2003). *Psychology and the question of agency.* State University of New York Press.

Moore, K. (2019). *Wellbeing and aspirational culture.* Palgrave Macmillan.

Sugarman, J. (2015). Neoliberalism and psychological ethics. *Journal of Theoretical and Philosophical Psychology, 35,* 103–116.

Sugarman, J., & Martin, J. (2020). *A humanities approach to the psychology of personhood.* Routledge.

8

Philosophical Hermeneutics and Psychological Understanding

A Conversation with Frank C. Richardson

Interviewed by Jeff Sugarman
Jeff Sugarman and Frank C. Richardson

Introduction

Frank C. Richardson has been consumed by the deep questions of human existence. While the questions that vex Frank have traditionally been relegated to the disciplinary territories of philosophy and theology, he sees addressing them as vital to any adequate understanding of human psychology. For Frank, it is self-evident that a credible account of psychological life must give due consideration to the meaning and significance we experience and bestow on our lives. Further, it also requires what that meaning and significance consist of, the sources from which they spring, how they orient us to life, and the way they form us as the persons and selves we are capable of being and becoming. Fundamental to Frank's perspective is the hermeneutic insight that there is a tacit horizon of understanding that contains our defining convictions about the meaning and significance of human life and against which all our actions and experiences are made intelligible. But to reveal this horizon and its psychological implications for individual and collective life is not simple.

   The long and winding intellectual road Frank has taken in search of means to grapple with these weighty matters has compelled him to venture off the beaten track of mainstream psychological methodology. In fact, a considerable portion of Frank's work (e.g., Richardson et al., 1999) has been devoted to revealing the deficiencies of psychological theories and methods – namely, the scientism, determinism, instrumentalism, reductionism, and hypertrophied individualism on which they are founded and how these and other problematic assumptions shackle

DOI: 10.4324/9781003280033-9

psychological thinking in ways that distort what persons are, turning us into creatures mutated to an extent found only in science fiction. As Elms (1996) makes the point, in a way Frank no doubt would appreciate, "I haven't met a psychologist yet who could put together a live person from those statistical body parts and honestly cry out, 'It's alive!'" (p. 13).

However, to amend the failings Frank finds in a psychology that has sanitized humanity of its moral, ethical, spiritual, and ontological significance necessitates journeying beyond psychology's disciplinary confines and reading widely – philosophy, theology, sociology, social and cultural theory, political studies, history, and literary theory. With undergraduate degrees in philosophy and divinity, Frank is better equipped than most psychologists to make these forays, and over the long course of his scholarly career he has traversed a large swath of the landscape of thought. It shows. Conversing with Frank, one quickly becomes aware not only of the scope of what he has studied but, moreover, of the great depth of his understanding and command of ideas.

Some of his ideational encounters have stuck and form cornerstones of his thought: the philosophical hermeneutics of Hans-Georg Gadamer (e.g., Richardson & Woolfolk, 1994), Richard Bernstein's (1983) critique of objectivism and relativism (e.g., Richardson, 2000), the moral philosophy of Charles Taylor (e.g., Richardson et al., 1999), Aristotelean virtue ethics (e.g., Richardson, 2012), a conception of social theory as practice (e.g., Richardson & Christopher, 1993), the cultural criticism of Christopher Lasch (e.g., Richardson et al., 2019), the theology of René Girard (e.g., Richardson, 2009), and relational ontology (e.g., Richardson & Woolfolk, 2013). There are many others. However, all of them are of a piece woven together by Frank into a powerful perspective that speaks to the rich complexity and profundity of individual and collective life and portrays psychology as simply one among an array of practices human beings have developed for interpreting themselves.

In this light, Frank asserts that psychologists need to return to the perennial question of "the good" and restore a conception of persons as inescapably moral beings because we are constituted psychologically by our moral understanding. Moreover, examining our notions of the good furnishes a hermeneutic opening to the recovery of moral and ethical responsibility, civic virtue, and the relationality by which we are "permeated by otherness," a phrase Frank (Richardson, 2014, p. 362) borrows from

Dunne (1996, p. 143) that pertains not only to what we are but also to the transcendence of which we are capable.

The importance Frank places on dialogue should not go unremarked (Richardson & Manglos, 2012). A key feature of hermeneutics to which Frank wholeheartedly subscribes is "dialogic understanding" (p. 191). Understanding psychological life cannot be achieved by treating it akin to natural phenomena that can be studied neutrally and objectively with scientific methods. Rather, a more appropriate approach suited to the social, cultural, historical, moral, ethical, political, and religious constitution of psychological phenomena, hermeneutic understanding is modeled on "a process of mutual communication, influence, negotiation, accommodation, and struggle, as in a conversation or a relationship" (p. 191).

However, the hermeneutic model of dialogue is not formulated in terms of interaction between isolated independent interlocuters. As dialogical beings, persons are formed in their mutuality, constituted relationally in the ongoing and ever-present swirl of human discourse and language into which they are thrust from birth and that structures their modes of thought and psychological existence. We are dialogical and relational "all the way down." Thus, dialogue is the condition of possibility for understanding. It is through dialogue that we are able to comprehend the manifold and dynamic nature of our moral and cultural values, aided by the recognition that we are embedded in a living history of human interpretations of the good, their differences, and their limitations. Only through dialogue, and critically interrogating our moral visions and ends, can they and the assumptions on which they rest be examined and evaluated for their merits and shortcomings. As such, hermeneutic dialogue holds the possibility not only for understanding the assumptions and commitments that form our horizon of understanding, but also for engagement with other forms of life and, in turn, the potential they pose for our individual and collective betterment. But, as Frank has made clear, hermeneutic dialogue demands much of us. Courage, humility, civility, respect, fair-mindedness, and open-mindedness are but some of the virtues required for productive dialogue with others in pursuing the self-critical questioning and rethinking of the moral commitments by which human lives are defined.

An octogenarian who has retired from professorial chores, Frank continues ceaselessly to explore the questions that vex him, and, as you will see evidenced in our interview, he admirably embodies the virtues and ethics of hermeneutic dialogue.

Jeff Sugarman (JS):   I want to start by saying that it's a particularly special honor for me to be conducting this interview. I consider you to be one of the most important contemporary theoretical and philosophical psychologists. You have contributed greatly to my thinking, as well as that of many others. Over the course of your career, you've produced an impressive oeuvre of what is refined, insightful, and innovative scholarship. But unlike many, you're not just a critic. Your work is replete with all kinds of positive proposals for how psychology could be improved as well as serve the betterment of human life.

But your work and contributions go far beyond what can be found in print. I don't know of anyone else who has done as much as you in expanding the horizons of the discipline by engaging scholars outside of it, by inviting them to participate in events, by generously mentoring students and young scholars with what is invariably astute advice, by giving consistent encouragement, and by lighting the way by example.

You're someone who doesn't just talk the talk. Many, including myself, are deeply indebted to you for your guidance, for your unwavering support and, indeed, for having careers.

So, I just want to start by thanking you.

Frank C. Richardson (FR):   Thank you.

JS: So, to start: How did you come to take up a philosophical/theoretical approach to your work in psychology?

FR: Well, thank you for the compliments, Jeff. I hope I half deserve them. Perhaps I am a big frog in a small pond. It's been a real pleasure to be involved in our field and to have friends and colleagues like you. It's been one of the two or three greatest joys in my life.

In some ways, it's fairly simple for me. I had one year in graduate school in philosophy at Yale University. Then, I got a degree from Yale Divinity School. I worked for a year in Chicago in community organization, Saul Alinsky-type community organization. The same kind of thing former President Obama did, only almost two decades earlier. At the end of that rather exciting year, I really had no idea what I wanted to do with my life. I did realize that I had to make a living. I had a child on the way to support. So, I went to graduate school in counseling psychology at Colorado State, which turned out to be a fine place. That was the heyday of the early upswing in counseling psychology.

During my time there, I met Richard Suinn, my major professor, ultimately president of APA. Dandy fellow. Easygoing. Helpful. Smart. He helped me get a job at the University of Texas teaching in the counseling psychology PhD program. I actually taught behavior therapy. That was part of my background (training under Suinn) and my early research, even though I didn't have a behavioral bone in my body. It was practical, it was interesting, and it was a wonderful way to engage people. It avoided what seemed like, at least to an outsider, some of the mystifications and pointless wordiness of psychoanalytic or psychodynamic thinking. So it seemed to me at the time.

In my second year, I started teaching theories of counseling psychology and theories of personality. That quickly became my academic specialty, my academic love. I was promoted early because I published a bunch of research on desensitization and behavioral treatments for anxiety and similar topics. Pretty far away from where we are now. But it was fun. It seemed pleasingly practical.

For me, the big turning point was when I fell in love with teaching theories of counseling psychology and theories of personality. I loved the theories; they were windows to reality, windows to human purpose and meaning.

But I can remember the day that all changed. We used to make an effort to compare and contrast theories. How were they different? Along what dimensions did they differ? What were their main points of conflict? We supposedly had about 260 theories of therapy at the time. It's now up into the 500s or more. But it hit me like a bolt of lightning one day. I was doing a little bit of outside reading, beginning to get back in touch with some of my philosophical training, and it hit me in a big way that what was interesting about this array of personality and psychotherapy theories was not their differences, not their points of conflict, but, weirdly enough, what they had in common.

They all had an underlying stratum of what today we would call individualism and instrumentalism. They all saw the person as a separate self, somehow able to get in touch with and actualize and empower itself and then, it was thought, to enter into the world and do things of a largely instrumental sort. Even existential psychotherapy involves getting in touch with your capacity for radical freedom and then implementing it in the world in a quasi-instrumental way, however you wish. Anyway, that insight just hit me like a bolt of lightning.

Subsequently, I started to read more widely and started to bring some of these critical perspectives into my teaching in counseling theories and elsewhere. That worked very well for four or five years, and I'm proud of the fact that, even though those interests were not common among my colleagues, I had a handful of students that took a real interest in and picked up on them. Some of them went on to have academic careers, which I was also proud of because it was not a mainstream focus.

But after about four or five years, the whole field was changing. I don't know how to explain it other than the fact that counseling psychology became more careerist. It became less critical and intellectual. We were no longer the kind of people who would just speculate broadly about anything with a sense of confidence that we had a lot to offer the world. That went away. Anxiety about getting jobs, anxiety about whether we were "scientific" or not, anxiety about our professional future burgeoned.

I hung on for, I don't know, five or six years more. I can tell you a brief story that I know you will enjoy, Jeff. We had a particularly unappealing class one year, and I recall one day in the counseling theories class when I quit trying to push some of my new ideas for a while. I got along well with students; I was a good teacher and enjoyed the work. But they were resistant; they didn't want to talk about what I wanted to explore. So, I just sat back and listened for about half an hour to their chatter. Eventually, a theme arose in the conversation, one they milked for about 20 or 30 minutes that went something like this, "When you graduate, when you get your PhD in counseling psychology and you have a practice, how long after you have quit your personal therapy can your former therapist begin to refer you clients?" That was the exciting matter they got into, in a graduate theories class! I think that speaks for itself. To me it felt dreary, petty, and pretentiously self-involved, as if they were living entirely within the world of the therapy room. A couple of years later, I began getting involved in Division 24. I read Philip Cushman's (1990) "Why the Self Is Empty" article in the *American Psychologist*. I called him up and talked to him on the phone. I met Phil in person at the next APA convention, right after giving my first Division 24 paper. Unfortunately, it was a dreadfully weak paper, barely comprehensible, and I was very upset that Phil had heard it. But he was a generous soul, we hit if off immediately, and the rest is history. I recall another now well-known theoretical psychologist delivered a paper on Heidegger at that same meeting that was enormously dense and also barely comprehensible. But we were a hardy band, courageous and sincere if still tutored to only a limited extent in the philosophy of social science and related matters. Within just a few years, we were all getting a lot clearer and fairly astute, I think, and soon theoretical and philosophical psychology became a respectable field of inquiry.

JS: Was this early 1990s?

FR: Yes. I identified with philosophical psychology more and more. About four years after that, I spoke to my chair, who was a good friend and I said, "I want out of counseling psychology." No one had ever jumped ship like that, and it was not immediately clear that there was any place for me in the department. But, in fact, I only had to change one course and teach an ethics course in school counseling rather than the theories course in counseling. The transition went smoothly. Students liked me, for the most part, and as long as I didn't pressure them to do what I was doing or get involved in hard-nosed critical thinking, colleagues tolerated me well. In fact, from time to time they liked to corner me in the hall or their offices to express their doubts and worries about their own research and the field as a whole – so long as I didn't ask them to read any big books or challenging material that called into question the whole enterprise.

So, I got assigned to an office on the fifth floor with the methodological faculty (a bit narrow in their outlook, also, but considerably less pretentious than the counseling and clinical types). I started teaching undergraduate honors courses, a great treat, as well as graduate courses, and had a pretty good time for the rest of my career. I became extensively involved in Division 24, rewarding papers and beginning to publish in our field and making extremely good friends and colleagues like yourself.

In my view, the history of my intellectual wanderings revolved around moments of insight like those, when some vivid, more or less distressing revelation took place. I saw my colleagues as likeable and sincere – many were good friends – but dreadfully fearful of thoroughly questioning the assumptions that we all operated on as social science academics and professionals. Too much was at stake for them – tenure and promotion, a steady income, and the smidgeon of prestige that society granted us. We have talked about that. I can't explain it, but a few of us seem to not have the ability to keep from asking uncomfortable questions and trusting blindly that something will work out for us. In fact, they did work out fairly well. We eat regularly, can support our families, and have a hell of a lot of fun together. (Interspersed only occasionally, of course, with brief bouts of depression and fleeting thoughts of suicide.)

JS: How people like us ended up where we are is much more a story of happenstance than deliberative planning. None of us decided, "I'm going to be a theoretical philosopher-psychologist" in our undergraduate program and end up where we are. It just didn't happen that way. We felt compelled by certain ideas and followed our insights. How has the field of psychology responded to your work? Has there always been resistance that you alluded to earlier?

FR: Well, do you mean like my department or the wider field as far as I can discern?

JS: You can differentiate between them.

FR: I know that question was on the list for this talk, but it's really difficult to say. My experience personally seems fairly clear. In terms of our field, I'm not entirely sure. I believe that they tolerate us. Perhaps they kind of like having philosophically minded people around. It adds a little bit of prestige or cultural window dressing to the field of psychology, as long as we don't ask too much of them, as long as we don't pillory them to any great extent. I think it salves their conscience because we raise some of the questions they at least subconsciously worry about but can't really discuss openly.

So, I think we're appreciated and have respect in a number of ways. That is gratifying. But I think our real impact is quite minimal. I see the field as declining into – it's not even empiricism, it's technicism. It's simply a business. Society at large comforts itself with the idea that we are uncovering important truths about human life, and we pretend to be doing so! I think I have had more impact on people through relationships with just a few students at the University of Texas and with a few faculty and graduate students in the philosophy or English departments, or even in the business school. There are some critically minded people in business, believe it or not. Those associations have been more rewarding and successful in terms of people picking up on some of my ideas and making use of them in their work.

JS: Within the world of theoretical and philosophical psychology, you've had some landmark works, like *Re-Envisioning Psychology*, cited pretty much by everyone who was also working on the topics with which you were grappling. I was wondering about the "Why Is Multiculturalism Good?" piece in *American Psychologist* which, also was widely read, but quite controversial. It must have stirred some lively conversation.

FR: It actually stirred less animus than I expected. There were no assassination attempts. There was no pressure from my department. Many of my colleagues were even impressed. Said so, sincerely, but typically did not want to converse about it much further. They didn't have the tools or perhaps the nerve to do so. At one point, the very first theoretical dissertation in our department, by a student of mine on Kohut's self-psychology, actually won the university dissertation prize for that year. Different though it was, I had the impression that evaluation committees at the department, college, and university levels read it and said to themselves something like, "OMG, this is human thought!" which is apparently somewhat of a novelty. No one in my department hassled me after that.

I don't actually consider that article on multiculturalism or most of the material in *Re-Envisioning Psychology* as terribly original. I regard it as a very good recapitulation and perhaps creative application of ideas from the two or three schools of thought or traditions that I value most – hermeneutic philosophy, virtue ethics, and some specific theorists, Hans-Georg Gadamer and Charles Taylor, for example. I'm very proud of our ability to get it right, add a little to those perspectives, and communicate those ideas in a way that may have some impact on our field.

So, what I'm most proud of is more doing careful communication of important intellectual traditions to our field and some others rather than breaking a terrible amount of new ground. There's something special about that, in my view. We wonder what we are in theoretical psychology. Are we applied philosophers? Are we social theorists? Are we psychologists? It's not entirely clear. However, it seems to me, as thinkers who are serious social theorists keenly interested in ethical theory or moral philosophy, more than most philosophers we talk about and elaborate some of the details of ground-level behavioral dynamics, normal and pathological. They don't talk much about personality dynamics, about the miserable, neurotic dynamics that afflict us in our everyday choices and the human interactions that make up the stuff of life. In terms of hermeneutic thought, we're not happy just talking broadly about dialogism or interpretive perspectives. We want to know how this plays out in everyday life and in the human struggle, moral and existential struggles. We give voice to that to some extent. I think that's valuable and perhaps our unique contribution.

JS: We identify as psychologists, but disciplinary boundaries exist mostly for administrative purposes.

FR: That's right.

JS: You read political theory, economics, theology, and cultural theory, among other areas. Serious scholars, in this day and age, need to read outside of their disciplinary enclave.

FR: Yes. Most don't.

JS: You raise hermeneutics. I know that hermeneutics and virtue ethics are very important aspects of your thinking. I was wondering if you could elaborate their importance in your thought and something of the connection between the two.

FR: [Sighs.]

JS: Did you think this was going to be easy?

FR: Well, you know, it took me about a year to read Gadamer's (1989) *Truth and Method* carefully with students. We had lots of other things to do. I don't know how widely it's known or commented on that Hans-Georg Gadamer – who I got to meet; I got to stand in his living room and shake his hand and spend 10 minutes with him – did not intend to publish *Truth and Method* at all. It was a series of lectures from his classes. His students ganged up on him and forced him to publish it. Then it became what many people think as one of the two or three most important books of philosophy of the 20th century across the humanities, not just in philosophy or social theory, which is a lovely story about a great but modest individual.

Gadamer regarded the whole of his broad hermeneutic perspective, ontological hermeneutics, as in large part a deepening and a generalizing of Aristotle's *Nicomachean Ethics*. According to Aristotle, we have an understanding of justice, but we can't deduce from that what to do in particular situations. That requires interpretation and judgment and a creative application of our understanding to date to a partly novel case.

The understanding or insight that we achieve going through this process of interpretation and judgment feeds back and gives us a somewhat richer understanding of justice in general or more theoretically, but not a final or complete one. Then we confront particular problems again and apply our richer understanding to it. We figure it out, as another matter of judgment or interpretation, and that feeds back into our general understanding once more. And so on, indefinitely. That is an instance of the hermeneutic circle that Gadamer generalizes to the pursuit of understanding meaning across the board in everyday life and the human sciences, not just the realm of moral judgment. In the hermeneutic view, we have no good reason to dismiss such interpretations as merely subjective or relative. In fact, at any given point in time or history we do in fact hold understandings and convictions that we take seriously as true or right, even if we remain open and humble in these convictions. At the same time, we cannot we find or lay claim to any standard by which to evaluate them as final, complete, or certain.

So, this may sound trite or dated in an academic context, but Richard Bernstein wrote an interesting and much-discussed book, *Beyond Objectivism and Relativism*, in 1983. I used his view as an organizing idea for several of my analyses and projects and in teaching. A number of people make reference to the idea of beyond objectivism and relativism – it's clearly exposited by Bernstein, an exceptionally fine writer. I know many people have articulated that idea and sort of babble about how we need to go "beyond objectivism and relativism." But they are unable to say clearly what that amounts to. Bernstein himself had some difficulty figuring that out, although that is another story.

Anyway, relativism is the idea that all of our beliefs, ethical principles, moral values, cultural meanings, and values simply *are* relative. They are just part of one or another form of life. There is no possibility of counting them as valid or true or more or less worthwhile in any general or objective way. Objectivism means you can somehow step out of those particular forms of life or particular contexts and access some kind of principles or ideas or standards that swing free of any of the historical particularities.

Neither one of those will work for a number of reasons that can be clearly adduced. They're both unsatisfactory, so where do you go from there? I see ontological hermeneutics as providing a credible way beyond objectivism and relativism. This means there are better and worse interpretations in everyday life, in academic affairs, and in making sense out of everyday human behavior and cultural life, but no final or certain ones. If that seems to make (albeit sophisticated) common sense, so much the better so far as I'm concerned.

It may seem that this kind of interpretive social science is very close to social constructivism or to familiar postmodern and poststructuralist viewpoints, similar to their kind of relativism. But it is significantly different. That kind of relativism insists that *all* cultural and moral values, meanings, ideals, etc., are strictly relative. None of them can rightly claim *any* sort of truth as compared to any others (except, of course, paradoxically, their own, historically embedded, relativistic theory!). So, contest or argument among them is simply a matter of emotional or ultimately arbitrary persuasion or power. But notice! These relativists are also objectivists! How do they know that all meanings and values are strictly relative? They simply announce that from a seemingly thorough objective, almost God's-eye point of view. Many kinds of social scientists and social theorists mangle Bernstein's search for a way beyond objectivism and relativism in a similar way. For example, many empirical social scientists are cognitive objectivists (about their findings) and moral relativists (about extrascientific meanings and values).

Here's the thing that's hardest to articulate about the interpretive approach. This ongoing process of interpretation is something that we can't avoid or escape. It is human finitude, the human condition, itself. As Taylor (1989) says, we all make inescapable "strong evaluations." We always already harbor some self-defining convictions about moral and political and spiritual matters. We take them into interactions with each other in everyday life and they inevitably color our investigations in social science.

This process of living is one of co-constituting influence and dialogue between person and person, individual and society, past and present. It is an ongoing existential process that is ontologically basic in the human life world. Living that out is what we're all about in everyday life and in the right kind of social inquiry. There is an idea that captures this well. Foucault has a version of it, as many of us know. So does Taylor. For reasons I have written about, I prefer Taylor's version. They use the same phrase. It is that "social theory is a form of practice." It's quite a radical idea. It means what we do as social scientists – collecting and interpreting data, theorizing, even higher-order critical theorizing – is different in degree or type, not fundamentally in kind, from what happens in the moral, political, existential, and spiritual struggles of everyday life.

If we absorbed that idea and took it seriously, it would turn our world on its head. We would be as much cultural practitioners, citizens, and politicians in a way as we were social scientists. The kind of psychology and psychological theorizing we do is based on a singular mammoth illusion – that somehow, we are different from the street corner preachers, moralists, parents, politicians, anyone in ordinary life, because we were able to proceed by way of a scientific methodology that gave us a superior truth of a higher order rather than just another biased angle of vision on human struggles.

For me, trying to work these issues through and rethink social inquiry from the ground up, there are certain simple ideas that became essential touchstones. I also found them very useful in teaching. One is in Brent Slife and Richard Williams' (1995) book *What's Behind the Research?*, which was one of the books that got our subfield really going in the early 90s. They start the book with a very simple notion, which is that in psychology "we test our ideas by our methods." But then, what if our methods presuppose certain ideas about the way the world is, about cultural and moral values? So much for pure objectivity or value freedom. We are blind concerning where we're coming from, what we're really doing, and why we are doing it. As a result, we are bound to come up with things that are relatively trivial and largely irrelevant to the ongoing struggles around us.

That's a pure hermeneutic notion, in my view. The best philosophical representation of that notion is Charles Taylor's (1995) great essay, "Overcoming Epistemology," which I notice appears as either the first or the last chapter in several major edited volumes of philosophy. It's as if everyone knows that Taylor may be top dog, may have said it best for our time.

I don't know if I've said enough about hermeneutics, but anyway, it speaks to serious questions that many have raised about the proper nature of social and psychological inquiry, questions that led one famous philosopher of social science (Taylor, 1995) to ask why such inquiry seems often to issue in just "wordy elaborations of the obvious." I could be wrong, of course, but I think of the hermeneutic view as somewhat analogous to quantum physics. It's been around for quite a while and it's going to be a predominant perspective for at least a few more centuries, maybe a lot of it forever. It certainly is not everything. It's a sketch of our functioning in a broad way. There are all kinds of things that aren't discussed there or made explicit ethically, theologically if you're inclined, and so forth. It's a comprehensive perspective that does not ask you to depart from common sense or the realities of everyday life. It does not ask you to endorse one theory as opposed to all or most others in an "I'm right and you're wrong" fashion. It's friendly and inclusive and touches on many of the heartfelt concerns of most major theories or metatheoretical viewpoints. They all illuminate some matters or contain some truth.

I can go into a few details about that. I have written about it extensively. We did in *Re-Envisioning Psychology* and tried to argue that qualitative research and phenomenological approaches, critical theory approaches, including the work of the great Jürgen Habermas, social constructionist points of view, all have something important to say and are at least somewhat illuminating. But all have a few serious contradictions, flaws, or inadequacies. Of course, I can't help but think that hermeneutics helps identify those and presents a coherent and clear alternative. It's a generous, open-minded, and flexible perspective. Whether that is a stunning virtue or simply a

matter of being so open-minded that one's brains fall out is something that everyone has to determine for themselves.
Did that help?

JS: Yes. As you point out, psychologists don't like to be told that psychology is just one more attempt over the history of humanity to try and understand something of what we are. But it belongs to that broader history. It doesn't have any special status when placed in a historical context even though calling it "psychological science" might prompt many to elevate it over other forms of understanding.

FR: That's a very nice way to put it.

JS: Psychologists are very ahistorical. They typically don't want to talk history but when they do talk about it, it's conveyed in terms of the triumphs of the past by which we've come to where we are now, assumed to be the pinnacle of human understanding of matters psychological: psychological science. And that, I think, is one impediment, the ahistoricism of psychology, to accepting the kind of work we do. What other sources of resistance and impediments to your work do you see in the wider sphere of psychology?

FR: I also think, social scientists are inordinately attached to method, to "methodologism," as Gadamer (1989) terms it. I used to joke with my students. I would say, "You have signed up for a PhD program in counseling or social or personality psychology, but when you walked into the education building, the first thing you did was check your brain at the door. You may no longer think for yourself. Your familial and cultural traditions need to be set aside. Subsequently, you are only allowed to firmly embrace those kind of things that you discover through your impersonal empirical methods. Henceforth, let your methods do your thinking for you."
I mean, it's borderline crazy, in a way, although it's sincere, and of course it incorporates some good values – autonomy, freedom, some kinds of criticalness, modern liberty, that kind of thing. Most students understood at least some of what I had said. A few took offense, I must admit.
What was your question? What's a barrier?

JS: So, methodologism is one barrier. What are some other barriers to psychology as a field?

FR: I think that my work is just a sliver of serious, and hopefully fairly clear, hermeneutic take on things. It's not only that, but that's part of it. I think the really interesting question is: How have hermeneutic points of view and the perspectives of Gadamer's and Taylor's work impacted the wider academic scene and culture? Not everyone has signed on for their enterprise, but they are widely honored, read in many places, and continue to be regarded as distinguished and important and paragons of philosophy and culture more broadly. I don't know how to say it other than that. People like Charles Taylor rise to the top, and their ideas and wisdom continue to trickle down. But I don't think the establishment of academic social science can ever reform itself in any way that would incorporate critical perspectives like the ones we are discussing. As you indicated earlier, that would be the end of disciplinary boundaries. Some of our colleagues have written about how foolish it is to have psychology, sociology and political theory, and economics in different compartments. Isn't that true? Most of us nowadays have absolutely no sense of how these things might be recast in an academy of the future.

JS: Yes, I mean, there's that, and then, with respect to the education of future psychologists and what that would involve, we're headed in the opposite direction, toward increasing specializations and increasing isolation as a discipline and entrenchment of our disciplinary boundaries. I honestly don't know what such recasting would require.

FR: Doesn't a lot of that have to do with the corporatizing of the whole enterprise, and with the decline of interest in the humanities, and with trying to make psychology into a science, technology, engineering, and math (STEM) discipline? The whole modern age – according to some interesting theorists like Gadamer, like Habermas, like Husserl, like Christopher Lasch, who I've been reading recently with great interest and appreciation, suggest that the whole modern age has been about power and control and advancing them first and foremost. Any refurbished discipline of psychology is going to have to say no to that and focus on a whole different kind of meaningfulness in living, not unlike what happens when somebody becomes a Benedictine monk, or goes back to their Quaker roots, or just decides that giving back to the community or service is more important than more or less conspicuous consumption.

We have no idea how such a transformation would occur. One way or another, we have to live qualitatively different and much more modest lives without giving up much at all in the way of medical or other kinds of valuable and useful technology, or creativity or entrepreneurship, for that matter.

There's an old-fashioned term for it in virtue ethics. It means you live for what was traditionally called "higher pleasures," for a qualitatively different kind of meaningfulness that, when you live for it, puts a cap on the restless, endless quest for power, control, success, prestige, comfort, or pleasure in the ordinary sense of them because you don't have time for it; your time and your energy has to, wants to, focus on qualitatively different things like love, friendship, the common good, and philosophic wisdom, secular or religious. A simple analogy is, if you want to play the violin well, you have to practice a whole lot and give up a whole lot of other things in your life for a singular, deep, qualitatively different kind of pleasure than being successful, making money, and spending it on things that entertain and puff up your life.

You asked about virtue ethics. That's my commonsense rendering.

JS: It's a pretty tall order.

FR: Well, yes, you and I talk about that sort of thing, don't we? On the surface we may be, very pessimistic about these things and or a bit cynical, but really, in the end, I'm kind of an incurable optimist. However, if you scratch the surface, I fall into periodic deep despair and you keep going in a cheerful manner. We are all human paradoxes, human puzzles.

By the way, that's where lots of these ideas we're discussing come from and are grounded for me. I find I anchor a lot of these ideas in the personalities and the faces and the manners and the styles of people that I know and care about, like you and others. These ideas only have meaning to me when they come to me reflected in the demeanor or manifest sensibility of a Jeff Sugarman or a Mark Freeman or a Brent Slife. I think that makes them truer rather than merely personal and unscientific.

So, I don't know. I do despair about the prospect for those sorts of ideals, especially in the context of this neoliberal condition that you have gotten a number of us to think and write about recently. One of the things that virtue ethics teaches is that we do not need anything like a perfect world to enact and "enjoy" moral excellences. There is such a thing as learning from suffering, sometimes called redemptive suffering, as well as finding strength and meaning in standing against shallowness and evil, even if they are not vanquished.

My simplest idea about that is, things are not supposed to work out, and may not in this life. We're just supposed to love. It doesn't really matter how that works out in worldly terms. Joan of Arc kept going. So did Socrates, the Buddha, Jesus of Nazareth, the Old Testament prophets, most of whom were murdered, slaughtered, you might recall. But we remember them and we honor them, not Attila the Hun or Nero or whomever.

JS: Yes, if you're a parent or a grandparent, or in the field of education, you're in the hope business. You can afford to be only so pessimistic and cynical. You have to harbor or look for some source of hope.

FR: I think that's very important and well said. For many of us in psychology, existential philosophy was an intriguing perspective. There was a survey done in the *American Psychologist* in the middle 1980s, a number of clinicians divided roughly equally among adherents of cognitive therapy, psychoanalysis, behavior therapy, and some other points of view. But for about 80% of them, existentialism was their second favorite theory! It seemed to undergird their standard therapy theory in a way that gave it more depth. I found this fascinating.

I spent some time trying to figure out existentialism and existential therapy and their appeal. Intellectually, it was very exciting and interesting for me to figure out exactly what is wrong as well as what is illuminating about Sartre and existentialism, about the idea of values and meanings becoming important or meaningful to you because you choose them. They're really valid only and precisely because you choose them. That's what gives them weight and "truth" for you. Not any tradition or authority or outside thing of any kind.

If you look closely, it's really a crazy idea; it doesn't work at all because your choice is ultimately arbitrary and whimsical and does not amount to the kind of conviction you are seeking to ground or justify. Also, most existentialism advocates turned out to be completely unoriginal in their cultural and moral values. They were liberal democrats or liberals who celebrated personal freedom, hated domination and discrimination, and believed in democracy. Big deal. Nothing original there.

So, I felt it was important to think through all this intellectually. But for me, my sense of this perspective as wanting was also anchored in personal experience, just the sort that you nicely described. I can remember when my children were young feeling particularly down about everything for a few hours and thinking, well, you know, maybe the existentialists are right, that it's all meaningless. Then I would think of my kids. There was no way I could deem their lives as meaningless in precisely the sense that I was being asked to embrace by the theory. I don't believe the existentialists could do so either. So, when I would talk to people drawn to that view, I would pose that issue, and they would either be quite taken by the idea or quickly change the subject.

JS: The overall social arrangement in our society is significantly unjust, yet many of us assume that all people, regardless of the conditions in which they live, should arrive at the same moral conclusions as those who have wealth and power. How should psychologists take up the issue of moral obligation and civic duty? The assumption that individuals have the freedom to make their own choices is complicated when conditions are so unjust.

FR: In reply, could I read a few paragraphs from your paper on neoliberalism to be delivered later today? I don't know how much more I could say about that topic.

JS: Well, you've written about it.

FR: Yes. I do think that social scientists or thinkers, if they want to speak to today's realities, have to engage with neoliberalism and the terrible and growing inequality in wealth and income among citizens in our kind of society, as you have argued. But they are going to have to greatly expand their intellectual horizons to do that.

Robert Bellah (1983) wrote an essay on the state of social science in the late 1980s entitled "The Ethical Aims of Social Inquiry." I particularly liked that essay. Although very much a gentleman, Bellah did something unusual for him in that chapter and got rather nasty. He did so appropriately, I thought, in dismantling the position of a particularly aggressive positivistic sociologist who insisted that experimental "science" was the only pathway to truth in his discipline. But Bellah said something else in that essay that stuck with me. It posed a tough challenge, a hard one for me to acknowledge as I am aware of my limitations. He wrote that what we do not need in social inquiry – in his case sociology, but he meant in all the social sciences – was to engage in what he called "cross-disciplinary" work, which was well-meaning but insufficient. We can't, you might say, take two buckets of mud and make a chocolate cake out of it. We can't take two shallow fields and somehow cross-fertilize them in a fruitful manner. Instead, we need to engage in "transdisciplinary" work in which psychologists and sociologists are somehow willing to become part-time competent philosophers. Philosophers have got to take a much keener interest than they commonly are inclined to do in the concrete issues and messy problems in social disciplines like psychology and sociology if we are going to make any real progress over time.

One of the things I am proud of is that I was able to involve several philosophers in serious work in our discipline, Charles Guignon and Robert Bishop, for example. They have rolled up their sleeves, gotten to work, and tried to figure out what the heck these interesting but also seemingly confused psychologists are doing. What do the psychologists mean by method? Look at all the things they blithely assumed as they charged on ahead. The philosophers dug in, gave us critical feedback, and published some of their findings in our journals to our benefit, work greatly appreciated by many in our field.

One indication of the need for this kind of transdisciplinary endeavor, and the death of high-quality versions of it, is how hard it is to find a really good philosophy of social science text to learn from or use in teaching in psychology. When I investigated this some 10 years ago, looking for a text for my "Understanding Social Inquiry" graduate seminar, I could find only two books that I could use. One was Robert Bishop's 2007 book *The Philosophy of the Social Sciences*; the other was a quirky but really insightful book *Philosophy of Social Science* by Michael Root (1993). Psychologists avoid the topic, and the relatively few philosophers that have tackled the matter usually twist themselves into confusing knots trying to figure out what kind of "science" is or should be involved in social inquiry.

What that means is that a transdisciplinary approach is essential. Without it, we won't have much of value to say about the neoliberal condition, including such things as the subtle pressure on the poor as well as the rich to think the same way about how the world works. That was the idea, right?

JS: Yes.

FR: I think we have to become part-time political philosophers. Plain and simple.

JS: You've borrowed Hannah Arendt's (1958) idea about citizenship. This is a significant aspect of who we are as persons – our immersion in social and political institutions – that psychology ignores. Psychology is concerned largely with the enhancement and empowerment of individuals. It doesn't prepare people to inculcate a sense of civic virtue and collective responsibility. It might deal with people's feelings of inequality. But it doesn't heed Arendt's insight that equality is acquired through citizenship. Psychologists don't prepare people to be citizens. They prepare them to be individuals governed by their self-interest and self-reliance.

FR: Yes, they seek to become autonomous individuals who are proficient technicians. We now have powerful critiques of psychology's slant in this regard, including *After Virtue* by Alasdair MacIntyre (1981) and, someone I am now revisiting with fascination, Christopher Lasch. Lasch's (1995) last book of short, penetrating essays, *The Revolt of the Elites*, I read in the late 1990s with great interest. I did not appreciate it fully at the time, however. Like so many other people, I'm revisiting Lasch now as neoliberalism advances in the godforsaken age of Trump. That book is perhaps the most exciting thing I have read – reread, really – in recent years. Lasch, you alluded to it, quotes Hannah Arendt, who says that the Enlightenment got it wrong. You do not make citizens by granting them equality and rights. They have to be people of some degree of character and ethical depth for equality to mean anything. Then she referred in just a few sentences to this existential underpinning of that idea. She said equality is not sameness, which really means that we're all cogs in the social and political machine and of no consequence as individuals, really. There's a whole other sense of equality. She calls it equality before death or equality before God. You have to deal with that level and range of things to honestly confront and cope with the actual human situation, including suffering, evil, tragedy, and their overcoming, with greater ethical and possibly spiritual depth. That, obviously, presents a mammoth challenge to the human sciences. As you know, I have written a few things on the topics of tragedy and human suffering in the last several years.

Lasch presents another idea in *Revolt of the Elites* that might seem simple or obvious, but I think it cuts very deep. He says that one particular conception has dominated modern secular thought. Lasch was very uncomfortable with the fact that he started reading modern theologians and found himself drawing on some of their ideas. He noted that he had no religious background and little interest in religion or theology until recently. He died of cancer at age 62, which is most unfortunate. Many of us would dearly love to see where his last thoughts might have taken him. Lasch contended that most modern thought was organized around a core idea of drawing an analogy between the development of an individual from childhood to adulthood and the advancement of the human race from early times to Middle Ages to the modern era as if we are the adults, the superior ones, the ones that really know things. We have left behind the silliness of Plato and Aquinas, or whatever, for something that is much more securely grounded, especially the successful natural sciences being one prominent example.

That conception, unfortunately, Lasch said, is just wrong. The way he puts it, and I'm being colloquial and oversimplifying it here, is that in modern times we have been on a kind of protracted power trip. He discusses this as our overriding ideal of "progress" in his great book *The True and Only Heaven: Progress and Its Critics* (Lasch, 1991). He chronicles how over the last 250 years or so critics from Thomas Jefferson to some contemporary Reagan Democrats, a surprising example of his, have sharply and often insightfully critiqued our overweening notions of progress at all costs. They protested that life is not just about endless, expanding control. Of course, this parallels the famous "critique of instrumental reason" proffered by the Frankfurt School in the early part of the 20th century. It was the original source of penetrating critiques of the kind of "instrumentalism" that is the uncritically assumed ideal of rational thought for much of 20th century social science (Richardson & Manglos, 2012). Few of these critics, often quite insightful, had plausible, constructive alternatives to offer. Jefferson toyed with the idea of having all manufacturing, which we needed the fruits of, be done in Europe. In America, we would all be farmers and craftspeople in small towns, be able to practice civic republican local politics, and not be tainted by big factories that atomize and depersonalize individuals. It was obviously not going to work, and he abandoned the idea.

Eventually, we gave up on alternatives and settled in on the ideal of progress, progress essentially consisting in the pursuit of "more." That became almost our national civic religion. It may be the one faith that the well-off and the poor-off, the top 1% or 10% and all the rest of us, including many of the poor, have in common. We have to question this ideal as social theorists and social scientists, investigate how that works out in the psychology of individuals, in relationships, and in everyday life. This is something philosophers tend not to do but for which we are fairly well qualified, if we can break the grip of individualism and instrumentalism on our social imaginations.

Individualistic, hypercompetitive neoliberalism isolates us socially and emotionally, as you have argued. It generates inequality, inevitably and automatically, because meritocracy means that those who are most successful in pursuing control, popularity, goods, and money, only a small minority, can succeed and flourish, albeit materialistically. The rest will suffer, and many will resent it and turn to authoritarian populism, which, guess what, is happening to one degree or another right now all over the Western world.

I don't know if that speaks to your question?

JS: It does very well. Given that you raised the idea of meritocracy, can you speak to the tension between meritocracy and inequality?

FR: Well, there are some good resources for elaborating on that issue. Some of my friends and colleagues have read, hot off the press, a book called *Why Liberalism Failed* by Patrick Deneen (2018). He's not a conservative attacking liberalism in the conventional sense. By liberalism, he means the kind of isolating individualism that lies at the root of both conventional conservative and liberal thought. Both of them have to do with advancing autonomy and human rights. They simply have a different conception of human rights. So-called conservatives focus on property rights; liberals focus on a wider range of social and economic rights. But they're still all about rights and the empowerment of the individual and have little conception of the common good beyond an accumulation of such empowered individuals delighting in their pleasure and possessions.

Deneen offers one of those simple but clear and deep-cutting ideas. He says that liberty in premodern times had no meaning apart from character, moral maturity, and ethical depth. Such liberty that was anchored in character and moral depth was the only thing that could deter tyranny, the only thing that would lead people to reject populist tyranny, reject attaching themselves to some hero or would-be dictator, and give them the moral force and influence to shame those who would seek such excessive power and perhaps laugh them out of town.

Deneen writes that there was a major transition, gradual but profound, that redefined liberty at the beginning of modern times. It was redefined largely in negative terms.

Autonomy now meant that we are "free from," as Erich Fromm put it – free from arbitrary authority, free from now pointless traditions, free from the control of others. What we are "free for" was left largely to individual preference or choice. We also – Machiavelli was the great voice of this – bought in to a great deal of skepticism about human nature. We saw humans as incurably selfish and greedy and power-driven. It was deemed hopeless to have most or even a large percentage of the human race counter those propensities with strength of character. That's just not plausible, we came to believe. So, we have to just unleash self-interest and the pursuit of money, success, pleasure, and power, and then institute controls of that through the political state and through the law and ultimately police power. Deneen termed this a new kind of politics, which he described as based on the reliability of "the low" rather than aspiration to "the high."

So, that is what "liberty" now means. If you think about it – this is my comment, not Deneen's – this view is a wild combination of deep cynicism about human nature and incredible, facile optimism about how we can channel it and control it and keep it in balance for our good. It's a bizarre perspective. It makes some kind of common sense, I suppose, because we want or need somehow to be realistic and at the same time, we also treasure all the fruits of individualism, autonomy, progress, and "more."

If I've characterized it at all clearly, I think Deneen's analysis helps us appreciate the idea that personality, social, and clinical psychology need to get political and take account of the human and moral dynamics he discusses. Such dynamics contribute to shaping us as persons and relationships greatly, from the inside out. As a result, we have to become, in part, historians of these ideas and political theorists.

JS: I want to get you to augment the critique a bit. You've often criticized the ideal of liberal individualism. But liberalism has given us a lot of good things: the idea that rights set a limit on legitimate power, that government must respect the liberty of individuals, that religious groups should be tolerant of each other. The belief that all people in an economically successful nation should have the opportunity to lead a decent life; that society should ensure the security of children, of old people, disabled people and people out of work for reasons not of their own doing; the protection of civil rights, the universality of civil rights. These are all liberal ideas. So, can you explain the problem with liberalism? What do you see as the preferred alternatives to it? That's the simplest question I have for the day.

FR: Well, I hope I just spoke to that by recapitulating a few of Deneen's ideas. But it's a very important question. Most of us are really torn between deep attraction to some much more traditional ideas of character and community along with a profound attachment to a radical or very one-sided sense of undoing discrimination and domination, a profound anti-authoritarianism that almost forbids us to talk about such things and character or the common good. Such ideals should be seen as merely "subjective" and be strictly left to the individual. Few of us have healed that split; we just have to live with it and do what we can.

Most of those profound ethical and social ideals concerning discrimination, equality, and the erasure of arbitrary authority, the gift of modern, are precious beyond words. They're somewhat stained by individualism, excessive individualism, the thing Tocqueville talked about, empowerment without being clear where we're supposed to go with that empowered self. So, those are incredibly precious ideals, on the one hand. On the other hand, many traditional ideals, the notions of character, virtue, the common good, genuine civic republican politics, seem equally important to many of us. I discuss some of that in a recent article on neoliberalism. I know that all those ideals and their instantiations in culture and history were stained with paternalism, insensitivity, various kinds of discrimination, sexism, and slovenly complacency. All this with the inherited or achieved high status without realizing that the reason you were the king or the noble or owned the company or whatever, was largely because you were a lucky son of a gun, not because you necessarily had any more intelligence or competence than the lowest worker in your regime. They're stained and colored by these wicked things, just as our worthy modern ideals are stained and colored with a one-sided individualism.

We have to sort that out. None of us know exactly how it will evolve or should evolve. Among people that I know and hang out with, many have some kind of spiritual side that is exceptionally important to them. It is to me, although I am as much a creature of doubt as I am of faith or belief. I just live with the tension and will never resolve it in this lifetime.

Other folks we know and admire are quite secular and have the same kind of ethical depth we supposedly do and share many of our concerns. They are free to interpret me as somewhat interested in spiritual things because I'm a good guy, but just a little confused. We don't really need that spiritual edge they feel. I am free to interpret them as being deeper than they know and possibly drawing on traditional and spiritual resources that they've forgotten, even though in some ways they may be a better person than I am. That's hermeneutics. We're free to interpret one another in searching dialogue.

That's what we have to do more of as citizens. I see this happening in some places, but it's hard to come by. Most people don't have anything like the education or the knowledge or the tools to deal with these issues in everyday life or politics. However, they're no more barren of those resources than most academics.

JS: So, there is a fundamental tension between individual freedom to pursue fulfillment in one's own way and obligations for civic virtue. There are some people, like Amy Gutmann (1990), who would say you're never going to resolve that tension and the best you can do is deal with issues on a case-by-case basis. Should the government be allowed to monitor our cell phones, or should child pornography be permitted? When individual freedoms conflict with the collective good, you're going to have to debate and argue over the issues and try to come to some rational decision, and that's the best we can ever do. You're never going to come up with some universal principle with which to resolve the tension. But I hear you saying something different, that if you have a common good that people could buy in to, maybe it would tip the balance in favor of civic virtue.

FR: That's very nicely put. Amy Gutmann is certainly a great liberal thinker and political philosopher. I read Professor Gutmann a number of years ago and admire her greatly. Her point of view is challenging, to be sure. I have no easy answer as to how more communitarian social thought or hermeneutic philosophy might put a slightly different spin on these questions. But here are a couple of thoughts.

I like Gutmann's idea that we can't simply appeal to universal principles. That means that we can't simply rely on Kant's categorical imperative or Rawls's principle ethics. Let us say that she rejects that kind of "objectivism." But when you or she indicates that we have to discourse with one another on a matter and come up with some sort of "rational" decision, then you or she has to explain just what the heck "rational" means and why she is not simply embracing some kind of moral "relativism," which I am sure neither of you would want to do. You and she have to say something credible about the basis, in some sense, upon which you ground, again in some sense, your deliberations. In other words, you are also faced with the challenge of finding some way of going "beyond objectivism and relativism."

So, I think Gutmann's approach and my hermeneutic or more communitarian approaches overlap considerably, a credit to both, I would say. Hermeneutics would zero in on the process of the serious dialogue about questions of right and wrong, good and evil, and the like. It puts those processes of mutual influence and dialogue at the very center of the ethical picture. In this view, we always enter into that dialogue or interactions, which we are always involved in some way, with some convictions about not only human rights but also about the common good and the good life or the best way to live. As the philosopher Georgia Warnke (1987) puts it, one has to grant one's interlocutor "provisional authority" to challenge one's most basic beliefs and values in order to search for the best understanding of the situation and what, ethically speaking, should be done.

It is not easy to allow oneself to be challenged at the root by another. It should be obvious that such dialogue or search requires much in the way of moral excellences like vulnerability, character, depth, and humility. It is not easy to allow ourselves to be challenged by people who may see things quite differently and who at first blush we find really quite annoying and irritatingly off the mark.

Moreover, you know, even that is only part of the story. It seems to some of us that what life is all about is not just getting those things correct and making reasonable compromises so we can order a workable liberal democracy. It is also about appreciating and dealing with the fact that being equal before death or equal before God (or Brahman or Tao) means having to figure out what life is all about in some deeper ways, having to face our mortality, having to deal with tragedy and suffering, our own death, sometimes the death of a child, the immense amount of suffering that pervades human experience and human life. We just have to come to terms with that in some way. Having some of that sense of things as part of our cultural life and built into the character of a lot of our citizenry may be a *condition* of having a workable liberal democracy.

JS: This is why I think your work on conversational virtues is so important, particularly for deliberative democracies. You need to have respect for the truth, respect for culture and history, open-mindedness toward difference, perseverance for the sake of understanding, and so forth. That's part of why I think your work on multiculturalism is so interesting. You argued that we shouldn't value multiculturalism simply because we have to be nice to other people. The value of multiculturalism is when you engage people with differing beliefs and practices, and you don't assimilate their worldview too quickly to your own, it casts your own horizon of understanding into relief. The contrast can be an opportunity for individual and collective enhancement. You see the assumptions on which you operate and then you become open to the possibility that there's a different way of thinking about this, or doing that, which might be better. That's why multiculturalism has merit.

FR: That's very nice. I'm very proud of Blaine Fowers's and my article (Fowers & Richardson, 1996) "Why Is Multiculturalism Good?" Clever title, eh? You know, today there is an angry critique and real condemnation of what many in politically correct academic and social circles call "cultural appropriation." It is the eleventh commandment: Thou shalt never culturally appropriate. Maybe it is even the first commandment now. In a recent article, David Frum made the point, a very hermeneutic point, I would say, that cultural appropriation is what life is all about! We talk to one another, we influence one another, we challenge, deepen, enrich, and humble one another. You mean I can't have books on Buddhist metaphysics on my shelf? I have been reading some of them lately and find it stimulating, uprooting, deepening, and immensely helpful in the business of living. Why would those dweeby little people want to deprive me of that? If they had their way, the only thing I would be allowed to read would be treatises condemning cultural appropriation! That would be my only culture.

One last point about that. One of the most exciting things happening in the world of religion and theology these days, I think, is what is called interspirituality. It involves a deep and searching conversation among Buddhism, Christianity, Judaism, Islam, and other spiritual traditions. The idea of moralizing about and condemning cultural appropriation is borderline insanity and puts a cap on this kind of life of the mind and the spirit. The challenge is to accept the humbling fact of such quite inevitable cross-cultural cross-fertilization and do it properly. Of course, it can be distorted or misused. Anything can. There is always a great danger that we will take their stuff and make it a subordinate part of our stuff, or we will make them serve our goals and dominate them intellectually or politically. Or, we might flee the riches and challenges of our own best traditions and hide out in a false and idealized picture of the other. So, I guess, we need to walk that fine line between domination and "going native." There is no life without risk.

JS: One more?

FR: Sure.

JS: So, when we call you up on your 103rd birthday, what do you expect to be working on? What do you expect or imagine to be the future directions of your thought? Where do you think you might go from here?

FR: Me? Or any of us?

JS: You can talk about any of us. But I'm mostly interested in you.

FR: Well, that's a distressing question, in some ways. I'm shooting for 87, for some reason. We'll see what happens. There are six or eight things I can imagine working on, even with my many limitations. I can't alter the mistakes I've made in the past, but I can broaden myself a bit in the future if I have the time. If I were to do it over, I'm not sure I would go into psychology, although I am proud of what our subfield of theoretical psychology has made of the many predicaments of social science.

I am keenly interested in Buddhist metaphysics and ethics, as I indicated. I have a young friend who's quite a scholar in the area. We're working on a paper that compares and contrasts Tibetan Buddhism and hermeneutic thought in several ways. I would like to dig deeper into these critiques of liberalism. Much has been done on the topic, and I think there is more to explore and clarify there. I dearly love some brands of philosophy, especially continental philosophy and moral philosophy. There is new work on virtue ethics that I would like to absorb and see what could be done with it.

Also, I am very interested in this whole new area of interspirituality, so-called, of deep and searching dialogue between all the major religious traditions. I have no idea where it will go, how it will develop. It is fascinating, and I think it's completely open-ended and undecided as to where it will go. I would love to be able to read 15 or 20 of those books and perhaps contribute a little to that exploration, including how it might impact psychology and what our kind of theoretical psychology reflections might add to the mix.

I may not get a chance to take on but half of one or two of those projects. I regret that, but I know I should not complain about it. I'm very lucky. So, I'll stop complaining.

References

Arendt, H. (1958). *The human condition.* University of Chicago Press.

Bellah, R. (1983). The ethical aims of social inquiry. In N. Haan, R. Bellah, P. Rabinow, & W. Sullivan (Eds.), *Social science as moral inquiry* (pp. 300–381). Columbia University Press.

Bernstein, R. (1983). *Beyond objectivism and relativism.* University of Pennsylvania Press.

Bishop, R. (2007). *The philosophy of the social sciences.* Continuum.

Cushman, P. (1990). Why the self is empty. *American Psychologist, 45,* 599–611.

Deneen, P. (2018). *Why liberalism failed.* Yale University Press.

Dunne, J. (1996). Beyond sovereignty and deconstruction: The storied self. In R. Kerney (Ed.), *Paul Ricoeur: The hermeneutics of action* (pp. 137–148). SAGE.

Elms, A. (1996). *Uncovering lives: The uneasy alliance of biography and psychology.* Oxford University Press.

Fowers, B. J., & Richardson, F. C. (1996). Why is multiculturalism good? *American Psychologist, 51*, 609–621.

Gadamer, H.-G. (1989). *Truth and method* (2nd rev. ed.) (J. Weinsheimer & D. Marshall, Trans.). Crossroad.

Gutmann, A. 1990). Democratic education in difficult times. *Teachers College Record, 92*, 7–20.

Lasch, C. (1991). *The true and only heaven: Progress and its critics.* W. W. Norton.

Lasch, C. (1995). *The revolt of the elites and the betrayal of democracy.* W. W. Norton.

MacIntyre, A. (1981). *After virtue.* University of Notre Dame Press.

Richardson, F. C. (2000). Fragmentation in psychology: A hermeneutic approach. *Journal of Mind and Behavior, 21*, 289–304.

Richardson, F. C. (2009). Mimesis and hermeneutics: René Girard and theoretical psychology. In T. Teo, P. Stenner, A. Rutherford, E. Park, & C. Baerveldt (Eds.), *Varieties of theoretical psychology: International philosophical and practical concerns* (pp. 30–39). Captus.

Richardson, F. C. (2012). On psychology and virtue ethics. *Journal of Theoretical and Philosophical Psychology, 32*, 24–34.

Richardson, F. C. (2014). Investigating psychology and transcendence. *Pastoral Psychology, 63*, 355–365.

Richardson, F. C., Bishop, R., & Slaney, K. L. (2019). Politics and moral realism. In B. D. Slife & S. C. Yanchar (Eds.), *Hermeneutic moral realism in psychology: Theory and practice* (pp. 97–115). Routledge.

Richardson, F. C., Fowers, B. J., & Guignon, C. B. (1999). *Re-envisioning psychology: Moral dimensions of theory and practice.* Jossey-Bass.

Richardson, F. C., & Manglos, N. D. (2012). Rethinking instrumentalism. *Journal of Consciousness Studies, 19*, 177–201.

Richardson, F. C., & Woolfolk, R. L. (1994). Social theory and values: A hermeneutic perspective. *Theory & Psychology, 4*(2), 199–226. https://doi.org/10.1177/0959354394042003

Richardson, F. C., & Woolfolk, R. L. (2013). Subjectivity and strong relationality. In R. W. Tafarodi (Ed.), *Subjectivity in the 21st century: Psychological, sociological, and political perspectives* (pp. 11–40). Cambridge University Press.

Root, M. (1993). *Philosophy of social science.* Blackwell.

Slife, B., & Williams, R. (1995). *What's behind the research? Discovering hidden assumptions in the behavioral sciences.* SAGE.

Taylor, C. (1989). *Sources of the self: The making of the modern identity.* Cambridge University Press.

Taylor, C. (1995). Overcoming epistemology. In C. Taylor (Ed.), *Philosophical arguments* (pp. 1–18). Harvard University Press.

Warnke, G. (1987). *Gadamer: Hermeneutics: Tradition, and reason.* Stanford University Press.

Index

individualism/individualization 72,
119, 206, 208–210, 220–221, 231,
248–250
inequality 38, 246; income and wealth
72; meritocracy and 248
infinite greed 162–183
injustice 220
innovative scholarship 229
institutional antipathy 26
institutional power 118
institutional psychiatry 220
instrumentalism 209, 220–221, 226,
231, 247–248
instrumental thinking 76
intellectual wanderings 233
interdisciplinary/interdisciplinarity
107, 133, 176, 186
International Society for Theoretical
Psychology 212–213
interpretation, process of 237–238
interpretative phenomenological
analysis (IPA) 176
interpretive perspectives 235
interspirituality 254
intersubjectivity 77–78
*In the Ruins of Neoliberalism: The
Rise of Antidemocratic Politics in
the West* (Brown) 4
investment, emotional returns on
133–134
IPA *see* interpretative
phenomenological analysis (IPA)
irreligious psychoanalysis 190
Islam 254

James, W. 116
Johnston, A. 10, 162
Jolly, M. 214
Josselson, R. 101
Journal of Humanistic Psychology
(Becker) 218
Judaism 254

Kaepernick, C. 157–158
Kant, I. 30, 169–170
Kaplan, B. 102, 109, 118
kindness 198

Kinget, G. M. 212
King, M. L. 36, 85
King, R. 158
Kirschner, S. R. 3, 8–9, 84–86
knowledge 111; critical 76–77;
psychological 63; traditional 76–77
Koch, S. 207, 212
Kohut's self-psychology 234
Kraidy, M. 125
Kuhn, T. S. 64, 66

Lacanian psychoanalysis 168
Lacan, J. 10, 149, 162, 165–168, 171,
174–178
language, Democratic position 196
lapsed history 23
Lasch, C. 241, 246–247
law-abiding citizenship 137
Layton, L. 132, 192
legitimization, forms of 3
Levinas, E. 145, 192
LeVine, R. 89
liberals/liberalism 248, 255;
deliberative democracy 33–34;
democracy 253; individualism 250;
legitimate critique of 195
liberty 249
life failures 220
life positioning analysis (LPA) 11,
214–217, 222
lifestyle discourse 132–133
life writing 207, 214
"listening" posture 159
living, process of 238
LPA *see* life positioning analysis
(LPA)

Macdonald, H. 10
MacIntyre, A. 1, 246
mainstream psychology 101
map of aspirations 126
Marecek, J. 88
marginalized communities 61, 111
Maritain, J. 164
market rationality 31–32
market values, ideology of 5
Martin, J. 3, 18